HISTORICAL AND CONTEMPORARY PHILOSOPHIES OF EDUCATION

HISTORICAL AND CONTEMPORARY PHILOSOPHIES OF EDUCATION

Frederick C. Gruber

University of Pennsylvania

Thomas Y. Crowell Company
New York Established 1834

Preface

Education is one of the most controversial subjects today. Some claim our educational system is no longer relevant to our age, that it is a rudderless ship on a sea of confusion. Answers to many of the perplexing problems of education are sought in science and in philosophy. The purpose of this book is to present the thoughts of some of the great educators from Plato to the present time.

The "science" of education, based upon studies in psychology and the behavioral sciences, points to practical applications. It encompasses much in the domain of metaphysics and epistemology, having no absolute answers, only probabilities. Discussion about education can be divided into the theoretical and the philosophical. General theories of education are frequently based upon dogma, belief, or tradition, and are often concerned with rationalizing or justifying them.

Philosophy of education is either normative (speculative) or analytical. Normative or speculative philosophy of education involves a comprehensive philosophical and theoretical line of reasoning derived from a metaphysical position, and is concerned with judgments of a qualitative nature involving the aims and purposes of education. Analytical philosophy of education, on the other hand, busies itself with the explication and clarification of the basic terminology and concepts used in educational discourse. The great contributions of philosophy of education today have been made in the study of normative or value judgments in education and in the examination of the language in which the science of education is expressed.

The world in crisis looks for new ways to meet its present perplexities. Modern educators insist that education should be relevant to our age, and look for innovations to chart new paths out of present dilemmas. This is not unique to our present age. Over two thousand years ago Aristotle remarked that *as things were* men are not agreed about the things to be taught.*

With the rise of conflicting political, social, and economic ideologies, and the formation of new nations from those that had been dominated by the Western powers, educators might well ask themselves these questions: "What is the relation of the individual to the state?" "What should be the aim of education in American democracy?" "What should be the objectives of vocational education in an age where advances in technology make many jobs obsolete before students have been trained for them?" "What is the nature of the learner, and do modern instructional resources hinder or further his self actualization?"

This textbook uses a chronological organization for ready reference, but through the use of the index students may explore what answers have been given to some of these questions in the past. The relation between the individual and the state may be briefly sketched in this manner, for example.

Man and the State

Does the citizen make the state or the state the citizen? Hegel, the German philosopher taught that the state was an organism, that each individual contributed whatever the state needed to sustain itself and to evolve toward perfection, much as each organ in the body fulfills its own purpose and not that of another. Out of Hegel's idealism,—process of intellectual evolution through the reconciliation of opposites—grew the doctrine of Karl Marx which led to communism on the one hand, and to the totalitarianism of Nazism and Fascism on the other. Nietzsche's idea of a superman fits into this frame of reference. On the other hand the revolt of Kierkegaard, the Danish theologian, led to the development of modern existentialism with its religious and atheistic aspects,

*Aristotle, *Politics,* Book VIII, Chapter 2

which attempts to lead the individual to create his own identity over and against the conformity of "the establishment."

Erasmus, the great sixteenth century theologican, advocated a totalitarian state in which a Christian prince ruled his people in kindness, prosperity, and peace. Machiavelli, in the Renaissance, believed that a prince with absolute power, skilled in war, should rule in peace by resorting to any method to achieve his end. Tired of the perpetual wars between rival princes, he wished to unify Italy into a peaceful nation. Hobbes, in Elizabethan England, had justified the divine right of kings in his *Leviathan.* These ideas are reminiscent of Aristotle, who wrote that the chief purpose of education was to train citizens for the state, and of Plato, who envisioned a perfect, peaceful state ruled by philosopher kings wherein all fulfilled their duties as the gods had ordained.

On the other hand, there are those who strongly advocate a free and open-end society. Jefferson, in the *Declaration of Independence,* wrote "all men are created equal," "they are endowed ... with certain inalienable rights," and "governments are instituted ... by the consent of the governed." These ideas strongly echo those of John Locke who justified the Glorious Revolution of 1688 by declaring that the citizens who had entered into a political contract had the right to dissolve the government if it no longer guaranteed their rights and privileges and to establish a new one. Locke, of course, differed from Hobbes regarding the nature of the social contract. Hobbes maintained that a contract could not be broken without the consent of both parties, the ruler and the ruled. Rousseau, on the other hand, while realizing the sorry state into which society had fallen politically, still insisted that the individual must submit to the rule of the majority. Thus, while Hobbes and Rousseau gave a nod to democracy, both their systems imposed restrictions on the individual, the former by an absolute monarch, and the latter by the majority of the citizens.

Catholic scholars have also wrestled with this problem which is further complicated by a belief that man belongs to "two kingdoms": the kingdom of God and the kingdom of man. Maritain points out that there is a difference between the government as a political organization and the body politic which is made up of individual men having a double destiny, and that the laws of God and therefore humanity supersede those made by men for secular political purposes. We are reminded of St. Augustine who envisioned an eternal "City of God" and a transitory city of man subject to its ultimate destruction because of its own inherent weaknesses.

Paternalistic government is seen in various forms of totalitarianism, fraternalistic government in an open and democratic society, and theistic government with religious groups. Modern education must recognize each of these, and the authors discussed on the following pages indeed have much to say on this subject.

Ideas in education are slow in developing; they are often cyclic: hailed as great innovations and then forgotten, they are resurrected in slightly modified form. This only confirms the old adage that we climb on the shoulders of our predecessors. Whoever attempts to solve the educational problems of the present without a knowledge of the past deprives himself of over two thousand years of educational experience.

Since there is no single philosophy of American education, the study of educational theory and philosophy is an absorbing and productive enterprise. In keeping with the spirit of America which is pluralistic, dynamic, and committed to change, those who enter the field will dedicate themselves to continuous adventure.

The text includes short selections from the principal authors and there is a generous listing of easily available paperbacks. The volume concludes with examples of classroom teaching with which the student can compare his own experience and practice. A glossary of terms used in the text is appended.

In a short work such as this it is possible to treat only a few figures in each age. However, charts listing many philosophers who were contemporaries of those cited, with a brief statement characterizing their contributions to Western thought, are included in the text. They are: (1) The Ancient Greeks to St. Jerome; (2) St. Augustine to St. Thomas Aquinas; (3) Renaissance, Reformation, and Counter Reformation; (4) Rationalism and the Enlightenment; (5) Humanism, Idealism, and Realism, and (6) Post Hegelianism and the Century of Darwin.

Many thanks are due to the authors and publishers who have granted permission to quote from their works. Special thanks are also due to my colleagues at the University of Pennsylvania—Professors Dwyer and McMullin, and to Professor Maxine Greene of Teachers College, Columbia University, for valuable suggestions and criticism, and to James Bergin and Judith Mallinson of Thomas Y. Crowell and Company.

The work could not have been completed without the advice and forbearance of my wife, Alma H. Gruber, and the devotion and skill of my secretary, Miss Ruthe Potter. Thanks are also due to Miss Parvin Surti and Mrs. Elizabeth Doherty for typing the final copy. Whatever faults are found in the work are my own.

Frederick C. Gruber

Contents

CHAPTER ONE
ANCIENT GREECE AND ROME
Plato, Aristotle, and Quintilian   1

CHAPTER TWO
THE MIDDLE AGES
Augustine and Aquinas   29

CHAPTER THREE
THE RENAISSANCE
Machiavelli and Erasmus   45

CHAPTER FOUR
THE REFORMATION AND COUNTER REFORMATION
Luther, Calvin, and Loyola   59

CHAPTER FIVE
THE ENLIGHTENMENT
Comenius, Locke, Rousseau, and Jefferson   87

CHAPTER SIX
NINETEENTH-CENTURY INNOVATORS
Pestalozzi, Hegel, Herbart, and Froebel   123

CHAPTER SEVEN
IDEALISM AND NATURALISM
Emerson and Spencer   155

CHAPTER EIGHT
THE POST-DARWINIANS
James, Dewey, and Whitehead   173

CHAPTER NINE
NEO-THOMISM, EXISTENTIALISM, AND LOGICAL EMPIRICISM
Maritain, Buber, and Scheffler   207

APPENDIX
CONTEMPORARY PHILOSOPHIES IN THE CLASSROOM   237

GLOSSARY
247

HISTORICAL AND CONTEMPORARY PHILOSOPHIES OF EDUCATION

Chapter One
Ancient Greece and Rome: Plato, Aristotle, and Quintilian

"ALL WESTERN PHILOSOPHY," declared Whitehead, "is a footnote to Plato." To a large extent this is true for, aside from a few fragments, much of what we know of Plato's predecessors and contemporaries is from Plato's discussion of them in his dialogues, and much of subsequent thought has been written to support or to refute his works or those of his disciples.

This chapter will treat some of the educational ideas of Plato, his most distinguished pupil, Aristotle, and Quintilian, an outstanding teacher of rhetoric.

PLATO

The world of Plato (427-347 B.C.) included not only the Greek mainland but the islands adjacent to it in the Aegean and Mediterranean seas and settlements on the coast of Asia Minor, in Sicily, and along the coast of Italy. Athens stood at the crossroads for the exchange of goods and ideas. The atomists, notably Heraclitus (535-475 B.C.) and Democritus (460-370 B.C.), taught that the universe was constantly changing, while the Pythagoreans, notably Parmenides (*fl.* 495 B.C.), described a fixed universe of mathematical forms and relationships in which nothing changed. Plato tried to reconcile these two metaphysical points of view.

The early years of his life coincided with the Peloponnesian Wars (459-404 B.C.), which were marked by constant strife between Sparta and Athens and their vacillating allies, and by political intrigues between the democratic and aristocratic parties. Plato, who was of ancient aristocratic lineage, tried to envision a stable and happy state. Socrates (469-399 B.C.) Plato's principal teacher developed a method of asking yes and no questions to draw out truths by recollection. He died by drinking hemlock to show his respect for the law even when unjustly administered, an event that turned the young Plato from a political career to one of teaching and writing. To attempt to formulate his philosophy into a rigid system is a fruitless task, for both Plato and the protagonist of his *Dialogues,* Socrates, were willing to consider all sides of a complex situation in a search for the eternal truth they considered to exist behind the phenomenal world. Their search was not for information or isolated bits of knowledge, but for profound insight.

Plato conceived the thousands of fleeting phenomena of experience to be parts of a meaningful and ordered world. These ordering forces are reflected in the mind of man in a way that transcends his day-by-day observations and renders his mind capable of realizing meanings and interrelationships between himself and the psychic forces of the universe. This unity of ideas, this "logos," cannot be described so concretely as this pen or that chair, but for Plato it possesses a far greater reality than things we can see, or taste, or handle. Thus, for Plato, the greatest activity of man is the search for this eternal truth, not only to discover what really is, but what ought to be. It was in order to set up goals for social and moral conduct that he wrote *The Laws* and *The Republic,* two utopias which hold great interest for the educator.

Plato believed that the true aim of human existence is the attainment of the beautiful and virtuous man, the *aner kalos k' agathos,* and that the true conduct of life rested on four moral concepts: worth, wisdom, service, and political leadership. Thus, in his search for perfection, man was not to seek wisdom and knowledge alone, but was to transform them into reality in a social setting. The moral concepts were not only to be studied, but to be put into action. Man alone is given the blessing of perfecting himself through increasing insight into the essence of the world. Thus man alone can project himself beyond his own ego into the realm of the logos, and it is the duty of the elders to enable the

oncoming generation to fulfill the eternal mission of man. "Education," wrote Plato, "is the process of drawing and guiding children
towards that principle which is pronounced right by law and
confirmed as truly right by the experience of the oldest and most
just."[1]

The Greek democracy of Plato's day differed in certain important respects from ours. First, there was a sharp distinction between the Greek citizens and the slaves, who outnumbered them
about five to one. Second, the Greeks distinguished between those
who were citizens of the city-state and those who lived outside it.[2]
Finally, within the city-state itself, the relatively small group of
citizens was again divided into classes. Plato was either oblivious of
these differences or took them for granted. He even admitted a
double standard of morality. For example, rulers were permitted
to lie in the interest of the state, but a workman was to be
punished with the severest penalty for telling a falsehood.[3] The
following quotation from *The Republic* illustrates these points.

> We shall tell our people, in mythical language; You are doubt-
> less all brethren, or as many as inhabit the city, but the God
> who created you mixed gold in the composition of such of
> you as are qualified to rule, which gives them the highest
> value; while, in the auxiliaries, he made silver an ingredient,
> assigning iron and copper to the cultivators of the soil and the
> other workmen. Therefore, inasmuch as you are all related to
> one another, although your children will generally resemble
> their parents, yet sometimes a golden parent will produce a
> silver child, and a silver parent a golden child, and so on, each
> producing any. The rulers therefore have received this in
> charge first and above all from the gods, to observe nothing
> more closely, in their character of vigilant guardians, than the
> children that are born, to see which of these metals enters into
> the composition of their souls; and if a child be born in their
> class with an alloy of copper or iron, they are to have no
> manner of pity upon it, but giving it the value that belongs to
> its nature, they are to thrust it away into the class of artisans
> or agriculturalists; and if again among these a child be born

[1] Plato, *The Laws*, Bk. II, Sec. 659D, trans. R. C. Bury. Loeb Classical Library
(Cambridge: Harvard University Press, 1926).

[2] It is estimated that in the city of Athens one-fifth of the small group of free men
were citizens of other states, and, therefore, were not included in the small group of
Athenians of which Plato writes.

[3] Plato, *The Republic*, Bk. III, Sec. 389, trans. J. L. Davies and D. J. Vaughan (New
York: Macmillan, 1927).

with any admixture of gold or silver, when they have assayed it, they are to raise it either to the class of guardians, or to that of auxiliaries: because there is an oracle which declares that the city shall then perish when it is guarded by iron or copper.[4]

Thus, Plato recommended a state-controlled system of education with censorship of art, literature,[5] and music[6] so that society would reflect the true, the beautiful, and the good. He also recommended a type of communal life for the philosopher-kings so that they would not be influenced by possessions or family relationships in making judgments for the public welfare.[7] These ideas greatly affected the organization of the medieval church and form the basis for some present-day practices.

Generally speaking, Plato's educational ideas implied that the child belonged to the state, which would supervise his entire development. The earliest years were to be spent in public nurseries, developing physical health and absorbing accepted ideas of religion and patriotism. More formal education would begin at six and continue to eighteen, when a series of examinations would separate the iron and copper workmen from the gold and silver upper classes. For boys between eighteen and twenty, the courses would be military. The soldier class could be eliminated at the end of this course. For the philosopher-rulers, education would continue until thirty, when an examination would eliminate the less brilliant, who would be assigned administrative posts in the government. The next five years would be spent by the most brilliant in a study of pure abstractions with the goal of catching a vision of the "Idea of the Good." From, thirty-five to fifty, these philosopher-kings would rule the state in minor offices, and at fifty the most brilliant would be elevated to the full status of Guardian.[8]

Even better known than Plato's myth of the metals is his allegory of the cave. Plato imagines a number of persons chained in a cave with their backs to the entrance. A fire burns behind them, casting shadows of the objects passers-by carry on their heads. The inhabitants of the cave do not know reality, but only its shadow. One of the prisoners is released and taken outside. When he becomes accustomed to the light, he is able to see the reality he had experienced only in shadows. After a time, he

[4] *Ibid.,* Bk. III, Sec. 415.
[5] *Ibid.,* Bk. III, Secs. 392, 394-396.
[6] *Ibid.,* Bk. III, Sec. 399.
[7] *Ibid.,* Bk. III, Secs. 416-417; Bk. V, Sec. 449.
[8] *Ibid.,* Bk. VII, Sec. 540.

returns to the cave and resumes his former duties and occupations, but now he can interpret the shadows for his fellow prisoners in terms of the reality he has come to know. So it is with the philosopher-kings in Plato's aristocratic state, and so it is with the intellectual elite in any society whose education is based upon this concept of Plato.

Some philosophers, however, point out that Plato uses the state as a symbol for mankind, and that *The Republic* is itself an allegory of the education of man. Lamprecht points out that Plato considered the social classes to represent the three divisions of the human soul.[9] The desires or passions represent the lowest class; the dynamic, energetic force corresponds to the soldier class; and the intelligence or reason is symbolized by the philosopher-kings. Only as man is ruled by his intellect will he attain a state of perfection. Plato pursues this triadic grouping further when he maintains that justice is composed of three elements: temperance, courage, and wisdom.[10] He further states that a good education should comprise music, gymnastics, and dialectic.[11]

Music for Plato was an intellectual discipline that included literature and history. Gymnastics was not only for physical development, but for morals as well. It disciplined the will and developed manliness and courage. Dialectic was a determined effort to systematize knowledge and to bring its various elements into logical relations with each other. It was a discipline reserved for those who were to be trained as magistrates.

Knowledge for Plato was a recollection, for men's souls existed as pure forms before they descended to earth to be imprisoned in the body. The highest vocation of man, therefore, was to seek to understand, to reconstruct, to recollect these pure forms. While the artisan or soldier thinks of circles, the geometrician contemplates the nature of the perfect circle. The person of lofty thoughts attaches little importance to the petty details of life.[12]

For Plato, knowledge of things as they really exist constituted a comprehension of form which suggested a philosophical monism.[13] That is, ideas are entities that exist before and are independent of their discovery by the human mind. This popular concept of Plato's epistemology has been questioned in recent

[9] Sterling P. Lamprecht, *Our Philosopical Tradition* (New York: Appleton-Century-Crofts, 1955), pp. 37-43.

[10] *The Republic,* Bk. IV, Secs. 428, 429, 430.

[11] *Ibid.,* Bk. II, Secs. 376-383; Bk. III, Secs. 383-414.

[12] *Ibid.,* Bk. VI, Sec. 486.

[13] *Ibid.,* Bk. VI, Sec. 484.

years.[14] Be that as it may, however, reality for Plato existed in the realm of ideas in pure form. Thus, although Plato did not specifically deny the existence of things outside the realm of ideas and admitted the difficulties of coming to a complete understanding of knowledge, his theory of ideas has been a starting point for much of the idealism of the present day. This theory was developed, perhaps transformed, into a system of idealistic monism by Plotinus (A.D. 205-270), who taught in Rome and is credited with establishing the Neoplatonic tradition.

Other philosophers of Plato's time were Protagoras (481-411 B.C.), who is famous for his remark, "man is the measure of all things"; Epicurus (341-355 B.C.) who founded the Epicurean school "The Gardens" and who extolled the life of contemplation as the greatest happiness; and Zeno of Citium (340-265 B.C.) whose school, "The Stoa," taught the doctrine of stoicism, which became the religious philosophy of imperial Rome. Plato's most famous pupil was Aristotle (384-322 B.C.).

The genius of Plato was so great that it has been very difficult for lesser minds to comprehend it entirely, which probably accounts for the many misconceptions of some of his theories. His emphasis on the unreality of the physical world had a tremendous influence on the thought of the early Middle Ages, and his interest in ideas has caused many a schoolman even to the present day to develop an abstract and theoretical educational program, forgetting all the while that Plato insisted that these abstract ideas should be translated into social action. His class education has found a parallel in many existing forms of European educational systems with their rigid systems of examinations and their emphasis at the university level on pure philosophy and science. On the other hand, Plato's emphasis on individualism has had a great effect on the Renaissance mind. Humanism and Protestantism derive much from Plato.

Through the Academy he founded in Athens, his influence spread through the ancient world. It was carried to Rome by Cicero (106-43 B.C.) and through Plotinus's Neoplatonism, it influenced St. Augustine (A.D. 354-430) and the medieval schoolmen.

The readings included in the text are from some of the philosophers studied. They are put here so that the student can taste the flavor of their work. The study of these selections should serve as an introduction to a more extensive reading. To this end lists of easily obtained paperbacks are included.

[14] See Lamprecht, *op. cit.,* p. 48.

Meno*

In this dialogue, Plato describes an experiment by Socrates in which he causes a slave boy to develop a simple theorem of geometry by a process of the recollection of innate ideas. Some critics[15] believe that Plato wrote this episode with tongue in cheek because the questioner asks leading questions which actually put the right answers into the boy's mouth. But most authorities believe the dialogue is intended to show that knowledge comes by way of insight, which Plato calls "recollection."

Men: Yes, Socrates; but what do you mean by saying that we do not learn, and that what we call learning is only a process of recollection? Can you teach me how this is?

Soc: I told you, Meno, just now that you were a rogue, and now you ask whether I can teach you, when I am saying that there is no teaching, but only recollection; and thus you imagine that you will involve me in a contradiction.

Men: Indeed, Socrates, I protest that I had no such intention. I only asked the question from habit; but if you can prove to me that what you say is true, I wish that you would.

Soc: It will be no easy matter, but I will try to please you to the utmost of my power. Suppose that you call one of your numerous attendants, that I may demonstrate on him.

Men: Certainly. Come hither, boy.

Soc: He is Greek, and speaks Greek, does he not?

Men: Yes, indeed; he was born in the house.

Soc: Attend now to the questions which I ask him, and observe whether he learns of me or only remembers.

Men: I will.

Soc: Tell me, boy, do you know that a figure like this is a square?

Boy: I do.

Soc: And you know that a square figure has these four lines equal?

Boy: Certainly.

Soc: And these lines which I have drawn through the middle of the square are also equal?

[15] See for example, Jerome Eckstein, *The Platonic Method* (New York: Greenwood, 1968).

Source: Plato, *Meno*, trans. B. Jowett with an introduction by F. H. Anderson (Indianapolis: Liberal Arts Press, Bobbs-Merrill, 1949) pp. 37-45.

Boy: Yes.

Soc: A square may be of any size?

Boy: Certainly.

Soc: And if one side of the figure be of two feet, and the other side be of two feet, how much will the whole be? Let me explain: if in one direction the space was of two feet, and in the other direction of one foot, the whole would be of two feet taken once?

Boy: Yes.

Soc: But since this side is also of two feet, there are twice two feet?

Boy: There are.

Soc: Then the square is of twice two feet?

Boy: Yes.

Soc: And how many are twice two feet? Count and tell me.

Boy: Four, Socrates.

Soc: And might there not be another square twice as large as this, and having like this the lines equal?

Boy: Yes.

Soc: And of how many feet will that be?

Boy: Of eight feet.

Soc: And now try and tell the length of the line which forms the side of that double square: this is two feet—what will that be?

Boy: Clearly, Socrates, it will be double.

Soc: Do you observe, Meno, that I am not teaching the boy anything, but only asking him questions; and now he fancies that he knows how long a line is necessary in order to produce a figure of eight square feet; does he not?

Men: Yes.

Soc: And does he really know?

Men: Certainly not.

Soc: He only guesses that because the square is double, the line is double.

Men: True.

Soc: Observe him while he recalls the steps in regular order. (*To the boy.*) Tell me, boy, do you assert that a double space comes from a double line? Remember that I am not speaking of an oblong, but of a figure equal every way, and twice the size of this—that is to say of eight feet; and I want to know whether you still say that a double square comes from a double line?

Boy: Yes.

Soc: But does not this line become doubled if we add another such line here?
Boy: Certainly.
Soc: And four such lines will make a space containing eight feet?
Boy: Yes.
Soc: Let us describe such a figure: Would you not say that this is the figure of eight feet?
Boy: Yes.
Soc: And are there not these four divisions in the figure, each of which is equal to the figure of four feet?
Boy: True.
Soc: And is not that four times four?
Boy: Certainly.
Soc: And four times is not double?
Boy: No, indeed.
Soc: But how much?
Boy: Four times as much.
Soc: Therefore the double line, boy, has given a space, not twice, but four times as much.
Boy: True.
Soc: Four times four are sixteen—are they not?
Boy: Yes.
Soc: What line would give you a space of eight feet, as this gives one of sixteen feet—do you see?
Boy: Yes.
Soc: And the space of four feet is made from this half line?
Boy: Yes.
Soc: Good; and is not a space of eight feet twice the size of this, and half the size of the other?
Boy: Certainly.
Soc: Such a space, then, will be made out of a line greater than this one, and less than that one?
Boy: Yes, I think so.
Soc: Very good; I like to hear you say what you think. And now tell me, is not this a line of two feet and that of four?
Boy: Yes.
Soc: Then the line which forms the side of eight feet ought to be more than this line of two feet, and less than the other of four feet?
Boy: It ought.
Soc: Mark now the further development. I shall only ask him, and not teach him, and he shall share the inquiry with me; and

do you watch and see if you find me telling or explaining anything to him, instead of eliciting his opinion. Tell me, boy, is not this square of four feet which I have drawn?

Boy: Yes.

Soc: And now I add another square equal to the former one?

Boy: Yes.

Soc: And a third, which is equal to either of them?

Boy: Yes.

Soc: Suppose that we fill up the vacant corner?

Boy: Very good.

Soc: Here, then, there are four equal spaces?

Boy: Yes.

Soc: And how many times larger is this space than this other?

Boy: Four times.

Soc: But it ought to have been twice only, as you will remember.

Boy: True.

Soc: And does not this line, reaching from corner to corner, bisect each of these spaces?

Boy: Yes.

Soc: And are there not here four equal lines which contain this space?

Boy: There are.

Soc: Look and see how much this space is.

Boy: I do not understand.

Soc: Has not each interior line cut off half of the four spaces?

Boy: Yes.

Soc: And how many spaces are there in this section?

Boy: Four.

Soc: And how many in this?

Boy: Two.

Soc: And four is how many times two?

Boy: Twice.

Soc: And this space is of how many feet?

Boy: Of eight feet.

Soc: And from what line do you get this figure?

Boy: From this.

Soc: That is, from the line which extends from corner to corner of the figure of four feet?

Boy: Yes.

Soc: And this is the line which the learned call the diagonal. And if this is the proper name, then you, Meno's slave, are prepared to affirm that the double space is the square of the diagonal?

Boy: Certainly, Socrates.

Soc: What do you say of him, Meno? Were not all these answers given out of his own head?

Men: Yes, they were all his own.

Soc: And yet, as we were just now saying, he did not know?

Men: True.

Soc: But still he had in him those notions of his—had he not?

Men: Yes.

Soc: Then he who does not know may still have true notions of that which he does not know?

Men: He has.

Soc: And at present these notions have just been stirred up in him, as in a dream; but if he were frequently asked the same questions, in different forms, he would know as well as anyone at last?

Men: I dare say.

Soc: Without anyone teaching him he will recover his knowledge for himself, if he is only asked questions?

Men: Yes.

Soc: And this spontaneous recovery of knowledge in him is recollection?

Men: True.

Soc: And this knowledge which he now has must he not either have acquired or always possessed?

Men: Yes.

Soc: But if he always possessed this knowledge he would always have known; or if he has acquired the knowledge he could not have acquired it in this life unless he has been taught geometry; for he may be made to do the same with all geometry and every other branch of knowledge. Now, has any one ever taught him all this? You must know about him if, as you say, he was born and bred in your house.

Men: And I am certain that no one ever did teach him.

Soc: And yet he has the knowledge?

Men: The fact, Socrates, is undeniable.

Soc: But if he did not acquire the knowledge in this life, then he must have had and learned it at some other time?

Men: Clearly he must.

Soc: Which must have been the time when he was not a man?

Men: Yes.

Soc: And if there have been always true thoughts in him, both at the time when he was and was not a man, which only need to be awakened into knowledge by putting questions to him, his soul must have always possessed this knowledge, for he

always either was or was not a man?
Men: Obviously.
Soc: And if the truth of all things always existed in the soul, then the soul is immortal. Wherefore be of good cheer and try to recollect what you do not know, or rather what you do not remember.
Men: I feel, somehow, that I like what you are saying.
Soc: And I, Meno, like what I am saying. Some things I have said of which I am not altogether confident. But that we shall be better and braver and less helpless if we think that we ought to inquire than we should have been if we indulged in the idle fancy that there was no knowing and no use in seeking to know what we do not know—that is a theme upon which I am ready to fight, in word and deed, to the utmost of my power.
Men: There again, Socrates, your words seem to me excellent.

ARISTOTLE

Aristotle (384-322 B.C.) was born in the Greek colony of Stagira in Macedon. At seventeen, he became the pupil of Plato in the Academy at Athens, where he remained for almost twenty years. He left Athens to become tutor to Alexander the Great, but returned in 335 to found the Lyceum, which he conducted for twelve years. In 323, anti-Maccdenonian feeling caused him to flee to Calchis, where he died a year later. Aristotle's work represents one of the greatest achievements of the human mind in the Western world and has materially influenced the ideas of men over two millennia. For his chief instrument of thought, Aristotle developed a science of Logic, based upon the syllogism which he elaborated in considerable detail. Although his syllogistic logic is almost entirely deductive, his overall philosophy of science presents a well-balanced union of deductive and inductive reasoning.

Aristotle maintained that reality ultimately consisted of many concrete individual things.[16] These, he thought, were real in a primary sense. In a derivative sense, he considered that the qualities of these things, their forms, and the relations among them were also real. All substances, then, consist of matter and form.

---

[16] Aristotle, *Physics*, Bk. VIII, especially Chs. 4-6. References to Aristotle's works have been taken from *The Basic Works of Aristotle*, ed. Richard McKeon (New York: Random House, 1941).

Matter is not some formless stuff as the atomists maintained, but is a way that real things differ from imaginary things and is a locus of potentialities that become actual through the activity of form.

The form of a substance is what makes it intelligible and therefore able to be known. When a man knows a substance, it is the form of the substance that is in his mind. The entire substance does not enter into the man's mind, but the form does. Conversely, a man has no right to assume that a substance exists because he has the idea or form in his mind, but he must substantiate the idea with sensory evidence.

Our thinking about the world is controlled by the nature of the world itself, which exhibits certain universal traits and relationships. These Aristotle listed as ten fundamental categories, namely: substance, quality, quantity, relation, place, time, action, possession, position, and condition.[17]

For Aristotle the highest good, "summum bonum," is the contemplation of truth. He uses the word *eudaemonia*[18] (happiness) for the moral ends men ought to pursue. The soul is not a substance but an action. A particular man is a substance, but his soul is what he does. Virtue is, therefore, a condition; particular instances of virtue are actions. The virtue of justice is a condition— the condition of having a well-established habit.

Basing his whole system of ethics upon this point, Aristotle maintained that ethics and politics are mutually dependent. Ethics examines how men may live best, but as man is by nature a political animal, it is in society that he finds his noblest fulfillment. States are formed to enable men to live; they are perpetuated to make them live well. An important function of the state is to educate its citizens.[19] Basic to education in a cultural and political sense is the development of right habits, which Aristotle considers man's second nature. Human nature consists of two aspects: the irrational and the rational. The irrational is what a person has no control over; any natural excellence is a matter of good fortune or luck. But the part that can be controlled by reason is moral virtue. The possession of well-established habits is what we mean by character; and character is good or bad according to the nature of the habits.[20] Character is, thus, the outcome of a long and consistent period of moral training.

---

[17] Aristotle, Organon, *Categoriae*, Chs. 1-9.
[18] Aristotle, *Nicomachean Ethics*, Bk. I, Chs. 1-5.
[19] Aristotle, *Politics*, Bk. VIII, Ch. I.
[20] *Ibid.*, Bk. VII, Ch. 13; Book VIII, Ch. 3.

Twenty-five Centuries of Educational Thought   CHART 1: THE ANCIENT GREEKS TO ST. JEROME

B.C. 600 500 400 300 200 100   A.D. 100 200 300 400 500

THALES 624-550 — Water is the basic stuff of reality
ANAXIMANDER 611-547 — Naturalist; anticipated modern theory of energy
ANAXIMENES 588-524 — Naturalist; air the basic substance of reality
PYTHAGORAS 572-497 — Astronomy; right angle triangle
HERACLITUS 535-475 — Law, the rational principle, pervades the universe; change the fundamental principle
PARMENIDES fl. 495 — Basic doctrine of idealism
ANAXAGORAS 500-428 — Pluralism of realities
EMPEDOCLES c. 495-435 — Four irreducible substances: earth, air, fire, water
ZENO OF ELEA 490-430 — Plurality and change impossible
PROTAGORAS 481-411 — Man is the measure of all things; relativism
DEMOCRITUS 460-370 — Atomist; explained world in mechanical terms
SOCRATES 469-399 — Theory of Ideas; Socratic method; freedom of thought
PLATO 427-347 — Rationalism
ARISTOTLE 365-275 — Skepticism
PYRRHO 361-270 — Happiness is the goal of life
EPICURUS 340-270 — Stoicism
ZENO OF CITIUM 335-265 — Transmitted Greek culture to Rome
CICERO 106-43 — Salvation through Jesus
ST. PAUL ?-64 — "Institutes of Oratory"
QUINTILIAN 35-95 — Stoicism; human will is one thing under man's control
EPICTITUS 60-117 — God's rational power given to all
FLAVIUS JUSTINIUS (Martyr) 105-165 — Stoic emperor; "Meditations"
MARCUS AURELIUS 121-180 — Aristotelian; medical science
GALEN 130-200 — Knowledge without faith does not exist
CLEMENT OF ALEXANDRIA ?-216 — Studied Plato; put faith above reason
TERTULLIAN 160-230 — Neoplatonist
PLOTINUS 205-270 — Monotheism; the Son subordinate to the Father
ARIUS 280-336 — Trinitarian
ST. ATHANASIUS 298-373 — Opposed Arius; converted Augustine
ST. AMBROSE 340-397 — Retranslated Bible into Latin—The Vulgate
ST. JEROME 344-420

14

Other functions of the state are to stabilize socially profitable policies in laws and to allow some citizens to live the contemplative life. The laws, when good, should be supreme[21] but the right to criticize the judicial and legislative powers of the state should be reserved to both rulers and citizens. "The nature of the state is to be a plurality."[22] Aristotle believed that the best men should be placed in the highest positions and that a balance of authority among groups should be maintained. The unity of the state should not be sought by coercion, but by fostering common purposes among the interacting and cooperating groups.

Life for Aristotle is the process of nutrition and growth. Therefore psychology can scarcely be separated from biology because the soul is the principle of life, the primary actualization of a natural body, the form of a natural body potential possessed by life. There are two types of souls: the nutritive and propagational, and the sensitive, which includes imagination, reason, thought, knowledge, and opinion.[23] Imagination he defined as a combination of knowledge and opinion, and reason as the faculty of apprehending the universals and first principles involved in all knowledge. All plants and animals have nutritive souls, all animals have sensitive souls, the higher animals have imagination by which their apparent rational behavior is explained, but men alone, unless there are beings superior to men, have reason or intellect. Since the mind is to know, it cannot have a form of its own. It is actually nothing before it thinks, but by thinking it becomes like its object. In other words, life (or soul) is the form of the living body, as cutting is the form or soul of the axe and as sight is the form or soul of the eye.[24]

The educator leads his pupil to discover where and of what

Chart 1. Note that in the three centuries between 600 and 300 B.C. the basis of Western philosophy was laid in Greece. There is a fallow period so far as creative thought is concerned for more than a hundred years before Cicero brought Greek thought to Rome, followed by almost a century of silence until St. Paul wrote his epistles to give substance to Christian theology. From the first to the fourth centuries of our era, we can trace the rivalry between pagan and Christian thought and the doctrinal disputes among the Church fathers, especially regarding the Trinity. St. Jerome's translation of the Scriptures produced a document upon which the commentaries of the scholastics could be based for over a thousand years.

[21] *Ibid.*, Bk. III, Ch. II.
[22] *Ibid.*
[23] Aristotle, *De Anima,* Bk. II, Ch. 4.
[24] *Ibid.*, Bks. II and III.

kind his creative powers are and helps him to become a living form. This forming energy, entelechy, enables a person to grow organically toward the realization of his inherent form.

Education begins with health and a sound physique. Therefore, good diet and exercise are essential, as are heredity and good race, for they are basic to a sound body. The pupil must submit to all suggestions, exercises, and disciplines of the master, for these are necessary to the development of his moral and intellectual character. The master must also lead a disciplined life, for Aristotle maintains that the teacher learns what he teaches.[25]

Happiness (*eudaemonia*) comes only from a well-balanced, productive life. The teacher directs the unreflective energy of the young child so that the constructive powers are developed and the destructive are negated. The regulation of the passions is a matter of habituation or conditioning.

Methods of teaching properly begin with what is most knowable to man and develop toward what is most knowable in itself, from empirical observation to contemplation of form.

Education ends in reason, but the reason of the adult determines the method and material for the training of youth. Education teaches one to avoid excesses and to adhere to the golden mean. Wisdom is a combination of intuitive and scientific knowledge used as a guide to the solution of the practical problems of life.

Aristotle was inclined to consider himself a Platonist. Both men agreed that all nature could be explained teleologically. However, Aristotle did not believe, as Plato seemed to, that there was one supreme principle from which all knowledge of nature could be brought into one complete system. The difference here may be one of degree. Plato enumerates five fundamental relationships or categories based upon his theory of ideas, namely: being, same, other, rest, and motion; Aristotle developed ten based upon empirical observation, namely: substance, quality, quantity, relation, space, time, activity, possession, position, and passivity or condition.

Plato used mathematics as a model for thinking. His philosophy deals with universals and envisions ideal ends. Beginning with man, he viewed the world as a setting for man's search for the ideal. He recognized the science of his day only as it fitted in with his scheme of knowledge. He conceived of truth as a recollection.

Aristotle was a zoologist. He was fascinated by things, in-

[25] *Politics*, Bk. VII, Chs. 13-17; Bk. VIII, Chs. 1-7.

terested in particulars, and absorbed in present actualities. Beginning with nature, he viewed man as a specialized case, at once typical of and distinctive from nature's general ways. He advanced the cause of science by his detailed observation, studies, realistic analyses, and writings. He conceived of truth as a construct from first steps and observation, and by his system of philosophy lifted things up to ultimate truth.

The German poet Heinrich Heine considered Plato and Aristotle as representative of two different kinds of human nature, the former contemplative and mystical, and the latter practical and systematic. He assigns the individualistic, visionary, creative spirit to Platonism and the dogmatic, institutional spirit to Aristotelianism.[26] Although the distinctions between the two philosophers are not so sharp and plain as Heine would have it, in the main, the development of Western thought clearly shows an admixture of their two points of view. "Like a splendid sonnet sequence in literature, the moral and metaphysical movement of Greek life at its height passes from the quest of Socrates through the faith of Plato to the systematization of Aristotle."[27]

Politics*

Aristotle proposes that education be the business of the state for the training of its future citizens. He describes education in several Greek states and outlines what he considers a good educational program.

No one will doubt that the legislator should direct his attention above all to the education of youth; for the neglect of education does harm to the constitution. The citizen should be moulded to suit the form of government under which he lives. For each government has a peculiar character which originally formed and which continues to preserve it. The character of democracy creates democracy, and the character of oligarchy creates oligarchy; and always the better the character, the better the government.

[26]See Robert Ulich, *History of Educational Thought* (New York: American Book, 1945), pp. 25-26.
[27]T. V. Smith, *From Thales to Plato* (Chicago: University of Chicago Press, 1956), p. 70.
Source: Aristotle, *Politics*, Bk. VIII, Chs. 1-4, in *The Basic Works of Aristotle*, ed. with an introduction by Richard McKeon (New York: Random House, 1941).

Again, for the exercise of any faculty or art a previous training and habituation are required; clearly therefore for the practice of virtue. And since the whole city has one end, it is manifest that education should be one and the same for all, and that it should be public, and not private—not as at present, when every one looks after his own children separately, and gives them separate instruction of the sort which he thinks best; the training in things which are of common interest should be the same for all. Neither must we suppose that any one of the citizens belongs to himself, for they all belong to the state, and are each of them a part of the state, and the care of each part is inseparable from the care of the whole. In this particular as in some others the Lacedaemonians are to be praised, for they take the greatest pains about their children, and make education the business of the state.

That education should be regulated by law and should be an affair of state is not to be denied, but what should be the character of this public education, and how young persons should be educated, are questions which remain to be considered. As things are, there is disagreement about the subjects. For mankind are by no means agreed about the things to be taught, whether we look to virtue or the best life. Neither is it clear whether education is more concerned with intellectual or with moral virtue. The existing practice is perplexing; no one knows on what principle we should proceed—should the useful in life, or should virtue, or should the higher knowledge, be the aim of our training; all three opinions have been entertained. Again, about the means there is no agreement; for different persons, starting with different ideas about the nature of virtue naturally disagree about the practice of it. There can be no doubt that children should be taught those useful things which are really necessary, but not all useful things; for occupations are divided into liberal and illiberal; and to young children should be imparted only such kinds of knowledge as will be useful to them without vulgarizing them. And any occupation, art, or science, which makes the body or soul or mind of the freeman less fit for the practice or exercise of virtue, is vulgar; wherefore we call those arts vulgar which tend to deform the body, and likewise all paid employments, for they absorb and degrade the mind. There are also some liberal arts quite proper for a freeman to acquire, but only in a certain degree, and if he attend to them too closely, in order

to attain perfection in them, the same evil effects will follow.
The object also which a man sets before him makes a great
difference; if he does or learns anything for his own sake or for
the sake of his friends, or with a view to excellence, the action
will not appear illiberal; but if done for the sake of others, the
very same action will be thought menial and servile. The
received subjects of instruction, as I have already remarked,
are partly of a liberal and partly of an illiberal character.

The customary branches of education are in number four; they
are—(1) reading and writing, (2) gymnastic exercises, (3)
music, to which is sometimes added (4) drawing. Of these,
reading and writing and drawing are regarded as useful for the
purposes of life in a variety of ways, and gymnastic exercises
are thought to infuse courage. Concerning music a doubt may
be raised—in our own day most men cultivate it for the sake of
pleasure, but originally it was included in education, because
nature herself, as has been often said, requires that we should
be able, not only to work well, but to use leisure well; for, as I
must repeat once again, the first principle of all action is
leisure. Both are required, but leisure is better than occupation
and is its end; and therefore the question must be asked, what
ought we to do when at leisure? Clearly we ought not to be
amusing ourselves, for then amusement would be the end of
life. But if this is inconceivable, and amusement is needed
more amid serious occupations than at other times (for he who
is hard at work has need of relaxation, and amusement gives
relaxation, whereas occupation is always accompanied with
exertion and effort), we should introduce amusements only at
suitable times, and they should be our medicines, for the
emotion which they create in the soul is a relaxation, and from
the pleasure we obtain rest. But leisure of itself gives pleasure
and happiness and enjoyment of life, which are experienced,
not by the busy man, but by those who have leisure. For he
who is occupied has in view some end which he has not
attained; but happiness is an end, since all men deem it to be
accompanied with pleasure and not with pain. This pleasure,
however, is regarded differently by different persons, and
varies according to the habit of individuals; the pleasure of the
best man is the best, and springs from the noblest sources. It is
clear then that there are branches of learning and education
which we must study merely with a view to leisure spent in
intellectual activity, and these are to be valued for their own

sake; whereas those kinds of knowledge which are useful in business are to be deemed necessary, and exist for the sake of other things. And therefore our fathers admitted music into education, not on the ground either of its necessity or utility, for it is not necessary, nor indeed useful in the same manner as reading and writing, which are useful in money-making, in the management of a household, in the acquisition of knowledge and in political life, nor like drawing, useful for a more correct judgement of the works of artists, nor again like gymnastics, which gives health and strength; for neither of these is to be gained from music. There remains, then, the use of music for intellectual enjoyment in leisure; which is in fact evidently the reason of its introduction, this being one of the ways in which it is thought that a freeman should pass his leisure; as Homer says—

'But he who alone should be called to the pleasant feast',
and afterwards he speaks of others whom he describes as
     inviting 'The bard who would delight them all'.

And in another place Odysseus says there is no better way of passing life than when men's hearts are merry and

'The banqueters in the hall, sitting in order, hear the voice of the minstrel'.

It is evident, then, that there is a sort of education in which parents should train their sons, not as being useful or necessary, but because it is liberal or noble. Whether this is of one kind only, or of more than one, and if so, what they are, and how they are to be imparted, must hereafter be determined. Thus much we are now in a position to say, that the ancients witness to us; for their opinion may be gathered from the fact that music is one of the received and traditional branches of education. Further, it is clear that children should be instructed in some useful things—for example, in reading and writing—not only for their usefulness, but also because many other sorts of knowledge are acquired through them. With a like view they may be taught drawing, not to prevent their making mistakes in their own purchases, or in order that they may not be imposed upon in the buying or selling of articles, but perhaps rather because it makes them judges of the beauty of the human form. To be always seeking after the useful does not become free and exalted souls. Now it is clear that in education practice must be used before theory, and the body be trained before the mind; and therefore boys should be handed over to the trainer, who creates in them the proper habit of body, and to the wrestling-master, who teaches them their exercises.

QUINTILIAN

Between the death of Aristotle (322 B.C.) and the birth of Quintilian (A.D. 35) there is a span of some 350 years during which time Greece came under the political domination of Rome (146 B.C.). But though the Roman legionnaires trod the streets of Athens, it was the Greek mind and the Greek culture that conquered Rome. The great orator Cicero (106-43 B.C.) was among those who brought Greek philosophy and literature to the Roman citizens who adopted the Greek language and the philosophy of stoicism. The orations of Cicero are lasting monuments to the purity of the Latin language and have become models for all subsequent rhetoricians.

As the empire spread over the ancient world, Latin became impure by mixing with the dialects of the conquered peoples. Vespasian (Roman emperor, A.D. 69-79) recognized the importance of a standard language for the ruling class, and for this and other reasons established "a chair of oratory" in Rome, to which he called Quintilian from Spain in A.D. 70.

Quintilian (A.D. 35-95), the Roman rhetorician, has been called the Schoolmaster of the West. He followed in the tradition of the Stoics and the sophists and wrote the *Institutes of Oratory* for the practical training of orators. This work has been a standard textbook for teachers and orators since the Renaissance. Quintilian believed in accepting a situation as one found it, and taught that moral standards and responsibilities do not spring from meditation, but from action.

Quintilian suggested that a principle of order exists behind the visible world and that a thorough knowledge of the natural world is the basis for ethics. He insisted that a good orator must be a good man. Concerning education, he recommended that from his earliest years a boy should be surrounded by the affectionate care of family, friends, nurse, and tutor; in this environment he would learn to speak Greek and Latin. Formal education should begin at six or seven, in a school where the boy could have the benefit of associating with his peers. Here he should learn to read, write, and participate in games and nature study. The third phase of education, usually in a separate grammar school (but not recommended by Quintilian), included elementary mathematics, astronomy, music, literature, and grammar. When the boy was thoroughly prepared, usually at sixteen or a year or two before, he should enter the school of rhetoric. On the training of teachers of oratory Quintilian wrote that the ideal teacher should have the following qualifications:

1. He should assume a parental attitude toward his pupil.
2. He should be free from vice and refuse to tolerate it in others.
3. He should be strict but not austere.
4. He should be genial but not familiar.
5. He should speak of what is honorable, for the more he admonishes the less he will have to punish.
6. He should control his temper.
7. He should be free from affectation.
8. He should be possessed of great industry.
9. His demands on his class should be continuous, but not extravagant.

The Institutes of Oratory*

Quintilian sets forth in great detail the education of a perfect orator, who must first be a good man. After stating some general principles, he pleads for class instruction over individual instruction by a tutor. He remarks on the qualities of a good student and a good teacher, and condemns corporal punishment.

My aim, then, is the education of the perfect orator. The first essential for such a one is that he should be a good man, and consequently we demand of him not merely the possession of exceptional gifts of speech, but of all the excellence of character as well. ... The man who can really play his part as a citizen and is capable of meeting the demands of both public and private business, the man who can guide a state by his counsels, give it a firm basis by his legislation and purge its vices by his decisions as a judge, is assuredly no other than the orator of our quest ... wherever imaginative power and am-

Source: Quintilian, *The Institutes of Oratory*, Bk. I, Sec. 1-10, trans. H.E. Butler, Loeb Classical Library (Cambridge: Harvard University Press, 1953).

plitude of diction are required, the orator has a specially important part to play. . . .

As soon as speaking becomes a means of livelihood and the practice of making an evil use of the blessings of eloquence came into vogue, those who had a reputation for eloquence ceased to study moral philosophy; and ethics, thus abandoned by the orators, became the prey of weaker intellects . . . certain persons, disdaining the toil of learning to speak well, returned to the task of forming character and establishing rules of life. . . .

Let our ideal orator then be such as to have a genuine title to the name of philosopher: it is not sufficient that he should be blameless in point of character . . . he must also be a thorough master of the science and the art of speaking, to an extent that perhaps no orator has yet attained. Perfect eloquence is assuredly a reality, which is not beyond the reach of human intellect.

•   •   •   •   •

Without natural gifts technical rules are useless. There are, it is true, other natural gifts, such as the possession of a good voice and robust lungs, sound health, powers of endurance and grace, and if these are possessed only to a moderate extent, they may be improved by methodical training . . . these gifts . . . are no profit in themselves unless cultivated by skillful teaching, persistent study and continuous and extensive practice in writing, reading and speaking.

I would, therefore, have a father conceive the highest hopes of his son from the moment of his birth. If he does so, he will be more careful about the groundwork of his education. For there is absolutely no foundation for the complaint that but few men have the power to take in the knowledge that is imparted to them, and that the majority are so slow of understanding that education is a waste of time and labour. On the contrary you will find that most are quick to reason and ready to learn. Reasoning comes as naturally to man as flying to birds, speed to horses and ferocity to beasts of prey: our minds are endowed by nature with such activity and sagacity that the soul is believed to proceed from heaven. Those who are dull and unteachable . . . are but few in number . . . boys commonly show promise of many accomplishments, and when such promise dies away as they grow up, this is plainly due not to the failure of natural gifts, but to lack of the requisite care. But, it will be urged, there are degrees of talent. Undoubtedly,

I reply and there will be a corresponding variation in actual accomplishment: but that there are any who gain nothing from education, I absolutely deny.

•   •   •   •   •

It is no easy task to create an orator, even though his education be carried out under the most favourable circumstances. . . .

I prefer that a boy should begin with Greek, because Latin, being in general use, will be picked up by him whether we will or no; while the fact that Latin learning is derived from Greek is a further reason for his being first instructed in the latter. . . .

Some hold that boys should not be taught to read till they are seven years old . . . Those however who hold that a child's mind should not be allowed to lie fallow for a moment are wiser. . . .

Above all things we must take care that the child, who is not yet old enough to love his studies, does not come to hate them and dread the bitterness which he has once tasted, even when the years of infancy are left behind. His studies must be made an amusement: he must be questioned and praised and taught to rejoice when he has done well; sometimes too, when he refuses instruction, it should be given to some other to excite his envy, at times also he must be engaged in competition and should be allowed to believe himself successful more often than not, while he should be encouraged to do his best by such rewards as may appeal to his tender years. . . .

But studies, like men, have their infancy, and as the training of the body which is destined to grow to the fulness of strength begins while the child is in his cradle and at his mother's breast, so even the man who is destined to rise to the heights of eloquence was once a squalling babe, tried to speak in stammering accents and was puzzled by the shapes of letters. Nor does the fact that capacity for learning is inadequate, prove that it is not necessary to learn anything . . . Small children are better adapted for taking in small things, and just as the body can only be trained to certain flexions of the limbs while it is young and supple, so the acquisition of strength makes the mind offer greater resistance to the acquisition of most subjects of knowledge . . . even the earliest instruction is best given by the most perfect teacher . . . every man's child deserves equal attention.

. . . I am not satisfied with the course . . . of teaching small children the names and order of the letters before their shapes.

... It will be best therefore for children to begin by learning their appearance and names just as they do with men.

But the time has come for the boy to grow up little by little, to leave the nursery and tackle his studies in good earnest ... there are some who disagree with this preference for public education owing to a certain prejudice in favour of private tuition. These persons seem to be guided in the main by two principles. In the interest of morality they would avoid the society of a number of human beings at an age that is specially liable to acquire serious faults. ... Secondly they hold that whoever is to be the boy's teacher, he will devote his time more generously to one pupil than if he has to divide it among several. ... If it were proved that schools, while advantageous to study, are prejudicial to morality, I should give my vote for virtuous living in preference to even supreme excellence of speaking. ... I hold that no one can be a true orator unless he is also a good man and, even if he could be, I would not have it so. ...

It is held that schools corrupt the morals. ... But morals may be corrupted at home as well.

•   •   •   •   •

Would that we did not too often ruin our children's character ourselves! We spoil them from the cradle. That soft upbringing, which we call kindness, saps all the sinews both of mind and body. ...

In the first place there is nothing to prevent the principle of "one teacher, one boy" being combined with school education. And even if such a combination should prove impossible, I should still prefer the broad daylight of a respectable school to the solitude and obscurity of a private education. For all the best teachers pride themselves on having a large number of pupils. ... On the other hand in the case of inferior teachers a consciousness of their own defects reconciles them to being attached to a single pupil. ...

By far the larger proportion of the learner's time ought to be devoted to private study. The teacher does not stand over him while he is writing or thinking or learning by heart ... not all reading requires to be first read aloud or interpreted by a master ... consequently individual instruction can be given to more than one pupil. The voice of a lecturer is not like a dinner which will only suffice for a limited number; it is like the sun which distributes the same quantity of light and heat to all of us. So too with the teacher of literature. Whether he speak of style or expound disputed passages, explain stories or paraphrase poems, everyone who hears him will profit by his teaching. . . .

But a good teacher will . . . make his teaching not a duty but a labour of love.

• • • • •

For eloquence depends in the main on the state of the mind . . . the loftier and the more elevated the mind, the more powerful will be the forces which move it. . . .

The skillful teacher will make it his first care, as soon as a boy is entrusted to him, to ascertain his ability and character. The surest indication in a child is his power of memory. The characteristics of a good memory are twofold: it must be quick to take in and faithful to retain impressions of what it receives. The indication of next importance is the power of imitation: for this is a sign that the child is teachable. . . . For I have no hope that a child will turn out well who loves imitation merely for the purpose of raising a laugh. He who is really gifted will also above all else be good. . . .

I regard slowness of intellect as preferable to actual bad-ness. . . . My ideal pupil will absorb instruction with ease and will even ask some questions; but he will follow rather than anticipate his teacher. Precocious intellects rarely produce sound fruit.

• • • • •

I approve of play in the young; it is a sign of a lively disposition; nor will you ever lead me to believe that a boy who is gloomy and in a continual state of depression is ever likely to show alertness of mind in his work. . . .

I disapprove of flogging, . . . it is a disgraceful form of punishment and fit only for slaves. . . . Secondly, if a boy is so insensible to instruction that reproof is useless, he will, like the worst type of slave, merely become hardened to blows. Finally there will be absolutely no need of such punishment if the master is a thorough disciplinarian . . . what are you to do with him when he is a young man no longer amenable to such threats and confronted with tasks of far greater difficulty? . . . children are helpless and easily victimised, and that therefore no one should be given unlimited power over them.

• • • • •

I am not describing any orator who actually exists or has existed, but have in my mind's eye an ideal orator, perfect down to the smallest detail. . . .

It will be agreed that though our ideal of perfection may

dwell on a height that is hard to gain, it is our duty to teach all we know, that achievement may at least come somewhat nearer the goal.

BIBLIOGRAPHY

PLATO

Bosanquet, Bernard, *A Companion to Plato's Republic for English Readers* (London: Rivingtons, 1925).

Bryan, W. S., and C. L. Bryan, *Plato the Teacher* (New York: Scribner, 1897).

Dent, J. M. (ed.), *Socratic Discourses of Plato* (New York: Everyman Edition, Dutton, 1913).

*Eckstein, Jerome, *The Platonic Method* (New York: Greenwood, 1968).

Fehl, Noah Edward, *A Guide to the Study of Plato's Republic and the Socratic Dialogues* (Hong Kong: Chung Chi College, Chinese University of Hong Kong, 1965).

Field, Guy Cromwell, *Plato and His Contemporaries; a Study of Fourth Century Life and Thought* (New York: Dutton, 1930).

Livingston, Sir Richard Winn, *Plato and Modern Education* (Cambridge, England: University of Cambridge Press, 1944).

Lodge, Rupert Clendon, *Plato's Theory of Education* (London: L. Paul, Trench, Trubner, 1947).

Nettleship, Richard Lewis, *The Theory of Education in the Republic of Plato* (New York: Oxford University Press, 1933).

*Plato, *Great Dialogues of Plato*, trans. W. H. Rouse (New York: Mentor Books, New American Library, 1956).

*——, *Meno*, trans. B. Jowett with an introduction by F. H. Anderson (Indianapolis: Liberal Arts Press, Bobbs-Merrill, 1949).

*——, *Plato's Republic*, ed. I. A. Richard, (New York: Cambridge University Press, 1966).

*——, *Plato's Theory of Knowledge [Theaetetus; Sophist]* trans. F. M. Cornford (Indianapolis: Liberal Arts Press, Bobbs-Merrill, 1957).

*——, *Republic*, trans. H. D. Lee (New York: Penguin Books, 1966).

*——, *Republic*, trans. B. Jowett (New York: Vintage Books, Random House, n.d.).

ARISTOTLE

Anscombe, Gertrude E. M., *Three Philosophers* (Oxford, England: P. T. Geach, 1961).

*Aristotle, *Aristotle on Education: Extracts from Ethics and Politics*, ed. J. Burnet (Cambridge University Press, 1967).

*——, *Ethics One: Politics One* (Chicago: Gateway Editions, Regnery, 1963).

*——, *Introduction to Aristotle*, ed. R. McKeon (New York: Modern Library College Editions, Random House, 1947).

*——, *Philosophy of Aristotle*, ed. R. Bambrough (New York: Mentor Books, New American Library, 1967).

Davidson, Thomas, *Aristotle and Ancient Educational Ideals* (New York:

Scribner, 1907).

Ellis, William (ed.), *A Treatise on Government* (New York: Dutton, 1935).

*Frankena, William K., *Three Historical Philosophies of Education* (Chicago: Scott, Foresman, 1965).

Shute, Clarence William, *The Psychology of Aristotle* (New York: Columbia University Press, 1941).

QUINTILIAN

Butler, H. E. (ed.), *The Institutio Oratoria*, 4 vols., Loeb Classical Library (Cambridge: Harvard University Press, 1921).

Gwynn, Aubrey Osborn, *Roman Education from Cicero to Quintilian* (New York: Teachers College Press, 1966).

Horne, Herman Harrell (ed.), *Quintilian on Education* (New York: New York University Book Store, n.d.).

*Smail, William M. (ed.), *Quintilian on Education* (New York: Teachers College Press, 1966).

*Watson, John Selby, *Quintilianus, Marcus Fabius, On the Early Education of the Citizen Orator* (Indianapolis: Bobbs-Merrill, 1965).

*Paperback editions.

Chapter Two
The Middle Ages: Augustine and Aquinas

THE EARLY YEARS of the Christian era saw the gradual disintegration of Rome from a universal empire through barbarian invasions from the north and decay from within. The center of culture moved from Europe to the northern coast of Africa where Plotinus (A.D. 205-270), first at Alexandria and later at Rome, based an adjustment to the altered conditions of life in his time on the classical Greek philosophers, chiefly Plato. Starting from the super-rational, which he called God, he proceeded to build a scale of reality through mind and soul to matter. All things come from God. Matter, which is farthest from God, is the source of evil, but it is not wholly so, because it is derived from God. It is the better part of wisdom to treat the body and whatever partakes of matter with contempt and to concentrate on the things of the spirit, which are nearer the Source of Being. Philosophy, said Plotinus, is a way of salvation whereby men can climb, step by step, the steep road that leads from the evil world to the realm of absolute good. Plotinus also developed a theory of psychology dealing with sensation, imagination, memory, and thought. The good life consists of reflection, good works, and finally, the mystical experience, which is rarely given to men. His doctrine, edited by Porphyry (A.D. 233-304), was for many years a strong rival of Christianity.

Christian philosophy was rapidly gaining a foothold, first among slaves and freedmen, but eventually among the rich and well educated. The emperor Constantine accepted Christianity in 324 A.D. and moved his capital to Byzantium in 330. Pagan schools were closed by the decree of Theodosius in 390. It was during this period that St. Augustine transformed the philosophy of Plotinus into a Christian ethic and became the architect of the Christian church and its theology.

ST. AUGUSTINE

In St. Augustine (A.D. 354-430), considered by many to be the greatest of the Church fathers, the Platonic tradition and Christianity blended constructively. For him, knowledge of the self is immediate and indubitable. As in Plotinus, ideas are real entities and present themselves through revelation. "Divine illumination takes the place in Augustine's thought of reminiscence in the Platonic philosophy."[1]

"Plato," writes Lamprecht, "is the locus classicus in history for a vision of the spiritual values which define the ideal fulfillment of man's natural resources and powers, Plotinus is the locus classicus in history for the argument that in spite of the seeming multiplicity of finite existences everything has its respective status in one all inclusive and spiritual world, St. Augustine is the locus classicus in history for the faith that above and beyond all changes in the lives of men lie the wisdom and the goodness of one spiritual power."[2]

Through St. Augustine, Neoplatonism passed into the life of the Church and of the Western world. Amended by St. Thomas and restated by Luther and Calvin, its influence is felt to the present day. He held with Plato a belief in a super-sensible world. He believed in the depravity of man. "God created man upright. He is the author of all natures insofar as they are, but certainly not of the blemishes in them. But man, having become deliberately depraved and justly condemned begat depraved and condemned children."[3]

Since children are thus depraved, the pathway to true knowledge is hard. They must be disciplined for there is no learning

[1] Frederick Copleston, S.J., *A History of Philosophy* (London: Burns, 1950), II, 64.
[2] Sterling P. Lamprecht, *Our Philosophical Tradition* (New York: Appleton-Century-Crofts, 1955), p. 146.
[3] St. Augustine, *The City of God*, ed. Vernon J. Burke (Garden City, N.Y.: Doubleday, 1958), Bk. XII, Ch. 14.

without punishment. The birch, the strap, the cane are necessary
to subdue the child. Only by such means is it possible to overcome
ignorance and bridle evil desires—these evils with which we come
into the world.[4]

The main thrust of St. Augustine's educational philosophy is
stress on inwardness. Learning occurs not so much through
observation of the external world of nature as by looking inward
and upward to know God and His truth. In the beginning of the
Confessions he cries:

> For thou hast made us for
> Thyself and our hearts are restless
> till they rest in Thee. Grant me,
> O Lord, to know which is the soul's
> first movement towards Thee—
> to implore Thy aid or to utter
> its praise: and whether it
> must know Thee before it
> can implore. For it would
> seem clear that no one can
> call upon thee without
> knowing Thee, for if he did he
> might invoke another than
> Thee, knowing Thee not.[5]

The teacher's first task is to stimulate soul searching. The
student should strive for dignity of thought rather than eloquence.
Having been a teacher of rhetoric himself, St. Augustine remarks
that the classical ends of rhetoric are amusement or delight,
action, and thought. He recommends that man should take delight
in the thoughts of the inner man, asserting that man's true dignity
resides in reason and his motivation to do God's will. The gift of
God's grace makes this possible. Christ is the interior master or
teacher, the source of all truth, and illumination comes through
Him. The Christian man is free when he operates according to the
rules of his own spiritual nature. The liberal arts stimulate
thoughts that enable him to do this.

St. Augustine recommended that the learning of ancient Rome
be mastered for its use in living the Christian life. History, natural
philosophy, logic, grammar, rhetoric, arithmetic, even philosophy,
were recommended, because these studies, if carefully pursued,

[4] *Ibid.,* Bk. XXIII, Ch. 12, *passim.*
[5] St. Augustine, *The Confessions of St. Augustine,* trans. F.J. Sheed (New York:
Sheed and Ward, 1943) p. 3.

will show the difference between knowledge and superstition. "For it is one thing to say: If you bruise down this herb and drink it, it will remove the pain from your stomach; and another to say: If you hang this herb around your neck it will remove the pain from your stomach. In the former case the wholesome mixture is approved of, in the latter the superstitious charm is condemned."[6] Study of all these subjects must be carefully guarded and subject always to the authority of the Scripture and of the Church, because sense and reason without faith lead to error.

Although he supported the current belief that the aim of all education was to prepare man for the life after death through an understanding and practice of the Christian virtues, chiefly faith, hope, charity, and humility, he maintained that the truly educated man was one who was capable of forming a consistent unity out of all arts and knowledge and who could experience the essential unity between reason and faith. Only after merging with the great laws of the universe can man dare to behold the face of God. The rule of St. Augustine and his reliance on faith and revelation profoundly influenced the educational pattern of the Middle Ages.

Concerning the Teacher*

In the first selection, St. Augustine asks his son Adeodatus to summarize the discussion so far. He distinguishes between words and their meanings and signs and that which they signify. The student cannot learn except by direct contact with things or situations. The teacher's words will not teach him anything without this contact.

In the second selection he poses the interesting question of whether one can teach what he does not know by using the words of another who does comprehend them. He stresses the importance of the use of words in expression and communication. The dialogue ends with reference to Jesus as the Master Teacher: ". . . when He spoke among the people He reminded us that we learn whether things are true from that one only whose habitation is within us, whom now, by His grace, I shall so love more ardently as I progress in understanding."

[6]St. Augustine, *Of Christian Doctrine,* trans. Sister Thérèse Sullivan (Washington, D.C.: Catholic University of America, 1930), Bk. II, Ch. 26.

Source: St. Augustine, *Concerning the Teacher: On the Immortality of the Soul,* trans. George Leckie (New York: Appleton, 1938), pp. 26-29, 51-52.

Aug: Now I wish to review what we have discovered by means of this discussion.

Ad: I shall do it in so far as I can. I remember that first of all we asked for what reason we speak. And it was found that we speak for the sake of teaching or reminding, since when we question we only do it that he who is asked may learn what we wish to hear; and that singing, which we seem to do for pleasure, is not properly speaking; that in praying to God whom we cannot suppose to be taught or reminded, words are for the purpose either of reminding ourselves or that others may be taught or reminded through us. . . . We came to those things which are shown to the questioner by pointing the finger. I thought that these included all corporeal things, but we found that they are only the visible things. From here we went on, I do not know just how, to deaf men and actors who signify by gesture and without the use of words, not only things which can be seen, but also many others and almost everything that we say. Still we found that gestures themselves are signs. Then again we began to inquire how we can show without any signs the things themselves which are signified by the signs; since wall, and color, and everything visible that is shown by pointing the finger were all proved to be shown by a certain sign. I erred in having said that nothing of this sort could be found, and at length we agreed that those things can be shown without a sign, which we are not in the act of doing when we are asked about them and which we can do after being asked. But speaking does not belong to this genus. For if, while we are in the act of speaking, we are asked what speaking is, it is quite evident that it is easy to show it by means of itself.

By this we were reminded that either signs show signs, or they show other things which are not signs, or else without a sign are shown things which we can do after we are questioned. And we undertook to investigate and discuss the first of these three more thoroughly. In this discussion it was revealed that the signs are in part those which cannot in turn be signified by means of those signs which they signify, as in the four-syllable word conjunctio (conjunction); in part, the signs are those which can in turn be signified by means of those signs which they signify, as when we say "sign," we also signify word (verbum), and when we say "word" we also signify sign; for sign and word are both two signs and two words. It was shown, moreover, that in this genus in which signs signify each other mutually, some mean not as much, some mean just as much, and some mean exactly the same thing. For the two-syllable word sign (signum) signifies absolutely everything by means of which anything is signified. Word (verbum) is not, however, a sign of all signs, but only of those which are uttered by the articulate voice; consequently, it is clear that although word (verbum) is signified by sign (signum) and sign by word, namely, the two former syllables by the latter two and the latter two by the former two, yet sign (signum) means more than word (verbum), for more things are signified by the latter two. But word in general means just as much as noun in general. For our reasoning taught us that all parts of speech are also nouns; for pronouns can be added to them, and it can be said of all that they name something; and there is none of them which cannot make a complete proposition when a verb is added to it. But although word (verbum) and noun (nomen) mean just the same amount because all things which are words are also names, yet they do not mean the same thing. It was argued, and with sufficient reason, that things are called words for one reason and nouns for another, since the former were found to be impressed on the vibration of the ear, but the latter on the memory of the mind; and this can be understood from the fact that in talking we correctly say "What is the name of this thing?" when we wish to commit it to memory, whereas we do not say "What is the word of this thing?"

●   ●   ●   ●   ●

From what has been said it follows, therefore, that in the case of those things which are grasped by the mind, anyone who is unable to grasp them hears to no purpose the words of him who does discern them; though we may make an exception in regard to the fact that where such things are unknown there is a certain utility in believing them until they are known. On the other hand, whoever can discern those things which are grasped by the mind is inwardly a pupil of truth and outwardly a judge of the speaker, or rather of his statements. For often he knows what has been said, though the speaker himself does not know; as if, for example, someone who is a follower of Epicurus and so thinks that the soul is mortal, should recite the arguments on the soul's immortality expounded by men of greater wisdom. If someone who is versed in spiritual things hears the speaker state the argument for the immortality of the soul, he will judge that true things have been said, but the speaker does not know that they are true; for, to the contrary, he thinks that they are quite false. Can he be understood as teaching what he does not know? He does use, however, the very same words which one who understood would use.

Now, therefore, not even this is left to words, namely, that at any rate they express the mind of the speaker, since a speaker may indeed not know the things about which he speaks. Consider also lying and deceiving, and you will easily understand from both of them that words not only do not disclose the true intention of the mind, but that they may serve to conceal it. For I by no means doubt that by words truthful men try, and to some extent do contrive, to disclose their minds, which would be accomplished, as all agree, if liars were not allowed to speak. And yet we have had the experience both in ourselves and in others of words being expressed which were not about the thing being thought. It seems to me that this can happen in two ways: (1) either when something which has been committed to memory and often repeated is expressed by one who is preoccupied with other things, as often happens to us when we sing a hymn, (2) or when against our will we make a slip in speech, for in this case, too, signs are expressed which are not of the things which we have in mind. For indeed those who lie also think of the things which they express, so that, although we do not know whether they tell the truth, we do yet know that they have in mind what they are saying, if they do not do one of the two things cited above. If anyone contends that this only happens now and then, and is apparent when it happens, I do not object, though frequently it is not observed and has often deceived me.

FROM AUGUSTINE TO AQUINAS

The most famous monastic rule of the Middle Ages was set up by St. Benedict (480-543) at Monte Cassino in 520. The rule of St. Benedict enjoined upon this community the virtues of purity, charity, humility, and poverty. All things were owned in common and absolute obedience to the abbot was demanded of all. The day was divided into periods of work, reading, and worship, and midnight orisons and the prayer hours were regularly observed. Each monastery was in a sense a school for the service of God, and until the thirteenth century each was self-supporting and entirely autonomous. After this time many of the monasteries were federated. During the Middle Ages other monastic orders for men and women were formed. Among these were the Franciscans, founded by St. Francis of Assisi (1182-1226), and the Dominicans, founded by St. Dominic (1170-1221). St. Thomas Aquinas was a member of the latter order. These institutions were among the most important educational institutions of the period and not only preserved remnants of ancient culture but also advanced the cause of learning.

The Augustinian tradition in philosophy and education was carried on by such men as Alcuin (735-804), who taught at the palace school of Charlemagne, St. Anselm (1033-1109), famous for his ontological argument for the existence of God (that the Being than whom none greater can be thought must exist), and by most of the members of the Franciscan and Augustinian orders.

At the same time, the philosophy of Aristotle began to be reintroduced into the West by way of the Arabian culture. Al-Farabi (870-950) introduced Aristotle to the Arabs, and Averroes (1126-1198), another Arab, is said to have been the greatest medieval commentator on Aristotle. Rocellinus (1050-1120), a Breton canon called the founder of the new Lyceum, interpreted Aristotle and was the teacher of Abelard. He defended the nominalist position derived from Aristotle against the neoplatonic and scholastic realism of St. Anselm, Archbishop of Canterbury (1070-1089). Roger Bacon (1214-1294) at Oxford and Paris, valued Aristotle highly, condemned the deductive method, and advocated observation and experimentation in science. William

---

Chart 2. Note on this chart the development of scholasticism, the realist-nominalist controversy, and the beginnings of nationalism. Here again we see time gaps between Proclus, the last of the pagans, and St. Gregory, the strengthener of the papacy. Noteworthy is the gap of six centuries between Galen the Roman and al Farabi the Arab, both followers of Aristotle who was lost to the Western world during the intervening period. It was not until after the Muslim conquest of Spain in 711 that Aristotle re-entered Western thought by way of the north coast of Africa and Spain. The conflict between Platonism and Aristotelianism took almost half a millennium to be resolved. The great impetus to the study of "The Philosopher" came after the crusades in the twelfth century. The synthesis of St. Augustine and Aristotle was effected by St. Thomas almost two centuries before the fall of Contantinople, in 1453. Finally, the growth of nationalism and the desire for local autonomy among churchmen should be noted in Robert of Lincoln who objected to papal appointments without local consent about 300 years before Luther posted his ninety-five theses.

Twenty-five Centuries of Educational Thought   CHART 2: ST. AUGUSTINE TO ST. THOMAS AQUINAS

	ST. AUGUSTINE 354-430	Reconciled pagan learning with Christianity
	NESTORIUS fl. 428	Two natures in Christ
	PROCLUS 411-485	Last important Neoplatonic philosopher in Athens
	ST. GREGORY THE GREAT 540-604	Increased authority of the Holy See
	ALCUIN 735-804	Influenced by St. Augustine; taught at Charlemagne's palace Academy
	AL-KINDI 800-870	First great Arab philosopher
	JOHN SCOTUS ERIGENA 810-877	Neoplatonist
	AL-FARABI 870-950	Introduced Aristotle to Arabs
	AVICENNA 980-1037	Moderate realism; studied Aristotle, Neoplatonism, Medici
	BERENGER 999-1088	Influenced by St. Augustine
	ST. ANSELM 1033-1109	Platonic realist; followed St. Augustine
	THEODORE OF CHARTRES fl. 1121-1150	Neoplatonist
	WILLIAM OF CONCHES fl. 1122	Taught Platonic realism at Paris
	JOHN OF SALISBURY 1115-1180	Combined Augustinian and Aristotelian philosophy
	RICHARD OF ST. VICTOR fl. 1162-1173	Neoplatonist; all truth not confirmed by Scripture is suspect
	AVERROES 1126-1198	Greatest commentator on Aristotle
	ROBERT OF LINCOLN 1175-1253	Nationalist, Neoplatonist; opposed papal appointments
	ALEXANDER OF HALES c. 1180-1245	Attempted reconciliation of Augustine, Arabs, Aristotle
	ALBERT THE GREAT 1193-1280	Influenced by Alexander of Hales
	ROGER BACON 1214-1294	Aristotelian
	WILLIAM OF MOERBEKE 1215-1286	Translated Aristotle into Latin
	ST. THOMAS AQUINAS 1225-1274	Aristotelian; The Angelic Doctor; Synthesized current philosophies

37

Moerbeke (1215-1286) and Albert the Great (1193-1289) translated Aristotle into Latin from the original Greek.

Many medieval scholars attempted to reconcile the teachings of Plato and Aristotle, among them being Avicenna (980-1037), Abelard (1079-1142), Maimonides (1130-1204), John of Salisbury (1115-1180), and St. Bonaventura (1221-1274). But it was the monumental work of St. Thomas Aquinas that successfully dislodged neoplatonism and brought the philosophy of Aristotle and the doctrines of the Church into harmony with each other.

ST. THOMAS AQUINAS

St. Thomas Aquinas (1225-1274), the Angelic Doctor, reconciled Aristotelian reasoning with Christian concepts by showing the relationship between reason and faith through a logical synthesis of seemingly opposite views. The essential point of his theory of knowledge is that there is one level concerned with the facts of nature with which reason is competent to deal and another concerned with what is beyond nature and is revealed by faith. Faith begins when reason has reached its limit. Reason is largely inductive and begins with sensory data, passing through ever larger generalizations, through science to philosophy. Theology also has two divisions: the natural, understood by reason and the supernatural, revealed by faith. Universals exist *before* things in the mind of God, *in* things in the natural world, and *after* things in the mind of man.[7] Man himself is composed of soul and body, the one immortal and the other mortal, yet in this life essentially they are one as form and matter are in any material object.

St. Thomas wrote only one short treatise on education, "Concerning the Teacher," but, in a sense, all his works may be considered as dealing with the philosophy of education, for he wrote a complete philosophy of life, which certainly has implications for education. He maintained that the teacher is a vessel or agent who, with the help of God, can be said to teach just as a physician, with the help of nature, can be said to heal, and that teaching is a function of the contemplative as well as the active life. He believed that will and intellect elevate man above the brute and must be trained through discipline. He held that learning

[7] Albert E. Avery, *Handbook in the History of Philosophy* (New York: Barnes and Noble, 1955), p. 94.

about the physical world comes through the senses and he advocated sense training and the direct experimental approach. He placed the intellect and theoretical knowledge above practical knowledge. He stated that the purpose of education is to develop the total personality through drawing out the dormant capabilities and bringing them into complete harmony with each other. The final purpose of education is sanctity. Man is incomplete until the physical, social, and intellectual aspects of his nature have been crowned by faith and he submits joyfully to Divine Will as expressed through the Church. The philosophy of St. Thomas has for many years formed the basis for much Catholic education although other theological and philosophical points of view are included at the present time.

Of the Teacher*

In De Magistro *St. Thomas poses four questions: Can man be called a teacher or is God the only teacher? Can anyone teach himself? Can man be taught by an angel? Is teaching an activity of the active or the contemplative life? Article IV illustrates the method of the scholastic disputation and the method of teaching. St. Thomas first sets up four propositions after which he states objections to each by which he refutes or confirms the propositions. Some present-day authorities maintain that schoolmen of St. Thomas's day carefully chose propositions which they arranged in progressive order so that they could be refuted, while others believe that the propositions were merely random samplings of students' opinions which the "schoolman" wished to discuss. Note the reliance on "authorities."*

WHETHER TO TEACH IS A FUNCTION OF THE ACTIVE OR OF THE CONTEMPLATIVE LIFE?

1. In the fourth article the question is, Whether to teach is a function of the active or of the contemplative life. And it seems that it is of the contemplative life. "For the active life ebbs with the body," as Gregory says (*Super Ezechielem*, hom. III). But teaching does not cease with the body, for angels, who lack bodies, also teach. Therefore, it seems that it pertains to the contemplative life.

2. Moreover, as Gregory says, "He is busy with the active

Source: Aquinas, *Of the Teacher, De Veritate*, trans. Rev. I. F. Shannon (Chicago: Regnery, 1949), pp. 33-36.

life in order that he may come later to the contemplative life"
(*Super Ezechielem,* hom. XIV). But teaching follows and contemplation precedes. Therefore, to teach does not pertain to
the active life.

3. Moreover, as Gregory says in the same place, the active
life, while it is taken up with work, sees less. But he who
teaches must necessarily see more than he who simply contemplates. Therefore, to teach is more for the contemplative
than for the active life.

4. Moreover, it is by reason of the same perfection that
anything is both perfect in itself and that it gives a like
perfection to others; as, for example, it is through the same
perfection that fire is both warm in itself and the cause of
warmth in others. But for someone to be perfect by reason of
the divine elements in himself pertains to the contemplative
life. Therefore, teaching, which is the pouring out of the same
perfection into another pertains to the contemplative life also.

5. Moreover, an active life is concerned with temporal
things. But teaching is chiefly concerned with the things of
eternity, and the teaching of these things is more excellent and
more perfect. Therefore, teaching does not belong to the
active life but to the contemplative.

But, on the contrary, Gregory says in the same homily, "It
is for the active life to give bread to the hungry, and to teach
the ignorant with the word of wisdom" (*Super Ezechielem,*
hom. XIV).

Moreover, the works of mercy pertain to the active life.
But to teach is reckoned among the spiritual works of mercy.
Therefore, it is of the active life.

In reply I answer that the contemplative life and the active
life are distinguished from each other by their subject matter
and their end. For temporal affairs are the subject matter of
the active life, with which human activity is concerned; but
the knowable reasons of things are the subject matter of the
contemplative life and are the things on which the follower of
the contemplative life dwells. And this difference of subject
matter arises from the difference of ends, just as in all things
the material element is determined according to the demand of
the end. The end of the contemplative life is the consideration
of truth, according as we are now treating of the contemplative life. I speak here of the uncreated truth known
according to the ability of the one contemplating. This truth is
perceived only imperfectly in this life, but perfectly in the

future life. Hence Gregory also says (*Super Ezechielem,* hom. XIV, near the middle) that the contemplative life begins here so that it may be completed in the future life. But the end of the active life is activity that is directed toward the utility of one's neighbors. But in the act of teaching we find a twofold subject matter, in token of which the act of teaching is connected with a twofold act. One subject matter is the thing itself which is taught. The other is he to whom the knowledge is given. Therefore, by reason of the first matter, the act of teaching belongs to the contemplative life; but by reason of the second it belongs to the active life. But as regards the end, teaching seems to apply only to the active life, because its ultimate subject matter, in which it arrives at its proposed end, is the subject matter of the active life. Hence, it applies more to the active life than to the contemplative; although it also pertains to the contemplative life in a certain way, as is clear from what has been said.

Reply to the first objection: The active life fails with the body for this reason, that it is employed with labor, and that it succours the infirmities of one's neighbors. In which vein Gregory says in the same passage that, "The active life is a laborious one, because it sweats in its work; two things which will not be in the future life." Still there is a hierarchy of activity among the heavenly spirits, as Dionysius says (*De Caelesti et Ecclesiastica Hierarchia,* Chap. 9); and the other activity is of a different kind from the active life we now lead in this life. Hence, also that teaching which will take place there, will be far different from the teaching here.

Reply to the second objection: As Gregory says in the same place. "Just as it is a good ordering of life that is directed from the active to the contemplative life, so also is it useful for many to turn the mind from the contemplative to the active life in order that what has been contemplated might inflame the mind and so that the active life might be pursued more perfectly." Still it must be kept in mind that the active life comes before the contemplative life in regard to those acts that are not in agreement with the contemplative life; but as regards those acts that take their subject matter from the contemplative life, it is necessary that the active life should follow the contemplative.

Reply to the third objection: The vision of the teacher is a principle of instruction. But the instruction itself consists more in the transferring of the knowledge of the things seen than in the vision of them. Hence, the vision of the teacher relates more to action than to contemplation.

Reply to the fourth objection: That account proves that the contemplative life is a principle of teaching. And just as heat is not the same as the act of warming, but is only the principle of the act of warming, in so far as it directs it; so, conversely, does the active life arrange for the contemplative.

Reply to the fifth objection: From what has been said the solution is clear. For in regard to the first subject matter teaching fits in with the contemplative life, as has been said in the body of the article.

BIBLIOGRAPHY

AUGUSTINE

*Augustine, *City of God,* ed. V. J. Bourke with an introduction by E. Gilson, (New York: Image Books, Doubleday, 1958).
*———, *Concerning the Teacher: On the Immortality of the Soul,* trans. G. G. Leckie (New York: Appleton 1938).
*———, *Confessions of Saint Augustine,* trans. J. K. Ryan (New York: Image Books, Doubleday, 1960).
Crombie, Alastair Cameron, *Augustine to Galileo* (Cambridge, Harvard University Press, 1953).
Deane, Herbert Andrew, *The Political and Social Ideas of St. Augustine* (New York: Columbia University Press, 1963).
Dods, Marcus (ed.), *The City of God* (New York: Hafner, 1948).
Kevane, Eugene, *Augustine the Educator, a Study in Fundamentals of Christian Formation,* (Westminster, Md.: Newman Press, 1964).
McCabe, Joseph, *St. Augustine and His Age* (New York: Putnam, 1903).
Morgan, James, *The Psychological Teaching of St. Augustine* (London: Robert Scott, 1932).

AQUINAS

*Aquinas, *Of the Teacher, De Veritate,* trans. Rev. I. F. Shannon (Chicago: Regnery, 1949).
*———, *Treatise on Man,* trans. J. F. Anderson (Englewood Cliffs, N.J.: Prentice-Hall, 1962).
*———, *Treatise on the Virtues,* trans. J.A. Oesterle (Englewood Cliffs, N.J.: Prentice-Hall, 1966).
*———, *The Teacher, The Mind,* trans. J. V. McGlynn (Chicago: Gateway Editions, Regnery, 1959).
*———, *Wisdom and Ideas of St. Thomas Aquinas,* ed. E. Freeman and J. Owens (New York: Premier Books, Fawcett).
*Donohue, John W., S.J., *St. Thomas Aquinas and Education* (New York: Random House, 1968).

43

Foley, Thomas Aquin, *Authority and Personality Development According to Saint Thomas Aquinas* (Washington, D.C.: Catholic University Press, 1956).
Mayer, Mary Helen, *The Philosophy of Teaching of St. Thomas Aquinas* (St. Paul: Bruce, 1929).

*Paperback editions.

Chapter Three
The Renaissance: Machiavelli and Erasmus

THE RENAISSANCE was a slow spiritual awakening, which can be traced back to the twelfth century or even earlier, for some historians claim that there never was a time when contact between the Byzantine and Roman civilizations was completely lost. The fall of Constantinople and the discovery of the Greek and Roman authors gave added stimulus which began in Italy, spread to France, and then moved to Germany and northern Europe. Humanism, the revival of interest in the literature and thought of the ancients coupled with the growth of an individualistic and critical spirit, was born. With "Back to Plato" as its battle cry and its emphasis on secular concerns, it inspired high hopes for the liberation of man. It encouraged humanistic teachers to revolt against monkish schoolmasters and dislodged the sacred authority of "The Philosopher," Aristotle. It began with a new vitality and a new spirit of self-assertion and self-realization. It aimed at freeing the human spirit and developing the all-round cultivated citizen of the world, who should be litterateur, artist, diplomat, soldier, esthete, courtier, and polite conversationalist. Many secular princes were also in revolt against the temporal power of the Church. The movement toward national identity can be seen in the refinement of the vernacular as a medium of literary expression. Dante wrote *The Divine Comedy* in Italian, and Chaucer, Luther, and Montaigne established English, German, and French as literary languages.

The Renaissance was not a popular movement. It was completely class-conscious and confined to the aristocracy. Renaissance schools and educational writings were directed toward the education of the nobility or as with Milton, the wealthy gentry, an attitude derived from Socrates and Plato. The same class consciousness, confusion of ends and means, and love of words for their own sake that characterized the Renaissance are typical of present-day humanistic education.

Classical studies had an extremely practical value. Latin was the universal language and continued to be the language of scholarship well into the seventeenth century. Parents who had ambitions for their sons naturally wanted them to become fluent in the use of Latin because it was the intellectual passport to culture, business, and advancement in Church and state. Early Renaissance educators would probably have considered an abstract education utter nonsense.

Quintillian's *Institutes of Oratory*, rediscovered by Andrew Poggio in the Cloister of Saint Gall in 1417, became the model of the Renaissance schoolmaster. Cicero, whose *De Oratore* was discovered at Lodi in 1422, was a favorite author and his style supplanted that of the contemporary Latin not only in writing, but also in speaking. A number of humanists even insisted that parents speak only classical Latin with their children.

Among the earliest publications on education were *Good Morals and School Studies* by Pietro Vergerio (1349-1420), and *On The Liberal and Moral Training of Children* by Maffeo Vegio (1406-1458). Vittorino da Feltre (1378-1446) conducted a school at Mantua to inculcate Christian piety and to develop mind and body harmoniously through classical studies and self-expression. For the most part, however, the curriculum in other schools was still based upon the seven liberal arts and required a tremendous amount of memorization.[1]

Some humanists were ridiculously self-conscious and vainglorious, often lacking the quiet solemnity and pious dignity of the great scholastics. On the other hand, some were bookish and ascetic like the Italian poet Petrarch (1304-1374), who exemplified this type. They loved words so well that means became ends, and they became slaves to Cicero as the scholastics had been to Aristotle. Those humanists who remained in the Church, in-

---

[1] The seven liberal arts are divided into two groups. The lower group, the trivium, includes the three language arts: grammar, rhetoric, and dialectic. The upper group, the quadrivium, is made up of the four mathematical arts: geometry, arithmetic, music, and astronomy.

cluding many of the higher clergy, valued religion chiefly as a means of preserving the existing social order. When humanism was linked to the Reformation, it became the servant of super-naturalism and new theological orthodoxies. What had begun as a movement to set men free became but a new type of oppression.

On the positive side, we may say that humanism created a new concept of art and the art of living. By teaching the art of systematic observation and experimentation it modified the rela-tion of man to nature. The finest representative of the "universal man" is Leonardo da Vinci (1452-1519). There is probably no phase of life, art, or learning that has not been influenced by this great genius, who maintained that certainty comes only from mathematical formulation.

NICCOLÒ MACHIAVELLI

Da Vinci's contemporary, Niccolò Machiavelli (1467-1527), is most famous for his educational treatise, *The Prince*. Disillusioned by the corruption of the churchmen of his day, he made the *state* the *center* of human life. He was a thoroughgoing materialist, and advocated absolute monarchy. Another contemporary, Baldassare Castiglione (1478-1529), wrote a companion piece in the *Book of the Courtier,* in which he stressed the education of the nobility. Michel Montaigne (1533-1592) is perhaps the most famous of the French humanists. Like his Italian contemporaries, he was in-terested in the education of the gentlemen. In his *Essays,* he stated that the aim of education was to teach the young the art of living through observation and travel, rather than through memorization. "I would have his manners, behavior, and bearing cultivated at the same time with his mind. It is not the mind, it is not the body we are training; it is the man, and we must not divide him into two parts."[2]

The Prince*

In The Prince *Machiavelli describes the knowledge and skills needed by a prince, especially in military affairs, and cites ancient*

[2]Michel Montaigne, *The Education of Children,* trans. L. E. Rector, International Education Series No. 69 (New York: Appleton 1899), p. 61

Source: Niccolò Machiavelli, *The Prince and the Discourses;* ed. Max Lerner (New York: Modern Library, 1940), pp. 53-57.

authors to support his contentions. It is interesting to note the inverted parallel between Machiavelli's The Prince *and Aristotle's* Politics, *wherein Aristotle issues warnings which are admonitions to Machiavelli.*

THE DUTIES OF A PRINCE WITH REGARD TO THE MILITIA

A Prince should therefore have no other aim or thought, nor take up any other thing for his study, but war and its organisation and discipline, for that is the only art that is necessary to one who commands, and it is of such virtue that it not only maintains those who are born princes, but often enables men of private fortune to attain to that rank. And one sees, on the other hand, that when princes think more of luxury than of arms, they lose their state. The chief cause of the loss of states, is the contempt of this art, and the way to acquire them is to be well versed in the same.

Francesco Sforza, through being well armed, became, from private status, Duke of Milan; his sons, through wishing to avoid the fatigue and hardship of war, from dukes became private persons. For among other evils caused by being disarmed, it renders you contemptible; which is one of those disgraceful things which a prince must guard against, as will be explained later. Because there is no comparison whatever between an armed and a disarmed man; it is not reasonable to suppose that one who is armed will obey willingly one who is unarmed; or that any unarmed man will remain safe among armed servants. For one being disdainful and the other suspicious, it is not possible for them to act well together. And therefore a prince who is ignorant of military matters, besides the other misfortunes already mentioned, cannot be esteemed by his soldiers, nor have confidence in them.

He ought, therefore, never to let his thoughts stray from the exercise of war; and in peace he ought to practise it more than in war, which he can do in two ways: by action and by study. As to action, he must, besides keeping his men well disciplined and exercised, engage continually in hunting, and thus accustom his body to hardships; and meanwhile learn the nature of the land, how steep the mountains are, how the valleys debouch, where the plains lie, and understand the nature of rivers and swamps. To all this he should devote great attention. This knowledge is useful in two ways. In the first place, one learns to know one's country, and can the better see how to defend it. Then by means of the knowledge and experience gained in one locality, one can easily understand any other that it may be necessary to observe; for the hills and valleys, plains and rivers of Tuscany, for instance, have a certain resemblance to those of other provinces, so that from a knowledge of the country in one province one can easily arrive at a knowledge of others. And that prince who is lacking in this skill is wanting in the first essentials of a leader; for it is this which teaches how to find the enemy, take up quarters, lead armies, plan battles and lay siege to towns with advantage.

Philopoemen, prince of the Achaei, among other praises bestowed on him by writers, is lauded because in times of peace he thought of nothing but the methods of warfare, and when he was in the country with his friends, he often stopped and asked them: If the enemy were on that hill and we found ourselves here with our army, which of us would have the advantage? How could we safely approach him maintaining our order? If we wished to retire, what ought we to do? If they retired, how should we follow them? And he put before them as they went along all the contingencies that might happen to an army, heard their opinion, gave his own, fortifying it by argument; so that thanks to these constant reflections there could never happen any incident when actually leading his armies for which he was not prepared.

But as to exercise for the mind, the prince ought to read history and study the actions of eminent men, see how they acted in warfare, examine the causes of their victories and defeats in order to imitate the former and avoid the latter, and above all, do as some men have done in the past, who have imitated some one, who has been much praised and glorified, and have always kept his deeds and actions before them, as they say Alexander the Great imitated Achilles, Caesar Alexander, and Scipio Cyrus. And whoever reads the life of Cyrus written by Xenophon, will perceive in the life of Scipio how gloriously he imitated the former, and how, in chastity, affability, humanity, and liberality Scipio conformed to those qualities of Cyrus as described by Xenophon.

A wise prince should follow similar methods and never remain idle in peaceful times, but industriously make good use of them, so that when fortune changes she may find him prepared to resist her blows, and to prevail in adversity.

OF THE THINGS FOR WHICH MEN, AND ESPECIALLY PRINCES,
ARE PRAISED OR BLAMED

It now remains to be seen what are the methods and rules for a
prince as regards his subjects and friends. And as I know that
many have written of this, I fear that my writing about it may
be deemed presumptuous, differing as I do, especially in this
matter, from the opinions of others. But my intention being to
write something of use to those who understand, it appears to
me more proper to go to the real truth of the matter than to
its imagination; and many have imagined republics and prin-
cipalities which have never been seen or known to exist in
reality; for how we live is so far removed from how we ought
to live, that he who abandons what is done for what ought to
be done, will rather learn to bring about his own ruin than
preservation. A man who wishes to make a profession of
goodness in everything must necessarily come to grief among
so many who are not good. Therefore it is necessary for a
prince, who wishes to maintain himself, to learn how not to be
good, and to use this knowledge and not use it, according to
the necessity of the case.

Leaving on one side, then, those things which concern only
an imaginary prince, and speaking of those that are real, I state
that all men, and especially princes, who are placed at a greater
height, are reputed for certain qualities which bring them
either praise or blame. Thus one is considered liberal, another
misero or miserly (using a Tuscan term seeing that *avaro* with
us still means one who is rapaciously acquisitive and *misero*
one who makes grudging use of his own); one a free giver,
another rapacious; one cruel, another merciful; one a breaker
of his word, another trustworthy; one effeminate and pusil-
lanimous, another fierce and high-spirited; one humane, another haughty; one lascivious, another chaste; one frank,
another astute; one hard, another easy; one serious, another
frivolous; one religious, another an unbeliever, and so on. I
know that every one will admit that it would be highly
praiseworthy in a prince to possess all the above-named qualities that are reputed good, but as they cannot all be possessed
or observed, human conditions not permitting of it, it is
necessary that he should be prudent enough to avoid the
scandal of those vices which would lose him the state, and
guard himself if possible against those which will not lose it
him, but if not able to, he can indulge them with less scruple.

And yet he must not mind incurring the scandal of those vices, without which it would be difficult to save the state, for if one considers well, it will be found that some things which seem virtues would, if followed, lead to one's ruin, and some others which appear vices result in one's greater security and well-being.

DESIDERIUS ERASMUS

Desiderius Erasmus of Rotterdam (1466-1536) was the most outstanding humanist of the Low Countries. He became an Augustinian monk with reluctance because he was more inclined to literary studies than to the affairs of the Church. However, he fulfilled his obligations to the Church with great distinction and was frequently the arbiter in ecclesiastical matters. He was interested in reform within the Church, and, therefore, broke with Luther and the more radical group when it became apparent that a schism would develop because of their teaching. One of his most popular works was a biting satire on all classes of men, *Encomium Moriae* (In Praise of Folly), written with a play on the name of his friend, Sir Thomas More (1478-1535), who was an outstanding representative of Renaissance humanism in England, a lecturer on Augustinianism, and author of *Utopia,* which described an ideal commonwealth. In More's utopia the individual would be subordinate to the community which would own all natural resources, provide free education and "universal employment" for all. Many of these ideas had been expressed by Erasmus in his *Enchiridion or Manual of Christian Knight* (1503) and in the *Education of a Christian Prince* (1531). In these works Erasmus advocated a limited absolute monarchy as the best form of government. He believed that the ruler should live with a sense of honor and with self-discipline. The ruler, he thought, should control all the country's natural resources, should prevent crime by economic and political measures, and abolish wars against the spirit of Christ. In *Upon the Method of Right Instruction* (1511), Erasmus held that proper methods will increase learning, that a nation should supply trained teachers for all grades, and that the teacher should know the nature of the child and the psychology of learning. He believed that nature, training, and practice determined individual progress. "For it is not by learning rules that we acquire the power of speaking a language, but by daily intercourse with those accustomed to express themselves with expertness and refinement and by the copious reading of the best authors." He despised all types of physical exercise and the empirical method of science.

Although he spoke of abolishing all classes, his attitude toward the common people was paternalistic. His was an education for an aristocracy of brains and birth.

De Ratione Studii*

In De Ratione Studii *Erasmus stresses the close correspondence between the clarity of one's ideas and the use of language for expressing them. He also gives some specific directions for developing such skills.*[3]

THE TREATISE OF ERASMUS *DE RATIONE STUDII,* THAT IS, *UPON THE RIGHT METHOD OF INSTRUCTION,* 1511

Thought and Expression Form the Two-fold Material of Instruction.

All knowledge falls into one of two divisions: the knowledge of "truths" and the knowledge of "words": and if the former is first in importance the latter is acquired first in order of time. They are not to be commended who, in their anxiety to increase their store of truths, neglect the necessary art of expressing them. For ideas are only intelligible to us by means of the words which describe them; wherefore defective knowledge of language reacts upon our apprehension of the truths expressed. We often find that no one is so apt to lose himself in verbal arguments as the man who boasts that facts, not words are the only things that interest him. This goes to prove that true education includes what is *best* in both kinds of knowledge, taught, I must add, under the *best* guidance. For, remembering how difficult it is to eradicate early impressions, we should aim from the first at learning what need never be unlearnt, and that only.

Expression Claims the First Place in Point of Time. Both the Greek and Latin Languages Needful to the Educated Man,

Language thus claims the first place in the order of studies and from the outset should include both Greek and Latin. The

Source: William Harrison Woodward, *Desiderius Erasmus: Concerning the Aims and Method of Education* (New York: Bureau of Publications, Teachers College, Columbia University, 1964), pp. 162-166.

argument for this is two-fold. First, that within these two literatures are contained all the knowledge which we recognise as of vital importance to mankind. Secondly, that the natural affinity of the two tongues renders it more profitable to study them side by side than apart. Latin particularly gains by this method. Quintilian advised that a beginning should be made with Greek before systematic work in Latin is taken in hand. Of course he regarded proficiency in both as essential. The elements, therefore, of Greek and Latin should be acquired early, and should a thoroughly skilled master not be available, then—but only then—let the learner fall back upon self-teaching by means of the study of classical masterpieces.

The Subject-Matter and the Methods Which Are Most Suitable to Beginners

If it is claimed that Logic should find a place in the course proposed I do not seriously demur; but I refuse to go beyond Aristotle and I prohibit the verbiage of the schools. Do not let us forget that Dialectic is an elusive maiden, a Siren, indeed in quest of whom a man may easily suffer intellectual shipwreck. Now here is the secret of style to be discovered. That lies in the use of the pen; whatever the form, whether prose or verse, or whatever the theme, write, write and again write. Supplement writing by learning by heart. Upon this latter question, memory depends at bottom upon three conditions: thorough understanding of the subject, logical ordering of the contents, repetition to ourselves. Without these we can neither retain securely nor reproduce promptly. Read, then, attentively, read over and over again, test your memory vigorously and minutely. Verbal memory may with advantage be aided by ocular impressions; thus, for instance, we can have charts of geographical facts, genealogical trees, large-typed tables of rules of syntax and prosody, which we can hang on the walls. Or again, the scholar may make a practice of copying striking quotations at the top of his exercise books. I have known a proverb inscribed upon a ring, or a cup, sentences worth remembering painted on a door or a window. These are all devices for adding to our intellectual stores, which, trivial as they may seem individually, have a distinct cumulative value.

Lastly, I urge, as undeniably the surest method of acquisition, the practice of teaching what we know: in no other way can we so certainly learn the difference between what we know, and what we *think we know;* whilst that which we actually know we come to know better.

De Pueris Instituendis

In De Pueris Instituendis *Erasmus stresses the importance of formal education, especially in early childhood. He also comments on the qualities of a good leader.*

DE PUERIS STATIM AC LIBERALITER INSTITUENDIS LIBELLUS; or, THE ARGUMENT OF ERASMUS OF ROTTERDAM, THAT CHILDREN SHOULD STRAIGHTWAY FROM THEIR EARLIEST YEARS BE TRAINED IN VIRTUE AND SOUND LEARNING; 1529. Addressed to William, Duke of Cleves.

The Argument at Large

I desire to urge upon you, Illustrious Duke, to take into your early and serious consideration the future nurture and training of the son lately born to you. For, with Chrysippus, I contend that the young child must be led to sound learning whilst his wit is yet unwarped, his age tender, his mind flexible and tenacious. In manhood we remember nothing so well as the truths which we imbibed in our youth. Wherefore I beg you to put aside all idle chatter which would persuade you that this early childhood is unmeet for the discipline and the effort of studies.

The arguments which I shall enlarge upon are the following. First, the beginnings of learning are the work of memory, which in young children is most tenacious. Next, as nature has implanted in us the instinct to seek for knowledge, can we be too early in obeying her behest? Thirdly, there are not a few things which it imports greatly that we should know well, and which we can learn far more readily in our tender years. I speak of the elements of Letters, Grammar, and the fables and stories found in the ancient Poets. Fourthly, since children, as all agree, are fit to acquire manners, why may they not acquire the rudiments of learning? And seeing that they must needs be busy about something, what else can be better approved? For how much wiser to amuse their hours with Letters, than to see them frittered away in aimless trifling!

Education of Their Children is a Duty Owed by Parents to the Commonwealth and to God.

Straightway from the child's birth it is meet that he should begin to learn the things which properly belong to his wellbeing. Therefore, bestow especial pains upon his tenderest

years, as Vergil teaches. Handle the wax whilst it is soft, mould
the clay whilst it is moist, dye the fleece before it gather
stains. It is no light task to educate our children aright. Yet
think—to lighten the burden—how much comfort and honour
parents derive from children well brought up: and reflect how
much sorrow is engendered of them that grow up evilly. And
further, no man is born to himself, no man is born to idleness.
Your children are begotten not to yourself alone, but to your
country: not to your country alone, but to God. Paul teaches
that women are saved by reason that they bring up their
children in the pursuit of virtue. God will straitly charge the
parents with their children's faults; therefore except they bring
up their little ones from the very first to live aright, they
themselves will share the penalty. For a child rightly educated
is a comfort and a joy to his parents, but a foolish child brings
upon them shame, it may be poverty, and old age before their
time. Nay, I know not a few men of note and place who have
lost their sons by lamentable deaths, the results of evil life;
some fathers, indeed, which out of many children had scarce
one surviving. And this from no other cause than that they
have made portions for their sons, but have taken no heed to
train them. They are called murderers who kill their new-born
children: but such kill the mere body. How great, then, is their
crime who destroy the soul? For what other thing is the death
of the soul than to live in folly and sin? Such fathers do no less
wrong to their country, to which, as far as in them lies, they
give pestilent citizens. They do, equally, a wrong against God,
at whose hands they receive their offspring to bring it up to
His service.

The Disposition of the Teacher

Seeing, then, that children in the earliest stage must be be-
guiled and not driven to learning, the first requisite in the
Master is a gentle sympathetic manner, the second a knowledge of wise and attractive methods. Possessing these two
important qualifications he will be able to win the pupil to
find pleasure in his task. It is a hindrance to a boy's progress,
which nothing will ever nullify, when the master succeeds in
making his pupil hate learning before he is old enough to like
it for its own sake. For a boy is often drawn to a subject first
for his master's sake, and afterwards for its own. Learning, like
many other things, wins our liking for the reason that it is
offered to us by one we love. But, on the other hand, there is a

type of man of manners so uncouth, of expression so forbidding, of speech so surly, that he repels even when he by no means intends it. Now men of that stamp are wholly unfit to be teachers of children; a man who loves his horse would hardly put such a man to have charge of his stable. Yet there are parents who think such a temper as I have described well adapted to breaking in the young child, thinking, perhaps, that seriousness of that sort betokens a proper gravity. Therein may lie a great error, inasmuch as that demeanour may cloak a depraved nature, which, delighting in tyranny, cows and breaks the spirit of the pupil. *Fear is of no real avail in education:* not even parents can train their children by this motive. Love must be the first influence; followed and completed by a trustful and affectionate respect, which compels obedience far more surely than dread can ever do.

The Qualities Desirable in a Good Master

Although I have urged the need of gentleness, let it not decline into unwise familiarity towards the pupil; a degree of formal authority must be maintained, such as marked the relation of Sarpedon towards the young Cato, who rendered his master great affection and equal reverence. What would the master do who can only teach by flogging, if he were set up as tutor in a royal household where no such discipline is for a moment allowed? "Oh," he rejoins, "such pupils are not of the common order." "How then? Are not the children of a citizen *men*? Do not citizens love their sons no less than kings?" If they be poor men, the more need have they of learning in order to minister to their deficiency; if they be rich, in order to learn to govern their wealth aright. Not a few born in low estate are called to high station, as to Bishoprics. All men do not rise to so great distinction, yet ought all to gain by right education the opportunity of so rising. Now I have said enough of that evil class of schoolmaster which only knows how to beat: but I cannot too seriously deplore that the scandal is in our day so widely spread.

Conclusion

Now I have done. I make my appeal to that practical wisdom which you have always exhibited in affairs. Consider how dear a possession is your son; how many-sided is learning; how exacting its pursuit, and how honourable! Think how instinctive is the child's wish to learn, how plastic his mind, how responsive to judicious training, if only he be entrusted to instructors at once sympathetic and skilled to ease the first steps in knowledge. Let me recall to you the durability of early impressions, made upon the unformed mind, as compared with those acquired in later life. You know also how hard it is to overtake time lost; how wise, in all things, to begin our tasks in season; how great is the power of *persistence* in accumulating what we prize; how fleeting a thing is the life of man, how busy is youth, how inapt for learning is age. In face, then, of all these serious facts you will not suffer, I do not say seven years, but three days even, of your son's life to pass, before you take into earnest consideration his nurture and future education.

BIBLIOGRAPHY

MACHIAVELLI

*Machiavelli, Niccolò, *Art of War,* trans. E. Farneworth with an introduction by N. Wood (Indianapolis: Liberal Arts Press, Bobbs-Merrill, 1957).

*———, *History of Florence and of the Affairs of Italy: From the Earliest Times to the Death of Lorenzo the Magnificent,* with an introduction by F. Gilbert (New York: Harper Torchbooks, Harper & Row, 1966).

*———, *Prince and Selected Discourses,* (New York: Modern Library, 1940).

Montaigne, Michel, *Selected Essays* (New York: Modern Library, Random House).

*Woodward, William Harrison, *Vittorino da Feltre and Other Humanist Educators* (New York: Teachers College, Columbia University Press, 1963).

ERASMUS

*Erasmus, Desiderius, *Education of a Christian Prince,* ed. L. K. Born (New York: Norton, 1965).

*———, *Enchiridion of Erasmus,* trans. by R. Himelick, (Bloomington: Midland Books, Indiana University Press, 1963).

*———, *Praise of Folly* (Ann Arbor: Ann Arbor Books, University of Michigan Press, 1958).

*Huizinga, Johan, *Erasmus and the Age of Reformation* (New York: Harper, 1951).

*Woodward, William Harrison (ed.), *Desiderius Erasmus: Concerning the Aim and Method of Education,* with a foreword by C. R. Thompson (New York: Teachers College Press, 1964).

*Paperback editions.

Chapter Four
The Reformation and Counter Reformation: Luther, Calvin, and Loyola

THE REFORMATION

Just as Italy had been prepared over several centuries for the cultural flowering of the Renaissance, so the European mind was made ready for the tremendous events that marked the Reformation and Counter Reformation of the sixteenth century. Meister Eckhart (1260-1327), a Dominican monk, early in the fourteenth century began the philosophical German language through his preaching in the vernacular. Marsilius of Padua (1270-1342) laid the foundation for the Protestant revolt by asserting that, although God is the ultimate source of all power, it comes immediately from the people; therefore, law is the expression of the will of the people and not of the prince. William of Ockham (1280-1349), remembered chiefly because of Ockham's razor (that in understanding things one must not use more concepts than are necessary), maintained that belief in God and mortality were matters of faith, and wrote much in opposition to the temporal power of the pope. John Wycliffe (1320-1384) translated large sections of the Bible into English and argued in favor of nationalism in the control of religion. Among his followers, the most famous was John Huss (1370-1415), rector of the University of Prague, who was burned for heresy. Many felt that the old order with its entrenched institutions was passing, and that a new era was being born.

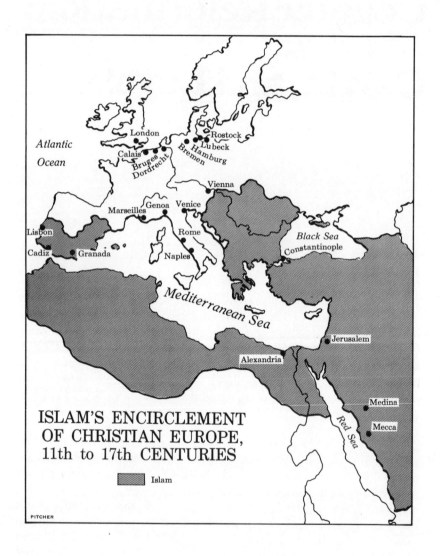

Atlantic
Ocean

London
Rostock
Calais
Lubeck
Bruges
Hamburg
Dordrecht
Bremen

Vienna

Marseilles
Genoa
Venice

Rome

Lisbon
Black Sea
Cadiz
Granada
Constantinople

Naples

Mediterranean Sea

Jerusalem

Alexandria

Medina

Red Sea

Mecca

ISLAM'S ENCIRCLEMENT
OF CHRISTIAN EUROPE,
11th to 17th CENTURIES

Islam

PITCHER

When the conquests of Islam made the established overland trade routes to India difficult, commerce turned to the German free cities with outlets to the North Sea. (See Figure 1, p, 14) The rich natural resources of central Europe stimulated manufacturing. The rising merchant middle class of the Hanseatic towns, the flourishing guilds, and the distance from Rome encouraged the growth of nationalism in both political and ecclesiastical affairs.

MARTIN LUTHER

It was into this age of striving toward nationalism, of growing individualism in thought and belief, of the rise of the middle class to wealth and power, especially in England, the Low Countries, and northern Germany, of the development and expansion of

---

Figure 1. This map shows the farthest reaches of Islam beginning with the conquests of North Africa and Spain in the eleventh century and culminating with the siege of Vienna in 1683.

As the house of Castile began its conquests in Spain, the might of Islam increased in the East. On May 29, 1453, the Crescent of the Moslems entered Constantinople and the Byzantine empire was irrevocably lost. The Balkans came under the political and religious domination of the "sons of the prophet," who were checked only at the gates of Vienna.

The Mediterranean became an inland lake, and commercial interests shifted from such important ports as Venice, Genoa, and Marseilles to the more accessible outlets on the Atlantic Coast and the Hansa cities along the North Sea.

Cultural, religious, and nationalistic interests followed trade. This period saw the rise of the guild, the development of a prosperous merchant middle class, and the assertion of feelings of nationalism which demanded freedom and local autonomy in religion, business, and politics.

The Renaissance in Italy was indeed not only a cultural movement, but had its commercial implications as well, as is reflected in the insistence of the humanistic educators on training world citizens rather than subjects of local lords. This movement along the Mediterranean, however, was kept in check by the area's proximity to the power of the Roman Pontiff and the Emperor of the Holy Roman Empire. But as the Renaissance dispersed through the mountains and the lush river valleys of central and northern Europe, as it stretched out in the age of discovery, beginning with the early voyage of the Portuguese, Spanish, Dutch, and British navigators, it became closely attached to the aspiring commercial middle classes, to the free cities of northern Europe, and to growing feelings of national unity and independence. Men such as Melanchthon played the double role of humanist and reformer. The Renaissance entered into an uneasy marriage with the reform church movement in Germany, Scandinavia, Great Britain, and the Low Countries, and the grand medieval unity of Christendom had come to an end.

commerce through the opening of new markets, following the discovery of America and the rounding of the Cape of Good Hope, that Martin Luther (1483-1546) was born.

It might be said that he contributed nothing new, but by the force of his character and by seizing upon the circumstances of the times, he brought ideas about understanding through faith, individualism of men and of nations, and the need for mass education in the vernacular into a system, and succeeded in implementing it.

Although Luther wanted to deliver the world from medieval institutionalism, he approached the educational situation as a religious reformer rather than as a humanist or a practical schoolmaster, for "as [Charles] Beard has well said Luther was Hebraic rather than Hellenic in spirit."[1] His contributions to education have been praised by some[2] and just as strongly criticized by others.[3] He denounced the medieval universities as "dens of corruption."[4] Yet he urged the study of the ancient languages[5] and urged Elector Frederick to establish several universities within his principality for the training of preachers, pastors, secretaries, and councilors,[6] adding that "if studying is to be good you must have not empty cloisters and deserted monasteries, and endowed churches, but a city in which many people come together and practice on one another and stir each other up and drive each other on."[7]

Luther's individualism did not rest in the feeling of rational autonomy, as the ancients believed, but in the Augustinian concept of the joyful experience of personal or individual salvation through faith in God's eternal grace. He hated Aristotle, who he thought had injected the venom of personal pride into the body of the Church. He was conservative in his theology and would have sided with the twelfth-century theologians against St. Thomas Aquinas.

[1] Frederick Eby, *Early Protestant Educators* (New York: McGraw-Hill, 1931), p. 43.

[2] See F. V. N. Painter, *Luther on Education* (St. Louis: Concordia, 1928); G. M. Bruce, *Luther as an Educator* (Minneapolis: Augsburg, 1928); T. M. Lindsay, *Luther and the German Reformation* (New York: Scribner, 1900); and Robert Ulich, *History of Educational Thought* (New York: American Book, 1945), pp. 114-129.

[3] Johannes Janssen, *History of the German People at the Close of the Middle Ages*, I, III, and XIII (London: K. Paul, Trench, Trubner, 1905); John I. von Dollinger, *Die Reformation* (Regensburg: Manz, 1851), L. 422; and F. Paulsen, *German Education Past and Present* (London: Unwin, 1908), pp. 76-77.

[4] Johannes Janssen, *op. cit.*, III, 335. Quoted in Frederick Eby and Charles Flinn Arrowood, *The Development of Modern Education* (New York: Prentice-Hall, 1934), p. 96.

[5] "Letter to Eeban Hess" in Frederick Eby, *op. cit.*, p.44.

[6] *Ibid.*, pp. 98-99.

[7] *Ibid.*, p. 99.

Unlike the humanists, Luther was much concerned with the education of the common man. In 1524 he issued a stirring appeal to the mayors and aldermen of the cities of Germany to revive their municipal schools.[8] Neither his theology nor his educational and social programs were entirely new, but the force of his personality and his great energy brought many of them to fruition. His belief in the supreme authority of the scriptures led him to compile a complete translation of the Bible from already existing texts and to put it into the hands of the common man. However, he wished to guard its interpretation and accordingly wrote the smaller and the larger catechisms that were to be used for religious instruction. He maintained that "the catechism is the right Bible for the Laitie."[9]

According to Luther the aim of education is to lead the young toward that degree of piety and understanding as will render a Christian community possible. In addition to his recommendation for the establishment of town and village schools he also urged stipends for the support of a few bright scholars. Luther is the first modern reformer to advocate compulsory school attendance. In his "Sermon on the Duty of Sending Children to School" (1530) he wrote, "If the government can compel such citizens as are fit for military service to bear spear and rifle, to mount ramparts, and perform other martial duties in time of war, how much more has it a right to compel the people to send their children to school, because in this case we are warring with the Devil."[10]

Luther also urged and participated in one of the earliest school surveys.[11] He was strongly opposed to parents who were indifferent about sending their children to school,[12] and though he pointed out the evils of lax discipline,[13] he was opposed to harsh methods.[14] His educational program included schooling for girls as well as boys. In 1520 he wrote "Would to God each town had also a girls' school in which girls might be taught the Gospel for an hour a day either in German or in Latin."[15]

[8] Painter, *op. cit.,* "Letter to the Mayors and Aldermen" pp. 169-209 and "Sermon on the Duty of Sending Children to School," pp. 218-271.

[9] Quoted in Eby, *op. cit.,* p. 97, from Capt. Henrie Bell, "Dr. Martin Luther's Divine Discourse at His Table."

[10] *Ibid.,* pp. 149-150.

[11] See Eby and Arrowood, *op. cit.,* p. 87.

[12] Eby, *op. cit.,* pp. 22-27. Original in George Walch, *Luther's Samtlich Schriften,* III, 1817-1825.

[13] *Ibid.*

[14] Quoted in Henry Barnard, *German Teachers and Educators* (Hartford, Conn.: Brown and Gross, 1878), p. 152. "Commentary on the Epistle to the Galatians," in *Dr. Martin Luther's Werke,* Weimar edition, XL, 529.

[15] Eby, *op. cit.,* p. 41.

Twenty-five Centuries of Educational Thought   CHART 3: RENAISSANCE, REFORMATION, AND COUNTER REFORMATION

Timeline	Figure	Description
1200 1300 1400 1500 1600 1700		
	MEISTER ECKHART 1260-1327	Combined Aristotelianism and mysticism; preached and wrote in German
	MARSILIUS OF PADUA 1270-1342	God the ultimate source of power; law expresses will of people; basis of Reformation
	WILLIAM OF OCKHAM 1280-1342	Ockham's Razor (Law of Parsimony); belief in God and immortality are matters of faith
	JOHN WYCLIFFE 1320-1384	English translator of the Bible; supported nationalist control of religion
	VITTORINO DA FELTRE 1378-1446	Humanist; founded school for boys in Mantua
	JOHN HUSS c. 1370-1415	Rector of University of Prague; follower of Wycliffe
	MARSILIO FICINO 1433-1499	Florentine humanist; translated Plato
	LEONARDO DA VINCI 1452-1519	Certitude comes only from mathematical formulation
	DESIDERIUS ERASMUS 1466-1536	Greatest humanist of northern Europe
	NICCOLO MACHIAVELLI 1467-1527	"The Prince"
	SIR THOMAS MORE 1478-1535	Humanist, lawyer; lectured on Augustine; wrote "Utopia"
	MARTIN LUTHER 1483-1546	Reformer; translated Bible into German; advocated free schools
	HULDREICH ZWINGLI 1484-1531	Humanist reformer; associated with Calvinism
	ST. IGNATIUS LOYOLA 1491-1556	Counter Reformation; founded Jesuits
	JOHN CALVIN 1509-1564	Reformer; advocated theocratic state
	ST. JEAN BAPTISTE DE LA SALLE 1651-1719	Founder of Christian Brothers; education of the poor

He maintained that the Christian endowed with faith in the grace of God does "all things gaily and freely," and because this becomes easier in a healthy mind and body, education has to take care not only of the religious and intellectual but of the total physical and emotional development of the child.[16] He was also interested in the continuing education of adults and recommended the establishment of libraries for the reading of good books.

Luther's ideal of a perfect state was a benevolent and patriarchal absolutism under enlightened princes. He supported the doctrine *cujus regio ejus religio* (whose territory, his religion) and enjoined all his followers to give their princes faithful obedience. All rulers were to acknowledge their responsibility to the spiritual kingdom of God, which was higher than all earthly kingdoms, and in this kingdom all individuals, whether high or low, were citizens of equal merit. These ideas of individual merit and Christian liberty have persisted in idealistic philosophy to the present day. By placing both school and church under the direct authority of the state he laid the foundation for popular state-controlled education throughout Germany.

Contrary to the period discussed in Chapter 3, important men and significant movements overlap each other historically. The years of Reformation and Counter Reformation saw many great contemporaries. There is an unbroken flow in the development toward Protestantism and nationalism. Two centuries before Luther, men such as Eckhart and Wycliffe advocated the use of the vernacular in the reading and interpretation of the Scriptures. At the same time a spirit of nationalism and of independence of foreign domination in church and state was growing.

The Renaissance preceded the Protestant revolt by more than a century. Leonardo da Vinci, acknowledged to be the greatest man of the Renaissance, died a few years after Luther had posted his ninety-five theses. The foundations of the earliest universities are lost in legend and tradition. Beginning in Italy, centers of culture and learning spread to France, Spain, and England. The Mediterranean lands and England knew more than thirty universities before the first foundation in central and northern Europe.

The Reformation stimulated the founding of Protestant universities in northern Europe. Within a hundred years as many new seats of learning were founded there as had been established in the four preceding centuries. The Reformation stimulated the growth of the common reading and writing schools with their emphasis on religion and Bible reading in the Protestant countries. It was not until a century after the death of Luther and Calvin that St. Jean Baptiste de la Salle founded his Brothers of the Christian Schools, whose aims were in many respects similar to the schoolmasters of the public schools already established in Germany, the Low Countries, and America.

[16] Ulich, *op. cit.*, p. 123.

Luther's Letter to the Mayors and Aldermen of All the Cities of Germany in Behalf of Christian Schools*

In his famous letter, Luther advocates that schools be supported and controlled by the municipality to develop learned, wise, upright, cultivated citizens, and that orphans and children of the poor not be neglected.

Grace and peace from God our Father and the Lord Jesus Christ. Honored and dear Sirs:

I beseech you all, in the name of God and of our neglected youth, kindly to receive my letter and admonition, and give it thoughtful consideration. For whatever I may be in myself, I can boast with a clear conscience before God that I am not seeking my own interest (which would be best served by silence) but the interest of all Germany, according to the mission, (doubt it who will) with which God has honored me. And I wish to declare to you frankly and confidently that if you hear me, you hear not me but Christ, and whoever will not hear me, despises not me but Christ. For I know the truth of what I declare and teach; and every one who rightly considers my doctrine will realize its truth for himself.

First of all we see how the schools are deteriorating throughout Germany. The universities are becoming weak, the monasteries are declining, and, as Isaiah says, "The grass withereth, the flower fadeth, because the spirit of the Lord bloweth upon it," through the Gospel. For through the word of God the unchristian and sensual character of those institutions is becoming known. And because selfish parents see that they can no longer place their children upon the bounty of monasteries and cathedrals, they refuse to educate them. "Why should we educate our children," they say, "if they are not to become priests, monks, and nuns, and thus earn a support?"

What would it avail if we possessed and performed all else, and became perfect saints, if we neglect that for which we chiefly live, namely, to care for the young? In my judgment there is no other outward offense that in the sight of God so heavily burdens the world, and deserves such heavy chastisement, as the neglect to educate children.

In my youth this proverb was current in the schools: "It is

*Source: F.V.N. Painter, *Luther on Education* (St. Louis: Concordia, 1928), pp. 169-171, 178-182, 208-209.

no less a sin to neglect a pupil than to do violence to a woman." It was used to frighten teachers. But how much lighter is this wrong against a woman (which as a bodily sin may be atoned for), than to neglect and dishonor immortal souls, when such a sin is not recognized and can never be atoned for? O eternal woe to the world! Children are daily born and grow up among us, and there are none, alas! who feel an interest in them; and instead of being trained, they are left to themselves. The convents and cathedral schools are the proper agencies to do it; but to them we may apply the words of Christ: "Woe unto the world because of offenses! Whoso shall offend one of these little ones which believe in me, it were better for him that a millstone were hanged about his neck, and that he were drowned in the depth of the sea." They are nothing but destroyers of children.

But all that, you say, is addressed to parents; what does it concern the members of the council and the mayors? That is true; but how, if parents neglect it? Who shall attend to it then? Shall we therefore let it alone, and suffer the children to be neglected? How will the mayors and council excuse themselves, and prove that such a duty does not belong to them?

Parents neglect this duty from various causes.

In the first place, there are some who are so lacking in piety and uprightness that they would not do it if they could, but like the ostrich, harden themselves against their own offspring, and do nothing for them. Nevertheless these children must live among us and with us. How then can reason and, above all, Christian charity, suffer them to grow up ill-bred, and to infect other children, till at last the whole city be destroyed, like Sodom, Gomorrah, and some other cities?

In the second place, the great majority of parents are unqualified for it, and do not understand how children should be brought up and taught. For they have learned nothing but to provide for their bodily wants; and in order to teach and train children thoroughly, a separate class is needed.

In the third place, even if parents were qualified and willing to do it themselves, yet on account of other employments and household duties they have no time for it, so that necessity requires us to have teachers for public schools, unless each parent employ a private instructor. But that would be too expensive for persons of ordinary means, and many a bright boy, on account of poverty, would be neglected. Besides, many parents die and leave orphans; and how they are usually cared for by guardians, we might learn, even if observation were not enough, from the sixty-eighth Psalm, where God calls himself the "Father of the fatherless," as of those who are neglected by all others. Also there are some who have no children and therefore feel no interest in them.

Therefore it will be the duty of the mayors and council to exercise the greatest care over the young. For since the happiness, honor, and life of the city are committed to their hands, they would be held recreant before God and the world, if they did not, day and night, with all their power, seek its welfare and improvement. Now the welfare of a city does not consist alone in great treasures, firm walls, beautiful houses, and munitions of war; indeed, where all these are found, and reckless fools come into power, the city sustains the greater injury. But the highest welfare, safety, and power of a city consists in able, learned, wise, upright, cultivated citizens, who can secure, preserve, and utilize every treasure and advantage.

In ancient Rome the boys were so brought up that at the age of fifteen, eighteen, twenty, they were masters not only of the choicest Latin and Greek, but also of the liberal arts, as they are called; and immediately after this scholastic training, they entered the army or held a position under the government. Thus they became intelligent, wise, and excellent men, skilled in every art and rich in experience, so that all the bishops, priests, and monks in Germany put together would not equal a Roman soldier. Consequently their country prospered; persons were found capable and skilled in every pursuit. Thus, in all the world, even among the heathen, school-masters and teachers have been found necessary where a nation was to be elevated. Hence in the Epistle to the Galatians Paul employs a word in common use when he says, "The law was our *school-master.*"

Since, then, a city must have well-trained people, and since the greatest need, lack, and lament is that such are not to be found, we must not wait till they grow up of themselves; neither can they be hewed out of stones nor cut out of wood; nor will God work Miracles, so long as men can attain their object through means within their reach. Therefore we must see to it, and spare no trouble or expense to educate and form them ourselves. For whose fault is it that in all the cities there are at present so few skillful people except the rulers, who have allowed the young to grow up like trees in the forest, and have not cared how they were reared and taught? The growth, consequently, has been so irregular that the forest furnishes no timber for building purposes, but like a useless hedge, is good only for fuel.

Yet there must be civil government. For us, then, to permit ignoramuses and blockheads to rule when we can prevent it, is irrational and barbarous.

Since God has so graciously and abundantly provided us with art, scholars, and books, it is time for us to reap the harvest and gather for future use the treasures of these golden years. For it is to be feared (and even now it is beginning to take place) that new and different books will be produced, until at last, through the agency of the devil, the good books which are being printed will be crowded out by the multitude of ill-considered, senseless, and noxious works. For Satan certainly designs that we should torture ourselves again with Catholicons, Floristas, Modernists, and other trash of the accursed monks and sophists, always learning, yet never acquiring knowledge.

Therefore, my dear Sirs, I beg you to let my labor bear fruit with you. And though there be some who think me too insignificant to follow my advice, or who look down upon me as one condemned by tyrants: still let them consider that I am not seeking my own interest, but that of all Germany.

Herewith I commend you all to the grace of God. May he soften your hearts, and kindle therein a deep interest in behalf of the poor, wretched, and neglected youth; and through the blessing of God may you so counsel and aid them as to attain to a happy Christian social order in respect to both body and soul, with all fullness and abounding plenty, to the praise and honor of God the Father, through Jesus Christ our Saviour. Amen.

JOHN CALVIN

John Calvin (1509-1564), stands slightly to the left of Luther's theology. He abolished all practices and doctrines that did not have direct biblical support. He gave much authority to the laity and established a Consistorium of lay elders and deacons in Geneva who were charged with inspecting not only the churches, but homes and municipal and business institutions as well. Writing from Geneva in 1610, Lutheran Pastor Andrea remarked, "Not

only is there in existence an absolutely free commonwealth, but
... a censorship of morals ... with investigations ... each week
into the morals and even into the slightest transgressions of the
citizens. ... As a result, all cursing, gambling, luxury, quarreling,
hatred, conceit, deceit, extravagance and the like, to say nothing
of greater sins, are prevented."[17]

While Luther recommended a state church where the civil
authorities were dominant, Calvin's system called for an organization where the regulation of both civil and religious affairs was
dominated by the clergy. "Civil government," he wrote, "is designed as long as we live in this world, to cherish and support the
eternal worship of God."[18] His recommendations had a great
influence in the establishment of church-state educational programs in Geneva, Holland, Scotland, and New England. Calvin
established his Academy at Geneva in 1559 with its classical
Gymnasium and theological school. All details of life and instruction were carefully planned and regulated and all teachers were
bound by oath to adhere to the profession of faith of the reformed church. The Academy was considered a model educational
institution and was widely copied. It influenced the Universities of
Leyden and Edinburgh, Emmanuel College of Cambridge University, and Harvard College.[19]

Calvin believed in the total depravity of man and in predestination: "... infants themselves as they bring their condemnation
into the world with them, are rendered obnoxious to punishment
by their own sinfulness, not by the sinfulness of another ... their
whole nature is ... odious and abominable to God. This depravity
never ceases in us. Our nature is not only destitute of all good, but
is so fertile to evil that it cannot remain inactive."[20]

Since man cannot set himself free from this original sin, every
man's salvation or damnation is therefore predestined, according
to the Augustinian theology from which Calvinism is derived. The
emphasis, then, is on the negative aspect of morality, which
consists of abstinence from evil acts and indulgence of bodily
passions through the exercise of man's free will. As Wheelwright
remarks: "Those Christian creeds which declare that God is
omniscient (in the precise sense of the word) and also that man
has free will (also in the precise sense) are trying to digest a hard
logical contradiction."[21]

[17] Felix Emil Held, *Johann Valentin Andrea's Christianopolis* (Urbana: University of
Illinois, 1914), p. 27. Quoted in Eby and Arrowood, *op. cit.,* p. 129.

[18] Eby, *op. cit.,* p. 127.

[19] *Ibid.,* pp. 252-253.

[20] John Calvin, *Institutes of the Christian Religion,* ed. John Allen (Philadelphia:
Presbyterian Board of Publications, n.d.), I, 229-231.

[21] Philip Wheelwright, *The Way of Philosophy* (New York: Odyssey, 1954), p. 305.

The movement stemming from the theology of John Calvin did much to establish state-supported systems of education in order to provide instruction in reading the Bible and other types of sacred literature. In the Netherlands, the church synods gave Calvinist civil magistrates the authority to establish and maintain orthodox Calvinist religious vernacular schools free to the poor. The curriculum included the vernacular, the catechism, prayers, and lessons in patriotism. Early attempts at a similar educational program were made by John Knox in Scotland, but a free system of parish education was not established until the eighteenth century. In colonial New England, the theocratic governments established systems of free schools as early as 1642 so that "all children might learn to read and understand the principles of religion and the capital lawes of this country."[22]

It is usually conceded that both Calvin and Luther derived their idealism, especially with regard to the freedom and integrity of the individual, from Plato through St. Augustine. This respect for the individual, although not always honored in the observance, is a basic principle of present-day idealism. "The weight of Protestant ethics has been upon the religious significance of the present life, . . . the bearing of religious faith upon the reorganization of economic and political practices, and the right of the Christian man to possess abundantly the natural goods of God's world.[23]

Institutes of the Christian Religion*

Calvin's Institutes of the Christian Religion *has been called "the supreme structure of the Protestant Reformation," and had a formative influence on the development of Reformed Protestantism. The first selection is a passage from the communion of saints, in which Calvin expands upon St. Paul's discussion of the vocations of Christians, among them teaching.*

Paul writes, that Christ, "that he might fill all things, gave some apostles, and some prophets, and some evangelists, and some pastors and teachers; for the perfecting of the saints, for the work of the ministry, for the edifying of the body of

[22]Quoted in Eby and Arrowood, *op. cit.*, p. 169.
[23]Sterling P. Lamprecht, *Our Philosophical Traditions* (New York: Appleton, 1955), p. 215.

Source: John Calvin, *A Compend of the Institutes of the Christian Religion*, Bk. IV, Ch. 21, Part 1, ed. Hugh T. Kerr (Philadelphia: Westminster, 1964), p. 154-155.

Christ: till we all come in the unity of the faith, and of the knowledge of the son of God, unto a perfect man, unto the measure of the stature of the fullness of Christ." We see that though God could easily make his people perfect in a single moment, yet it was not his will that they should grow to mature age, but under the education of the Church. We see the means expressed; the preaching of the heavenly doctrine is assigned to the pastors. We see that all are placed under the same regulation, in order that they may submit themselves with gentleness and docility of mind to be governed by the pastors who are appointed for this purpose. . . . He not only requires us to be attentive to reading, but has appointed teachers for our assistance. This is attended with a twofold advantage. For on the one hand, it is a good proof of our obedience when we listen to his ministers, just as if he were addressing us himself; and on the other, he has provided for our infirmity, by choosing to address us through the medium of human interpreters, that he may sweetly allure us to him, rather than to drive us away from him by his thunders. . . . Those who consider the authority of the doctrine as weakened by the meanness of the men who are called to teach it, betray their ingratitude; because among so many excellent gifts with which God has adorned mankind, it is a peculiar privilege, that he deigns to consecrate men's lips and tongues to his service, that his voice may be heard in them. . . . Many are urged by pride, or disdain, or envy, to persuade themselves that they can profit sufficiently by reading and meditating in private, and so to despise public assemblies, and consider preaching as unnecessary. But since they do all in their power to dissolve and break asunder the bond of unity, which ought to be preserved inviolable, not one of them escapes the just punishment of this impious breach, but they all involve themselves in pestilent errors and pernicious reveries. . . .

THE OFFICERS OF THE CHURCH AND THEIR DUTIES*

Those who preside over the government of the Church, according to the institution of Christ, are named by Paul, first, "apostles"; secondly, "prophets"; thirdly, "evangelists"; fourthly, "pastors"; lastly, "teachers." Of these, only the two

*Sources: John Calvin, *A Compend of the Institutes of the Christian Religion*, Bk. IV, Ch. 22, Part 2, pp. 163-165.

last sustain an ordinary office in the Church: the others were such as the Lord raised up at the commencement of his kingdom, and such as he still raises up on particular occasions when required by the necessity of the times. The nature of the apostolic office is manifest from this command: "Go preach the gospel to every creature."

Next follow "pastors" and "teachers," who are always indispensable to the Church. The difference between them I apprehend to be this—that teachers have no official concern with the discipline or the administration of the sacraments, or with admonitions and exhortations, but only with the interpretation of the Scripture, that pure and sound doctrine may be retained among believers; whereas the pastoral office includes all these things.

We have now ascertained what offices were appointed to continue for a time in the government of the Church, and what were instituted to be of perpetual duration. If we connect the evangelists with the apostles, as sustaining the same office, we shall then have two offices of each description, corresponding to each other. For our pastors bear the same resemblance to the apostles, as our teachers do to the ancient prophets. . . .

We may infer that the preaching of the gospel, and the administration of the sacraments, constitute the two principal parts of the pastoral office. Now, the business of teaching is not confined to public discourses, but extends also to private admonitions. Thus Paul calls upon the Ephesians to witness the truth of his declaration, "I have kept back nothing that was profitable unto you, but have showed you, and have taught you publicly, and from house to house, testifying both to the Jews, and also to the Greeks, repentance toward our Lord Jesus Christ." And a little after: "I ceased not to warn every one, night and day, with tears."

The Book of Discipline*

The following selection is taken from The Book of Discipline, *written by John Knox and others about 1560 to effect ecclesiastical and scholastic changes to further the religious reformation in Scotland. Some of these measures became part of Scottish law after severe opposition from certain noblemen who had acquired former church property. It shows the Calvinist reformers' concern for education and their conception of the close relation of church and state.*

FOR THE SCHOOLS

Seeing that the office and duty of the godly Magistrate is not only to purge the Church of God from all superstition, and to set it at liberty from the bondage of tyrannies; but also to provide, to the uttermost of his power, how it may abide in the same purity to the posterities following: we can not but freely communicate our judgements with your Honours in this behalf.

I. The Necessity of Schools

Seeing that God hath determined that his Church here in earth, shall be taught not by angels but by men; and seeing that men are born ignorant of all godliness; and seeing, also, how God ceaseth to illuminate men miraculously, suddenly changing them, as that he did his Apostles and others in the Primitive Church: of necessity it is that your Honours be most careful for the virtuous education, and godly upbringing of the youth of this Realm, if either ye now thirst unfeignedly the advancement of Christ's glory, or yet desire the continuance of his benefits to the generation following. For as the youth must succeed till us, so ought we to be careful that they have the knowledge and erudition, to profit and comfort that which ought to be most dear to us, to wit, the Church and Spouse of the Lord Jesus.

Of necessity therefore we judge it, that every several Church have a School-master appointed, such a one as is able, at least, to teach Grammar and the Latin tongue, if the Town be of any reputation. If it be Upland, where the people convene to doctrine but once in the week, then must either the Reader or the Minister there appointed, take care over the children and youth of the parish, to instruct them in their first rudiments, and especially in the Catechism, as we have it now translated in the Book of our Common Order, called the Order of Geneva. And farther, we think it expedient, that in every notable town, and especially in the town of the Super-intendent, [there] be erected a College, in which the Arts, at

Source: Daniel Calhoun (ed.), *The Educating of Americans* (New York: Houghton Mifflin, 1969), pp. 19-21.

least Logic and Rhetoric, together with the Tongues, be read by sufficient Masters, for whom honest stipends must be appointed: as also provision for those that be poor, and be not able by themselves, nor by their friends, to be sustained at letters, especially such as come from Landward.

The fruit and commodity hereof shall suddenly appear. For, first, the youthhood and tender children shall be nourished and brought up in virtue, in presence of their friends; by whose good attendance many inconveniences may be avoided, in the which the youth commonly falls, either by too much liberty, which they have in strange and unknown places, while they cannot rule themselves; or else for lack of good attendance, and of such necessities as their tender age requires. Secondly, the exercise of the children in every Church shall be of great instruction to the aged.

Last, the great Schools called Universities, shall be replenished with those that be apt to learning; for this must be carefully provided, that no father, of what state or condition that ever he be, use his children at his own fantasy, especially in their youthhood; but all must be compelled to bring up their children in learning and virtue.

The rich and potent may not be permitted to suffer their children to spend their youth in vain and idleness, as heretofore they have done. But they must be exhorted, and by the censure of the Church compelled to dedicate their sons, by good exercise, to the profit of the Church and to the Commonwealth; and that they must do of their own expenses, because they are able. The children of the poor must be supported and sustained on the charge of the Church, till trial be taken whether the spirit of docility be found in them or not. If they be found apt to letters and learning, then may they not (we mean, neither the sons of the rich, nor yet the sons of the poor,) be permitted to reject learning; but must be charged to continue their study, so that the Commonwealth may have some comfort by them. And for this purpose must discreet, learned, and grave men be appointed to visit all Schools for the trial of their exercise, profit, and continuance; to wit, the Ministers and Elders, with the best learned in every town, shall every quarter take examination how the youth have profited.

A certain time must be appointed to Reading, and to learning of the Catechism; a certain time to the Grammar, and to the Latin tongue; a certain time to the Arts, Philosophy, and to the [other] Tongues; and a certain to that study in which they intend chiefly to travel for the profit of the Commonwealth. Which time being expired, we mean in every course, the children must either proceed to farther knowledge, or else they must be sent to some handicraft, or to some other profitable exercise; provided always, that first they have the form of knowledge of Christian religion, to wit, the knowledge of God's law and commandments; the use and office of the same; the chief articles of our belief; the right form to pray unto God; the number, use, and effect of the sacraments; the true knowledge of Christ Jesus, of his office and natures, and such others, as without the knowledge whereof, neither deserveth [any] man to be named a Christian, neither ought any to be admitted to the participation of the Lord's Table: And therefore, these principles ought and must be learned in the youthhood.

II. *The Times Appointed to Every Course*

Two years we think more than sufficient to learn to read perfectly, to answer to the Catechism, and to have some entrance in the first rudiments of Grammar; to the full accomplishment whereof, (we mean of the Grammar,) we think other three or four years at most, sufficient. To the Arts, to wit, Logic and Rhetoric, and to the Greek tongue, four years; and the rest, till the age of twenty-four years to be spent in that study, wherein the learner would profit the Church or Commonwealth, be it in the Laws, or Physic or Divinity: Which time of twenty-four years being spent in schools, the learner must be removed to serve the Church or Commonwealth, unless he be found a necessary Reader in the same College or University. If God shall move your hearts to establish and execute this Order, and put these things in practice, your whole Realm, (we doubt not,) within few years, shall serve itself of true preachers, and of other officers necessary for your Commonwealth.

THE COUNTER REFORMATION

The appointment of the Commission on Reform in 1537 by Pope Paul III was a fitting beginning of the Catholic Counter Reformation. Some of the distinguished prelates of the Commission were devoted to the interests of the schools, . . . [such as] Cardinal Reginald Pole . . .in England . . . and Cardinal Jacopo Sadoleto, the author of a notable educational treatise: *De liberis recte instituendis liber* (1533) [which advocated] compulsory education by the state. . . . Their report was the basis of many of the reforms of the great Ecumenical Council of Trent held from 1545-1563 . . . [which] decreed that every diocese should have its own seminary for the preparation of ecclesiastical students. Regulations were also made regarding the courses and qualifications of the teachers. . . . The Council also [required] all masters [in universities] to engage upon oath to teach the Catholic faith according to the canons of the Council . . . instruction of the faithful by preaching and by the printed word, and the Sunday School, were subjects of legislation. . . . The parish school was to be reopened wherever it had declined; the religious orders founded for the instruction of the young were to be encouraged . . . one of the most complete treatises on the education of children appeared under the title *Dell' educatione christiano dei figliuoli by Cardinal Silvio Antoniano.* Written at the request of St. Charles Borromeo, the treatise was first published in 1584. . . . It aims to prepare man for his place in society as a Christian gentleman and to direct him to his supernatural destiny. The importance of the preschool years of the child, a sympathetic understanding of child psychology, vocational guidance and direct training for citizenship . . . are fundamental concepts in the educational theories of Antoniano.

The prescriptions of the Council of Trent convinced the churchmen of the period that before they could hope to bring about religious reforms they must first reform education. Accordingly, new fervor entered into older religious orders, and . . . younger orders and congregations came into existence under the auspices of the church.[24]

ST. IGNATIUS OF LOYOLA

While in his early thirties, St. Ignatius of Loyola (1491-1556), a Spanish soldier of noble lineage, was seriously wounded in the defense of the citadel of Pamplona against the French. During his long recovery he decided to abandon the profession of arms and to devote himself to a life of religion. After eleven long years of study and hardship, he was ordained to the priesthood. He and six companions founded the Society of Jesus (Jesuits) at Paris in 1534, and the order was approved by Pope Paul III in 1540.

[24]Patrick J. McCormick, *History of Education* (Washington, D.C.: The Catholic Education Press, 1946), pp. 407-410.

The Jesuits at first intended to convert Palestine and other parts of the world to the Church. St. Ignatius envisioned the education of only Jesuit postulants at the great centers of learning rather than in special educational foundations, but the great number of students who flocked to him for training forced him to make the general education of boys one of his principal purposes. The aim of the Society is well expressed in its motto: *omnia ad majorem Dei gloriam* (All for the greater glory of God).

The *Constitution* which set forth the guiding principles and organization of the Society and which was issued practically in its final form in the year of Loyola's death, originally consisted of ten parts, the fourth of which treats of studies and of the administration of colleges and the preparation of teachers. It promised a later document that would deal in detail with the method and order of studies. This document appeared as the *Ratio Studiorum* in 1584 and was published in its final form in 1599, after fifteen years of discussion and experimentation in the schools. It is a practical method or system of teaching and a code of laws for governing schools and colleges.

A. C. Beales writes:

The Jesuit basis, was not psychological or sociological but philosophical and religious. The schooling was not 'child centered'; the center was the Christian ideal. The teacher, though outwardly seeming at times to 'follow' the child, was there expressly to control and direct. The child's 'natural development' was deliberately restrained, in the interests of training and character-formation. The goal was not so much self-expression as self-control and self-formation. This is a vital point, and it lies at the heart of what St. Thomas had said in the *De Magistro*. The emotions had to be harnessed to the will, and the will trained by reason and the spiritual life.[25]

The *Ratio* can hardly be called a philosophy, but is rather a method of implementing a philosophy which the student accepts without question. Method consists in two types of class exercises, prelection and repetition. In the former the teacher gave a clear and detailed exposition of the material to be learned, after which the student committed it to memory or was otherwise drilled and questioned until he made it his own. Sometimes the prelection was merely a lecture followed by a summary.

[25] A. C. Beales, *Education under Penalty* (London: University of London, Athlone Press, 1963), p. 9.

Loyola said, "Man . . . was created to be happy by giving service and praise or glory to God. . . . All other creatures are created as means to aid man in attaining his end. . . . If faced with a choice between two creatures or courses of action, he should choose the one which is more conducive to his end. . . . In imparting such education and motivation, a director or teacher should endeavor to procure not passive absorption of his own statements or opinions, but intensive self-activity by which the learner acquires intimate understanding, personal conviction, and relish of the truth."[26]

Jesuit education was concerned with strengthening the Roman Catholic position and the authority of the pope against adherents of the Protestant revolt. It was directed, in the main, toward the sons of the wealthy and the aristocracy and was concerned with secondary and higher education almost exclusively. It accepted the Renaissance curriculum with few modifications and developed no new intellectual insights, but was designed to secure unwavering loyalty to the accepted doctrine of the Church. Jesuit educational method and organization have been of great influence not only in predominantly Catholic countries, but throughout the world.

The Constitutions of The Society of Jesus*

The Jesuit system of education is based upon the Constitutions of the Society of Jesus, *which St. Ignatius constantly revised until his death in 1556, and the* Ratio Studiorum, *published in 1559.*

CONCERNING THE METHOD AND ORDER OF TEACHING THE BE-FORE-MENTIONED SUBJECTS.

1. A suitable arrangement and order of treating both the lower faculties and the study of theology shall be kept both morning and evening.

2. Although a diversity (Explanation A) may arise because of differences in localities and of seasons in the order and in the fixed hours devoted to study, this will be the guiding principle: That everywhere these matters be arranged in that place which it is thought will best promote progress in letters.

[26]Quoted in George E. Ganss, S.J., *Saint Ignatius' Idea of a Jesuit University* (Milwaukee: Marquette University Press, 1954), pp. 19-20.

Source: Edward A. Fitzpatrick, *St. Ignatius and the Ratio Studiorum* (New York: McGraw-Hill, 1933), pp. 1102-1105.

(Explanation A) Concerning the stated hours for lectures, and the order and mode, and concerning the exercises both of compositions (which ought to be corrected by teachers) and of disputations in all the faculties and of giving public orations and odes, *all this will be treated separately in a certain treatise approved by the General, to which this Constitution refers us, giving however this admonition that these matters ought to be accommodated to the times*, places, and persons although as far as possible it would be advisable to follow this order.

3. Not only shall there be lectures, which shall be given publicly, but different masters (Explanation B) shall be secured according to the capacity and the number of students (Explanation C). These masters are to see especially to the progress of each one of his own students, and to demand an account of their lectures (Explanation D). They are to take care that these be repeated, and that the students of the classical languages cultivate their ordinary conversation by speaking Latin commonly; and their style, by writing; and their pronunciation, by carefully reading aloud their compositions; and for these, and more especially for the students of the higher faculties, they shall assign frequent disputations. For these disputations certain days and hours shall be appointed, when they shall dispute not only with fellow classmen, but lower classmen with little more advanced classmen in those subjects which they understand; and *vice versa* the upper classmen with lower classmen by descending to those subjects which the lower classmen are at the time studying; and some teachers will give demonstrations with other teachers, always observing that modesty which is fitting, and always with some one presiding who will check contentions, and determine what doctrinal conclusion ought to be drawn from the disputation.

(Explanation B) There will ordinarily be three instructors in the three different classes in grammar, a fourth will teach humane letters, and a fifth, rhetoric, and included in these last two there are classes in Greek, Hebrew, and any other language taught; so that always there will be five classes. But if any one of these classes demand so much work that one teacher is not sufficient, an assistant may be given to him. If the number of the students is so great that one teacher cannot give attention to all, although he has assistants, the class may be divided, so that for example there will be two "fifth" classes or two "fourth" classes. All the instructors, if possible, should be from the Society, although if necessity demands, they may be outsiders. If the number or the disposition of the students does not demand so many classes and so many instructors, then prudence in regulating the number and in assigning the number only which will be sufficient will have place.

(Explanation C) Whether besides the ordinary instructors who especially have the care of the students there should be one or several who lecture in the manner of public professors on philosophy, mathematical sciences, or any other discipline, with greater solemnity, than the ordinary lecturers, prudence will decide according to the localities and persons to be dealt with, keeping in mind the greater edification and service of God.

(Explanation D) Not only would there be repetitions of the last lecture but of the week's and of a longer time, as is judged advantageous.

4. It will be the function of the Rector either by himself or through a Chancellor always to see to it that new students be examined, and be located in classes and with professors to which they are suited, and that it may be left to his discretion (having heard the opinion of others delegated to this task) whether students ought to remain longer in a class or be promoted to a higher. He is to judge (Explanation E) in the case of the study of the languages, besides Latin, whether they shall be taught before or after the arts and theology and how much time each person ought to devote to them. So also in the higher sciences on account of the inequalities of talents and age and other things which are deserving of consideration it will belong to the same Rector to what extent each one shall study them, and how long he shall devote himself to them. In the case of those who are capable because of their age and talents, it is better that they strive to make progress in all subjects, and to be conspicuous in them for the glory of God.

(Explanation E) There may be some one of such an age and intelligence that the Latin language alone will be sufficient for him, and there will be need for him from the other faculties just as much as is necessary to hear confessions and deal with the neighbor; of this kind some are not capable of much learning but they can exercise the care of souls. Again there will be others who will progress to the higher sciences. It will be for the Superior to decide how far it is convenient to take these sciences or those; but in regard to outside scholars, if they wish to follow another course, they are not to be forced.

5. Just as diligence is necessary in literary exercises so also is relaxation from work necessary (Explanation F). How much this should be, and at which times, is left to the prudent consideration of the Rector, considering the circumstances of persons and locality.

(Explanation F) Every week one afternoon should be set aside for recreation; as for the rest let the Provincial be consulted as to what arrangement is to be made in the case of vacations and the ordinary intermissions from study.

The *Ratio Studiorum* of 1599*

RULES FOR THE PROFESSOR OF HUMANITIES

1. *Grade.* In the first rule, for such knowledge of language as consists especially in propriety and copiousness, let there be explained in the daily prelections Cicero alone of the orators in those books of his which contain his philosophy or morals; of the historians, Caesar, Sallust, Livy, Curtius, and others of the same kind; of the poets, especially Virgil, excepting some of the eclogues and the fourth book of the Aeneid.

Let a brief summary of the precepts of rhetoric from Cyprian be given in the second semester; during which time omitting the philosophic writings of Cicero. Some of his easier orations as the *Pro lege Manilea, Pro archia, Pro Marcello,* and others addressed to Caesar can be taken. Of the Greek language, that part belongs to this class which is properly called syntax, taking care in the meantime that they understand the Greek writers fairly well, and know how to write Greek somewhat.

2. *Division of Time.* The division of time will be this: The first hour in the morning Cicero and the art of versification will be recited by heart to the Decurions; the Preceptor will correct the written work which he receives from the Decurions, assigning in the meanwhile to the students various exercises mentioned below in Rule 4; at the end of the hour some will recite aloud, and the master will examine the marks

---

Source: Fitzpatrick, *St. Ignatius and the Ratio Studiorum,* pp. 216-219. The *Ratio Studiorum* has been revised several times since 1599. Many Catholic scholars prefer the revision of 1832.

given by the Decurions. In the second hour of the morning the last prelection will be repeated briefly, and a new one will be explained for a half an hour, or a little more, and will immediately be recited, and if there is any time left, it will be taken up in concertatio among the students. In the final half-hour at the beginning of the first semester, a historian and the art of versification will be taken on alternate days; but when the art of versification is finished, the historian will be taken briefly; then in the second semester every day the rhetoric of Cyprian will be either explained or repeated or disputation will be held on it.

In the first afternoon hour a poet and a Greek author will be recited from memory, the master looking over the marks given by the Decurions, and correcting the written work which had been assigned in the morning or which remained over from the written work done at home. At the end of the hour a theme will be dictated. The following hour and a half will be divided equally between reviewing and explaining some poet and in a Greek prelection and writing.

On a holiday let the matter of prelection on the last holiday be recited from memory; and let the papers which remain be corrected, according to custom. Let the second hour be used for some epigram, ode, or elegy, or something about metaphors, figures, and especially metrics, according to the custom from the beginning of the year; or let some theme or essay be explained and reviewed, or let there be a concertatio.

On Saturday let the prelections of the entire week be recited from memory during the first hour; let them be reviewed the second hour. During the last half-hour let either a declamation or prelection by one of the pupils be held, or let them go to hear a lecture, or let there be a concertatio.

During the first half-hour after lunch let a poet and the catechism be recited from memory while the master examines papers, if any remain from that week, and looks over the marks of the Decurions.

Let the following hour and a half be divided equally between the review of a poet, or the explanation and consideration of some short poem, and a study of Greek in the same way.

Let the last half-hour be occupied in an explanation of the catechism or in a pious exhortation unless this was held on Friday: but if it was, let the time be occupied by that subject in whose place the catechism had been substituted.

OTHER CATHOLIC EDUCATORS

Catholic education for the lower classes had been carried on for many years by parish priests and was often of poor quality. In order to strengthen the Catholic position and to combat Protestantism, about 30 teaching orders were established between 1525 and 1700. The Ursulines, founded by St. Angela Merici in 1535, are often credited with having been the first of the new orders. Other sixteenth century foundations were the Fathers of Christian Doctrine, which provided religious education for the young and for the blind; a free school for poor boys and girls founded 1597 by the Spanish priest St. Joseph Calasanctius; and the Sisters of Notre Dame, founded by St. Peter Fourier in 1598 for the education of poor girls.

Seventeenth-century France and, to a lesser extent, Italy and Germany, were active in establishing new orders, many of which exist today in various parts of the world. Orders particularly devoted to the education of girls and in some cases orphans include the Visitandines, the Sisters of the Presentation B.V.M., the Sisters of Charity, the Sisters of St. Joseph, and the Sisters of Mercy. For the most part these orders were concerned with educating girls to take their places in fashionable society and to direct the affairs of their households. This type of convent school was widely adopted for the education of girls even in Protestant countries, and greatly influenced the private girls' schools in America.

Four famous teaching orders for men were the Port Royalists (Jansenists), 1637-1661; the Vincentians of St. Vincent de Paul, 1625; the Sulpicians, founded at Paris by Jean Jacques Olier in 1642; and the Brothers of the Christian Schools, founded at Rheims in 1683 by St. Jean Baptiste de la Salle.

St. Jean Baptiste de la Salle (1651-1719) was born into a wealthy and influential family in Rheims, France. He studied for the priesthood, was appointed canon of the cathedral, and received his doctorate from the University of Rheims. His parents died while he was still a young man, leaving him in charge of the management of a large estate and the care of his younger brothers and sisters. Because of the low state of public school teaching in France, he agreed to help a friend establish a free school that she wished to endow. This activity probably marks his initial attempt to raise the standards of schools for the poor and to train teachers. He not only trained young men for elementary school teaching, but provided them with money, food, clothing, and shelter, and eventually took them into his home.

"In 1683 he resigned his office as canon of the Cathedral of Rheims, sold his patrimony and distributed his fortune gradually and judiciously to the poor."[27] Thenceforth he devoted his whole life to the training of teachers and the establishment of schools for the poor. During the following years he often endured poverty, disappointment, hardship, and persecution. At a retreat in 1684 the elements of rule for the order were drawn up, and annual vows were imposed until 1694 when perpetual vows of stability and obedience were required. The order was approved by Pope Benedict XIII in 1725. The movement has flourished greatly, and schools have been established on all grade levels both in Europe and America. St. de la Salle's contribution to the art of teaching and management has influenced both Catholic and Protestant schoolmasters.

The Renaissance developed education for the aristocracy. The Counter Reformation paid attention to the education of the upper classes, to the reform of the parish schools, and to the establishment of charitable foundations for the elementary education of the poor. Protestant education appealed most strongly to the rising commercial middle class. The Renaissance broke the hold of scholasticism on the European mind, but crystallized all too soon into a dry humanism that had little connection with the political, economic, and social changes taking place in western Europe. The Reformation, which began with an appeal to individual freedom, bound itself all too soon to an infallible Book. The Counter Reformation was in the main an attempt to hold the line and it relied upon an infallible church, especially after the Council of Trent (1534-1563). It remained for the next age to declare the doctrine of infallible reason.

BIBLIOGRAPHY

LUTHER

Bruce, G. M., *Luther as an Educator* (Minneapolis: Augsburg, 1928).
*Luther, Martin, *Luther's Commentary*, with an introduction by E. C. Nelson and a foreword by M. Hinderlie (Minneapolis: Augsburg).
*——, *Martin Luther: Selections from His Writings* ed. J. Dillenberger (New York: Anchor Books, Doubleday, 1961).
*——, *Three Treatises* (Philadelphia: Fortress, 1960).
Painter, F. V. N., *Luther on Education* (St. Louis: Concordia, 1928).
Paulsen, F., *German Educators Past and Present* (London: Unwin, 1908).

[27]McCormick, *op. cit.*, p. 489.

Richter, Friedrich, *Martin Luther and Ignatius Loyola, Spokesmen for Two Worlds of Belief* (Westminster, Md.: Newman, 1960).

CALVIN

*Calvin, John, *Compend of the Institutes of the Christian Religion* (Philadelphia: Westminster, 1964).

*——, *Institutes of the Christian Religion*, 2 vol. J. T. McNeill (ed.) (Philadelphia: Westminster, 1960).

*——, *On God and Man*, ed. F. W. Strothman (New York: Ungar, 1956).

*——, *On the Christian Faith: Selections from the Institutes, Commentaries and Tracts*, (Indianapolis: Liberal Arts Press, Bobbs-Merrill, 1957).

ST. IGNATIUS LOYOLA

Beales, A. C., *Education Under Penalty* (London: The Athlone Press, University of London, 1963).

Fitzpatrick, Edward A., *St. Ignatius and the Ratio Studiorum* (New York: McGraw-Hill, 1933).

Ganss, George E., S.J., *Saint Ignatius' Idea of a Jesuit University* Milwaukee: Marquette University Press, 1954).

Hughes, Thomas, *Loyola and the Educational System of the Jesuits* (New York: Scribner, 1892).

*Loyola, Saint Ignatius, *Spiritual Exercises of Saint Ignatius*, trans. A. Mottola, with an introduction by R. W. Gleason, (New York: Image Books, Doubleday).

McCormick, Patrick J., *History of Education*, (Washington, D.C.: Catholic Education Press, 1946).

*Paperback editions.

Chapter Five
The Enlightenment: Comenius, Locke, Rousseau, and Jefferson

THE ENLIGHTENMENT was a crucial period in the history of Western thought, in which men tried to free themselves from the shackles of the medieval mind. "Liberalism, tolerance, humanitarianism, natural law, the social contract, the social sciences—these are some of the fruits of this great period in human history."[1]

... "The thinkers of the Enlightenment rejected the three stately entrance ways of the Middle Ages—theology, philosophy, and deductive Logic—in favor of history, science, and inductive reasoning."[2]

Political theorists explored concepts of natural law, freedom, equality, and authority in the spirit of the science and mathematics of the day. Hobbes's *Leviathan* described an ordered state under an absolute monarch. Locke, in *The Second Treatise on Government*, wrote of a society of free men who formed a body politic in which they consented to delegate their police power to elected officials in order to preserve their inalienable right to life, liberty, and property, but they reserved the right to change the form of government and its leadership if the elected officials failed

---

[1] Louis L. Snyder, *The Age of Reason* (New York: Van Nostrand, 1955), p. 1.
[2] *Ibid*, p. 88.

to preserve those rights. In his *Social Contract* Jean Jacques Rousseau (1712-1778) tried to reconcile the freedom of the individual with government by declaring that the relation of the individual to the state is social rather than political.

Perhaps one of the greatest contributions of the age was the advancement in the theory and philosophy of education. Notions of innate ideas and original sin were exploded, the importance of the environment was stressed, emphasis was placed upon observation and education according to nature, and much attention was given to mass education, although education for the gentleman still found a prominent place in pedagogical writings. By common consent the greatest educator of the Enlightenment was John Amos Comenius (1592-1670), whose ideas of sense realism influenced later German and Swiss educators. This chapter concludes with a discussion of Thomas Jefferson, who applied the political and educational ideas of John Locke to the American scene.

JOHN AMOS COMENIUS

John Amos Comenius (1592-1670), called the first sense realist, was a bishop of the Moravian church. His life was fraught with persecution and disappointment, especially with regard to his "Pansophia," a plan for a college and research center of universal knowledge. His thought was influenced by Calvinism as well as by the writings of Bacon and Locke. Laurie rates him as the most eminent figure in the history of European education.[3] He combined the mysticism of the Moravians with empiricism, believing that life was a continuous state of development toward the divine. Man, he declared, is a rational creature, the lord of all creatures, the image and joy of his creator. He held that the human race could be improved since the seeds of knowledge, virtue, and piety are found in everybody. Unlike Milton and Locke, he was greatly concerned with the education and welfare of the common man. "We wish all men to be trained in all the virtues, especially in modesty, sociability, and politeness, and it is therefore undesirable to create class distinctions at such an early age, or to give some children the opportunity of considering their own lot with satisfaction and that of others with scorn."[4] He carried his pansophic

[3] S. S. Laurie, *Educational Opinion from the Renaissance* (London: Cambridge University Press, 1903), p. 157.

[4] John Amos Comenius, *The Great Didactic*, trans. and with biographical and historical notes by M. W. Keatinge (London: Adam and Charles Black, 1896).

idea into the realm of politics and advocated a league of nations with universal schools, books, and language.

He aimed to make method so definite that the length of time could be predicted accurately. His educational psychology was set forth in the *Great Didactic,* published first in Czech and later in Latin at Amsterdam in 1657. Briefly, his principles of method are as follows: Education should begin early, before the mind is corrupted. The mind should be duly prepared to receive instruction. Education should proceed from the general to the particular and from the easy to the difficult. Progress should be slow in every case, and the pupil should not be overburdened with too many subjects, nor should the intellect be forced to anything to which its natural bent does not incline it in accordance with its age and with the right method. "Let our maxim be to follow the lead of nature in all things, to observe how the faculties develop one after the other, and to base our method on this principle of succession."[5] Everything should be taught through one and the same method, that is, through the medium of the senses, and its use is continually to be kept in mind.

About the classical education of his day he writes: "Most men possess no information but the quotations, sentences, and opinions they have collected by rummaging about in various authors, and thus piece their knowledge together like a patchwork quilt."[6]

But for Comenius's pupils, "They will learn not from school but from life."[7] "Nothing should be learned solely for its value at school, but for its use in life."[8]

In his other great work, *Orbis Sensualium Pictus* (1658), he applied his theory to the teaching of Latin vocabulary by first presenting a picture of the object followed by a Latin statement with translation. For example, following a picture of a wolf is the sentence "Lupus ululat" with its translation, "The *wolf* howleth," the letter "l" and the sounds "lu" and "ulu."[9] It remained, however, for Pestalozzi (1746-1827) to realize that objects must precede pictures in learning.

In organizing formal education Comenius planned schooling up to the age of twenty-four. He divided this period into four segments of six years each: First, during infancy, birth to six years, the school should be the "mother's knee"; second, for childhood, ages seven to twelve, the vernacular school; third, for

[5] *Ibid.,* p. 409.

[6] *Ibid.,* p. 300.

[7] Quoted in Frederick Eby and Charles F. Arrowood, *The Development of Modern Education* (New York: Prentice Hall, 1947), p. 259.

[8] Keatinge, *op. cit.,* p. 341.

[9] John Amos Comenius, *The Orbis Pictus* (Syracuse: Bardeen, 1887), p. 3.

boyhood, ages thirteen to eighteen, the Latin school or gymnasium; and fourth, for youth, ages nineteen to twenty-four, the university and travel. Education in Europe follows this plan closely.

The influence of Comenius was widespread. Basedow (1723-1790) followed his lead in the use of pictures, Rousseau (1712-1778) stressed the education of the young in the things of nature, and Froebel (1782-1852) developed the concept of early childhood education and its implementation.

Comenius came to London in 1641 at the invitation of Samuel Hartlib and the other Commonwealth educators to present his idea of the pansophia. John Milton (1608-1674), who wrote his essay *Of Education* in 1644, was a prominent member of this group, but there is no known record that he and Comenius ever met. Unlike Comenius, Milton was not interested in sense realism or in universal education. Like John Locke, he advocated the education of the gentry for leadership and the revision of the English public schools along the lines of the European gymnasium.

The Great Didactic*

In The Great Didactic, *Comenius maintains that the greatest knowledge is to know God and through him to know oneself. Man is God's most perfect creation. Education directs him to God through knowledge, virtue, and piety. Method in education must be thorough and must follow the path of nature.*

MAN IS THE HIGHEST, THE MOST ABSOLUTE, AND THE MOST EXCELLENT OF THINGS CREATED

When Pittacus of old gave to the world his saying "Know thyself," the sentiment was received by the wise with so much approval, that, in order to impress it on the people, they declared that it had fallen from heaven, and caused it to be written in golden letters on the temple of the Delphic Apollo, where great assemblies of men used to collect. Their action was prudent and wise, but their statement was false. It was, however, in the interests of truth, and is of great importance to us.

Source: John Amos Comenius, *The Great Didactic*, trans. and with biographical and historical notes by M. W. Keatinge (London: Adam and Charles Black, 1896).

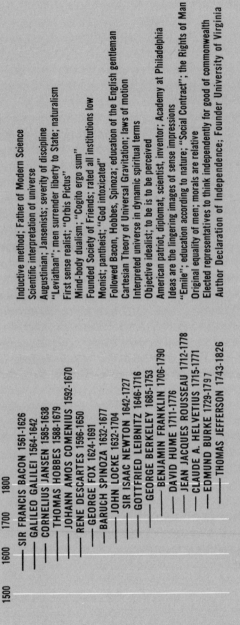

Twenty-five Centuries of Educational Thought   CHART 4: RATIONALISM AND THE ENLIGHTENMENT

Timeline	Person	Description
1500 1600 1700 1800		
	SIR FRANCIS BACON 1561-1626	Inductive method; Father of Modern Science
	GALILEO GALILEI 1564-1642	Scientific interpretation of universe
	CORNELIUS JANSEN 1585-1638	Augustinian; Jansenists; severity of discipline
	THOMAS HOBBES 1588-1679	"Leviathan"; men surrender liberty to State; naturalism
	JOHANN AMOS COMENIUS 1592-1670	First sense realist; "Orbis Pictus"
	RENE DESCARTES 1596-1650	Mind-body dualism; "Cogito ergo sum"
	GEORGE FOX 1624-1691	Founded Society of Friends; rated all institutions low
	BARUCH SPINOZA 1632-1677	Monist; pantheist; "God intoxicated"
	JOHN LOCKE 1632-1704	Followed Bacon, Hobbes, Spinoza; education of the English gentleman
	SIR ISAAC NEWTON 1642-1727	Cartesian Theory of Universal Gravitation; laws of motion
	GOTTFRIED LEIBNITZ 1646-1716	Interpreted universe in dynamic spiritual terms
	GEORGE BERKELEY 1685-1753	Objective idealist; to be is to be perceived
	BENJAMIN FRANKLIN 1706-1790	American patriot, diplomat, scientist, inventor; Academy at Philadelphia
	DAVID HUME 1711-1776	Ideas are the lingering images of sense impressions
	JEAN JACQUES ROUSSEAU 1712-1778	"Emile"; education according to nature; "Social Contract"; the Rights of Man
	CLAUDE A. HELVETIUS 1715-1771	Original equality of men; morals are relative
	EDMUND BURKE 1729-1797	Elected representatives to think independently for good of commonwealth
	THOMAS JEFFERSON 1743-1826	Author Declaration of Independence; Founder University of Virginia

For what is the voice from heaven that resounds in the Scriptures but "Know thyself, O man, and know Me." Me the source of eternity, of wisdom and of grace; thyself, My creation, My likeness, My delight. . . .

Would that this were inscribed, not on the doors of temples, not on the title-pages of books, not on the tongues, ears, and eyes of all men, but on their hearts! Would that this could be done to all who undertake the task of educating men, that they might learn to appreciate the dignity of the task and of their own excellence, and might bring all means to bear on the perfect realisation of their divinity!

•   •   •   •   •

THERE ARE THREE STAGES IN THE PREPARATION FOR ETER-
NITY: TO KNOW ONESELF (AND WITH ONESELF ALL THINGS): TO
RULE ONESELF: AND TO DIRECT ONESELF TO GOD.

1. It is evident, then, that the ultimate end of man is eternal happiness with God. The subordinate ends, also, at which we aim in this transitory life, are evident from the words of the divine soliloquy which the Creator uttered when about to make man. "Let us make man," He said, "in our image, after our likeness; and let them have dominion over the fish of the sea, and over the fowl of the air, and over the cattle, and over all the earth, and over every creeping thing that creepeth upon the earth." (Gen.i.26). 2. From which it is plain that man is situated among visible creatures so as to be

(i) A rational creature.
(ii) The Lord of all creatures.
(iii) A creature which is the image and the joy of its Creator.

These three aspects are so joined together that they cannot be separated, for in them is laid the basis of the future and of the present life.

•   •   •   •   •

THE EXACT ORDER OF INSTRUCTION MUST BE BORROWED
FROM NATURE, AND MUST BE OF SUCH A KIND THAT NO
OBSTACLE CAN HINDER IT.

1. Let us then commence to seek out, in God's name, the principles on which, as on an immovable rock, the method of teaching and of learning can be grounded. If we wish to find a remedy for the defects of nature, it is in nature herself that we must look for it, since it is certain that art can do nothing unless it imitate nature.

2. A few examples will make this clear. We see a fish swimming in the water; it is its natural mode of progression. If a man wish to imitate it, it is necessary for him to use in a similar manner the limbs that are at his disposal; instead of fins he must employ his arms; and instead of a tail, his feet, moving them as a fish moves its fins. Even ships are constructed on this plan; in the place of a tail, the rudder. We see a bird flying through the air; it is its natural mode of progression. When Daedalus wished to imitate it, he had to make wings (large enough to carry such a heavy body) and set them in motion.

[Hereafter follows a discussion of the origin of the flute, gunpowder, the syphoning of water, and methods of telling time and seasons.]

7. It is now quite clear that that order, which is the dominating principle in the art of teaching all things to all men, should be, and can be, borrowed from no other source but the operations of nature. As soon as this principle is thoroughly secured, the processes of art will proceed as easily and as spontaneously as those of nature. Very aptly does Cicero say: "If we take nature as our guide, she will never lead us astray," and also: "Under the guidance of nature it is impossible to go astray." This is our belief, and our advice is to watch the operations of nature carefully and to imitate them.

8. But some one may laugh at our expectations and may cast in our teeth the saying of Hippocrates: "Life is short, and art is long; opportunities are fleeting, experience is deceptive, and judgement is difficult." Here are five obstacles, the reasons why so few scale the heights of wisdom: (i) The shortness of life; through which so many are snatched away in youth before their preparations for life are finished. (ii) The perplexing crowd of objects which the mind has to grasp, and which makes the endeavour to include all things within the limits of our knowledge, very weary work. (iii) The lack of opportunities to acquire the arts, or their rapid departure when they occur (for the years of youth, which are the most suitable for mental culture, are spent in playing, and the succeeding years, in the present condition of mankind, bring far more opportunities for worthless than for serious matters); or if a suitable opportunity presents itself, it vanishes before we can grasp it. (iv) The weakness of our intellects and the lack of sound judgment. The result of this is that we get no farther than the outside shell, and never attain to the kernel. (v) Finally, the circumstance that, if any wish to grasp the true

nature of things by patient observation and experiments repeated as often as possible, the process is too wearisome, and is at the same time deceptive and uncertain (for instance, in such accurate observations the most careful observer may make an error, and as soon as one error creeps in, the whole observation becomes worthless).

9. If all this be true, how can we dare hope for a universal, sure, easy, and thorough road to learning? I answer: Experience teaches us that this is true, but the same experience teaches us also that the proper remedies can be found. These things have been ordained thus by God, the all-wise arranger of the universe, and are for our good.

•   •   •   •   •

11. God permits opportunities to be fleeting, and only to be grasped by the fore-lock, that we may learn to seize them the very instant they present themselves.

12. Experience is deceptive in order that our attention may be excited, and that we may feel the necessity of penetrating to the essential nature of things.

13. Finally, judgment is difficult, in order that we may be urged on to eagerness and to continual effort, and that the hidden wisdom of God, which permeates all things, may, to our great satisfaction, become ever more apparent.

"If, everything could be easily understood," says St. Augustine, "men would neither seek wisdom with keenness, nor find it with exultation."

•   •   •   •   •

THE PRINCIPLES OF THOROUGHNESS IN TEACHING AND IN LEARNING

1. It is a common complaint that there are few who leave school with a thorough education, and that most men retain nothing but a veneer, a mere shadow of true knowledge. This complaint is corroborated by facts. . . .

•   •   •   •   •

3. I maintain that a method can be found by means of which each person will be enabled to bring into his mental consciousness not only what he has learned, but more as well; since he will recall with ease all that he has learned from teachers or from books, and, at the same time, will be able to pass sound judgment on the objective facts to which his information refers.

4. This will be possible:
  (i) If only those subjects that are of real use be taken in hand.
  (ii) If these be taught without digression or interruption.
  (iii) If a thorough grounding precede instruction in detail.
  (iv) If this grounding be carefully given.
  (v) If all that follows be based on this grounding, and on nothing else.
  (vi) If, in every subject that consists of several parts, these parts be linked together as much as possible.
  (vii) If all that comes later be based on what has gone before.
  (viii) If great stress be laid on the points of resemblance between cognate subjects.
  (ix) If all studies be arranged with reference to the intelligence and memory of the pupils, and the nature of language.
  (x) If knowledge be fixed in the memory by constant practice.
  We will now consider each of these principles in detail.

First Principle

5. Nature produces nothing that is useless. For example, nature, when commencing to form a bird, does not give it scales, gills, horns, four feet, or any other organs that it cannot use, but supplies a head, a heart, wings, etc. In the same way a tree is not given ears, eyes, down, or hair, but bark, bast, wood, and roots.

6. Imitation in the arts.—In the same way no one who wishes to grow fruit in his fields, orchards, and gardens, plants them with weeds, nettles, thistles, and thorns, but with good seeds and plants.

7. The builder, also, who wishes to erect a well-built house, does not collect straw, litter, dirt, or brushwood but stones, bricks, oak planks, and similar materials of good quality.

8. And in schools.—In schools therefore
  (i) Nothing should be studied, unless it be of undoubted use in this world and in the world to come,—its use in the world to come being the more important (Jerome reminds us that knowledge, that is to be of service to us in heaven, must be acquired on earth).
  (ii) If it be necessary to teach the young much that is of value solely in this world (and this cannot be avoided), care

must be taken that while a real advantage is gained for our present life, our heavenly welfare be not hindered thereby.

9. Why then pursue worthless studies? What object is there in learning subjects that are of no use to those who know them and the lack of which is not felt by those who do not know them? Subjects, too, which are certain to be forgotten as time passes on and the business of life becomes more engrossing? This short life of ours has more than enough to occupy it, even if we do not waste it on worthless studies. Schools must therefore be organized in such a way that the scholars learn nothing but what is of value.

JOHN LOCKE

John Locke (1632-1704) was born of Puritan ancestry in the same year as Spinoza. He was only nine when Comenius came to England at the request of Hartlib and other Puritan educators. From fourteen to twenty, he was enrolled in Westminister School under the direction of Dr. Busby, the notorious flogger, where he studied Latin and Greek exclusively. From this experience he developed a revulsion to boys and schools which he carried throughout life. He obtained a studentship at Christ Church College, Oxford, where he remained as lecturer for over thirty years. He became confidential secretary to the Earl of Shaftesbury and tutor to his heir and grandson. He spent four years in France and then went to Holland where he wrote his principal philosophical and educational treatises. Returning to England with William of Orange, he held important government posts and received many honors.

Locke's thought was greatly influenced by Rabelais (1483-1553) and by Bacon's empiricism. Like Bacon and Hobbes, his interests were practical and social. His theory of the "tabula rasa" had been anticipated by Comenius, but it is doubtful whether Locke had ever read his great work on method. He followed Descartes in the belief that man is both a sensory and a rational creature, and his educational writings show the influence of Montaigne and the practice of the best English families.

Following the sensory origin of knowledge postulated by Bacon, he destroyed forever, in its older form, the theory of innate ideas as held by Descartes and the Cambridge Platonists. He argued that innate ideas could not conflict with each other and if they existed, should also be found in idiots, infants, and all primitive peoples. They should be in the minds of all peoples at all times and in all places and immediately perceived as necessary, self-evident propositions. However, as a physician and anthropologist he could find no evidence that this was true. Because both the history and the works of the greatest philosophers reveal such great variations in thought, he concluded that not a single idea known to the human mind can be said to be universal and therefore innate. By doing this he gave the science of education a new beginning.

He suggested a new explanation for the growth of knowledge, insisting that all knowledge comes from experience—chiefly from reflection and observation. He was inclined to nominalism since he held that general ideas, being framed by us, are nominal rather than real.

The mind in its original state he likened to a sheet of white paper, a "tabula rasa," a wax tablet upon which impressions are made through the senses, thus forming mental images. The "tabula rasa" theory discredited the rationalistic claims that all knowledge can be deduced from "first principles."

He justified the acceptance of Christianity as reasonable and useful in practical living, and is sometimes classified as a deist.

Locke concluded that we have an intuitive knowledge of ourselves, a demonstrative knowledge of the existence of God, and a sensitive knowledge of the material world.

His *Treatise on Government* (1690) advocated the rights of the individual and the need to limit the powers of the throne. He influenced the writings on constitutional government. He argued against the divine right of kings and declared that in a state of nature all men are free, independent, and equal, thus setting forth a naturalistic basis for the personal and civil rights of the individual. In a letter on toleration, he insisted upon the rights of conscience, saying: "Absolute liberty, just and true liberty, equal and impartial liberty, is the thing we stand in need of."[10]

Locke's principles of psychology and education are to be found in the *Essay Concerning Human Understanding* (1687), in *Some Thoughts Concerning Education* (1693), and a number of posthumous essays. He declared the doctrine of human depravity to be false since there were no innate ideas. If such ideas existed, the child would be a miniature adult, but since they do not, he differs radically from his elders. Locke's position thus opened the

[10] John Locke, "Letter on Toleration," quoted in Eby and Arrowood, *op. cit.*, p. 366.

way to a more realistic study of human development. He had, however, little notion of the function of heredity. Believing that all children are equal at birth, he maintained that whether they are good or bad, useful or worthless, depends on education.

Education, for Locke, was primarily a moral discipline based upon the habit of self-control rather than on a process of intellectual instruction. His observations regarding perception, reasoning, doubting, and other mental processes were keen. He thought that intellectual capacities were the result of habit. It appears that he did not believe in general powers of the mind, although Graves credits him with having first stated the doctrine of formal discipline.[11]

> We are born with faculties and powers capable almost of anything, such at least as would carry us farther than can easily be imagined: but it is only the exercise of those powers, which gives us ability and skill in anything and leads us toward perfection.... As it is in the body so it is in the mind: practice makes it what it is; and most even of those excellencies, which are looked on as natural endowments, will be found, when examined into more narrowly, to be the product of exercise and to be raised to that pitch only by repeated actions.[12]

"Strength of memory," he wrote, "is owing to a happy constitution, and not to any habitual improvement got by exercise."[13] He would train the powers of attention by having the learner "buckle" to the things to be learned, but he insisted that the teacher should have great skill in getting and maintaining attention through an appeal to the child's sense of usefulness and power. "The Great Skill of a Teacher is to get and keep the Attention of his Scholar; whilst he has that, he is sure to advance as fast as the Learner's Abilities will carry him."

He was among the first to recognize the factor of readiness. "The fittest Time for Children to learn any Thing is when their Minds are in Tune and well dispos'd to it."[15] Human actions, he believed, are motivated by inner needs such as hunger, cold and sleep, by desires to avoid pain or to experience pleasure, and by

---

[11] Frank Pierpont Graves, *History of Education during the Middle Ages and the Transition to Modern Times* (New York: Macmillan, 1920), p. 309.

[12] John Locke, *Conduct of the Understanding,* Secs. 4 and 6, quoted in Eby and Arrowood, *op. cit.,* p. 419.

[13] *Ibid.,* p. 410.

[14] *Ibid.,* p. 411.

[15] *Ibid.,* p. 414.

acquired habits such as the "itch" for power, and many others brought about by custom, example, and education.

Locke could not conceive of a society without an upper and lower class. His discussion of equality seems to have been confined to the upper classes. However, he was interested in improving the condition of paupers, as were the other philanthropists of his day. As King's Commissioner for the Board of Trade he drew up a plan for poor relief whereby children of the indigent were to be taken from their parents and to be kept in working schools from three to fourteen years of age after which they were to be apprenticed. They were to be fed on bread and gruel and taught religion, respect for their betters, habits of industry, and the simpler handicrafts. This formula of simple piety, handicrafts, and respect for superiors was repeated over and over in western Europe and had a considerable following in America.

His principle concern was with the education of future gentlemen, for he maintained that if they are once set right they will quickly bring the rest in order. With Milton he opposed and ridiculed the practices of the eighteenth-century grammar schools, and branded them as producers of vice, trickery, violence, and self-conceit. He recommended private tutoring as the best kind of pre-university education.

His curriculum included everything that would make a youth a gentleman of virtue, wisdom, breeding, and learning, for he maintained that a virtuous man is worth more than a great scholar. With Rabelais and Montaigne he insisted that all learning should be made not only pleasant, but easy. The guiding principle for curriculum building was usefulness, but usefulness to the future citizen, not to the child. He proposed the elimination of Greek for the general student and would retain only such study of Latin as would give the student the ability to read a Roman author. He stressed the study of English and foreign languages, especially French. There was no place for poetry or music in his plan. He criticized the linguistic education in his day, pointing out that children possess ability to learn words but frequently do not attach the right meanings to them. Rhetoric, he declared, was a powerful instrument of error and deceit.

He recommended the study of mathematics to improve children's ability to reason and to train in methods of consecutive and exact thought, for he insisted the method of mathematics, when learned, could be transferred to the learning of other subjects.

He urged the inclusion of physical education as basic to the development of a sound mind in a sound body. Boys were to swim and to exercise in the open air, and to engage in manual arts, gardening, and painting for health and recreation. Other subjects included geography, geometry, chronology, natural philosophy, ethics, and psychology. Travel in England and on the continent completed formal education.

Locke's views were so comprehensive that materialists and idealists, sensationalists, empiricists, and rationalists, formal disciplinarians and utilitarians found support in them. His influence in England can be readily seen in the writings of Hume and Berkeley. In France he influenced the Enlightenment, and in America, Franklin and Jefferson owe much to his writings. Basedow, Pestalozzi, and Herbart carried his ideas into education. He was not without his critics, among them Leibnitz, who wrote a rebuttal to "the Essay" but did not publish it because it was finished just at the time of Locke's death. It was published after the death of Leibnitz.

Locke transformed the ideas of men by declaring that many errors are due to mistaking words for things, that minds can be described as accurately as plants and animals, that the findings of philosophers should keep close to common sense, and that problems in philosophy are due more often to confusion among philosophers than to difficulties inherent in these problems.

Some Thoughts Concerning Education*

John Locke wrote Some Thoughts Concerning Education *as a series of letters giving advice on training a boy to become an English gentlemen. He stresses health, building a rugged body, and the necessity of a wise and well-bred tutor. Rewards and punishments should be carefully chosen, esteem and disgrace providing the best motivation. A good education should stress virtue, wisdom, breeding, and learning in that order.*

A sound mind in a sound body is a short but full description of a happy state in this world. He that has these two has little more to wish for; and he that wants either of them will be but little the better for anything else. Men's happiness or misery is most part of their own making. He whose mind directs not wisely will never take the right way; and he whose body is

Source: John Locke, *Some Thoughts Concerning Education,* ed. with an introduction by Howard R. Penniman (New York: Van Nostrand, 1947), pp. 210-388.

crazy and feeble will never be able to advance in it. I confess there are some men's constitutions of body and mind so vigorous and well framed by nature that they need not much assistance from other; but by the strength of their natural genius they are from their cradles carried towards what is excellent; and by the privilege of their happy constitutions are able to do wonders. But examples of this kind are but few; and I think I may say that of all the men we meet with, nine parts of ten are what they are, good or evil, useful or not, by their education.

· · · · ·

How necessary health is to our business and happiness, and how requisite a strong constitution, able to endure hardships and fatigue, is to one that will make any figure in the world, is too obvious to need any proof.

· · · · ·

The first thing to be taken care of, is, that children be not too warmly clad or covered, winter or summer. The face when we are born is no less tender than any other part of the body. 'Tis use alone hardens it, and makes it more able to endure the cold.

· · · · ·

I will also advise his feet to be washed every day in cold water, and to have his shoes so thin that they might leak and let in water, whenever he comes near it. Here, I fear I shall have the mistress and maids too against me. One will think it too filthy, and the other perhaps too much pains, to make clean his stockings. But yet truth will have it that his health is much more worth than all such considerations, and ten times as much more.

As the strength of the body lies chiefly in being able to endure hardships, so also does that of the mind. And the great principle and foundation of all virtue and worth is placed in this: that a man is able to deny himself of his own desires, cross his own inclinations, and purely follow what reason directs as best, though the appetite lean the other way.

· · · · ·

The great mistake I have observed in people's breeding their children has been, that this has not been taken care enough of in its due season: that the mind has not been made obedient to discipline and pliant to reason, when at first it was most tender, most easy to be bowed.

Those therefore that intend ever to govern their children

should begin it whilst they are very little, and look that they perfectly comply with the will of their parents.

•   •   •   •   •

Rewards, I grant, and punishments must be proposed to children, if we intend to work upon them. The mistake, I imagine, is that those that are generally made use of are ill chosen. The pains and pleasures of the body are, I think, of ill consequence, when made the rewards and punishments whereby men would prevail on their children; for, as I said before, they serve but to increase and strengthen those inclinations, which 'tis our business to subdue and master.

The rewards and punishments then, whereby we should keep children in order, are quite of another kind, and of that force that when we can get them once to work, the business, I think, is done, and the difficulty is over. *Esteem* and *disgrace* are, of all others, the most powerful incentives to the mind, when once it is brought to relish them. If you can once get into children a love of credit, and an apprehension of shame and disgrace, you have put into 'em the true principle, which will constantly work and incline them to the right.

In all the whole business of education, there is nothing like to be less hearkened to, or harder to be well observed, than what I am now going to say; and that is, that children should, from their first beginning to talk, have some discreet, sober, nay, wise person about them, whose care it should be to fashion them aright, and keep them from all ill, especially the infection of bad company.

Besides being well-bred, the tutor should know the world well; the ways, the humors, the follies, the cheats, the faults of the age he is fallen into, and particularly of the country he lives in. These he should be able to show to his pupil, as he finds him capable; teach him skill in men, and their manners; pull off the mask which their several callings and pretenses cover them with, and make his pupil discern what lies at the bottom under such appearances that he may not, as un-experienced young men are apt to do if they are unwarned, take one thing for another, judge by the outside, and give himself up to show, and the insinuation of a fair carriage, or an obliging application.

The only fence against the world is a thorough knowledge of it, into which a young gentleman should be entered by degrees, as he can bear it; and the earlier the better, so he be in safe and skillful hands to guide him. The scene should be gently opened, and his entrance made step by step, and the dangers pointed out that attend him from the several degrees, tempers, designs, and clubs of men. He should be prepared to be shocked by some and caressed by others; warned who are like to oppose, who to mislead, who to undermine him, and who to serve him. He should be instructed how to know and distinguish them; where he should let them see, and when dissemble the knowledge of them and their aims and workings. And if he be too forward to venture upon his own strength and skill, the perplexity and trouble of a misadventure now and then, that reaches not his innocence, his health, or reputation, may not be an ill way to teach him more caution.

·   ·   ·   ·   ·

That which every gentleman (that takes any care of his education) desires for his son, besides the estate he leaves him, is contained, I suppose, in these four things, *virtue, wisdom, breeding* and *learning.* I will not trouble myself whether these names do not some of them sometimes stand for the same thing, or really include one another. It serves my turn here to follow the popular use of these words, which, I presume, is clear enough to make me be understood, and I hope there will be no difficulty to comprehend my meaning.

I place *virtue* as the first and most necessary of these endowments that belong to a man or a gentlemen; as absolutely requisite to make him valued and beloved by others, acceptable or tolerable to himself. Without that, I think, he will be happy neither in this nor the other world.

Having laid the foundations of virtue in a true notion of a God, such as the creed wisely teaches, as far as his age is capable and by accustoming him to pray to Him, the next thing to be taken care of is to keep him exactly to speaking of truth, and by all the ways imaginable inclining him to be good-natured. Let him know that twenty faults are sooner to be forgiven than the straining of truth to cover anyone by an excuse. And to teach him betimes to love and be good-natured to others is to lay early the true foundation of an honest man; all injustice generally springing from too great love of ourselves and too little of others.

Wisdom I take in the popular acceptation, for a man's managing his business ably and with foresight in this world. This is the product of a good natural temper, application of mind, and experience together, and so above the reach of children.

The next good quality belonging to a gentleman is *good breeding*. There are two sorts of ill breeding: the one a sheepish bashfulness, and the other a misbecoming negligence and disrespect in our carriage; both which are avoided by duly observing this one rule, *not to think meanly of ourselves, and not to think meanly of others.*

You will wonder, perhaps, that I put *learning* last, especially if I tell you I think it the least part. This may seem strange in the mouth of a bookish man; and this making usually the chief, if not only bustle and stir about children, this being almost that alone which is thought on, when people talk of education, makes it the greater paradox. When I consider what ado is made about a little Latin and Greek, how many years are spent in it, and what a noise and business it makes to no purpose, I can hardly forbear thinking that the parents of children still live in fear of the schoolmaster's rod, which they look on as the instrument of education; as a language or two to be its whole business. How else is it possible that a child should be chained to the oar seven, eight, or ten of the best years of his life, to get a language or two, which, I think, might be had at a great deal cheaper rate of pain and time, and be learned almost in playing?

JEAN JACQUES ROUSSEAU

Eight years after the death of Locke, Jean Jacques Rousseau (1712-1778) was born in Geneva of a poor but highly respected Calvinist family. His mother died when he was a week old, and he was brought up by his father, an eccentric watchmaker with a passion for reading, which Rousseau soon acquired. When he was ten his father deserted him, and he was sent to boarding school for three years to receive the only systematic education he ever had. He was unsuccessful as an apprentice so he became a vagabond and wandered through France and Italy where he was converted to Catholicism, which he later deserted for deism. He went to Paris, where he earned a meager living as a copyist, musician, and writer, and in spite of his eccentricities he was accepted into the circle of the leaders of the Enlightenment. Although his reading was desultory it included the works of the principal philosophers from Plato to his own time. The works of Montaigne, Locke, Voltaire, and Defoe probably made the greatest impression upon him.

In 1762 he published two of his greatest works, in which he wrestled with two seemingly irreconcilable problems. "Man is born free, but everywhere he is in chains" is the opening cry of the *Social Contract.* "All is good as it comes from the hand of God" declares *Emile.* The problems might be joined thus: What is man's relation and responsibility to the state, and how can a child born into such a state be reared as to be uncorrupted by the vices of civilization?

Briefly, men become social beings only by associating with each other. This association, especially in its social and political aspects, is called the "state." In the course of time the state became corrupted and could no longer save itself. Society can only renew itself through the proper education of boys according to nature. Only thus can man develop fully and harmoniously. Up to the age of fourteen the child should be allowed free play and to have experience with nature without adult interference, except that the teacher should set up desirable situations to encourage the pupil to right action. At the age of fourteen there will come a great spiritual and moral awakening, and the youth will feel love and justice for himself. Girls should be trained to be docile, to serve men, and to make them happy.

Rousseau differed from Locke in many fundamental ways. With regard to the state, Locke offered a practical common-sense solution to justify the political, economic, and religious organization of his day. God created man, and not only gave him the whole world for his use but also endowed him with certain rights, such as life, liberty, and property, which could not be taken away from him. Men formed governments by social contract to guarantee (secure) these divine rights, which belong to all gentlemen, not only to kings. When governments no longer foster these natural rights, it is man's duty to rebel and to set up governments that do. Locke's theory is thoroughly individualistic, Protestant, and capitalistic. Private rights are morally grounded in the will of God, and are superior to law and order.

On the other hand, Rousseau contrasts the civil state with the state of nature. In the state of nature there is no justice because there are no laws; there is no equality because each man differs in his ability to grab and to retain; there is no freedom, only license, because each man strives to satisfy his own desires. There is no morality among men without government.

The state is primary. It creates conventions, civilization, culture, even reason. Social conventions decide between right and wrong, between good and bad behavior. Only by becoming a citizen can one become a man. The individual cannot be superior to the state of which he is a citizen. The only freedom that exists is *in* and *by* the state. The schools express the will and the wisdom of the community. The teacher is its agent and attempts to bring the individual into conformity with a pattern.

With regard to education, Locke's principal concern was with the English gentleman. Believing that the mind at birth was like a wax tablet, he considered the teacher's function to be to write desirable impressions of the outside world upon it. The purpose of education was practical in this sense and was designed to achieve the happiness of the individual through experience with nature and society by means of private tutors and travel.

Rousseau stated but did not solve the relationship between freedom on the one hand and imposed authority and required obedience on the other. He showed the necessity for attention to individual differences on the ground that unless we know what he is now, we cannot make a pupil what he ought to be. He recommended the elimination of terms of external coercion such as duty, obedience, and obligation from the vocabulary and advocated that from earliest infancy a child should learn to accept responsibility and be motivated by an internal sense of duty. His method was naturalistic, but his curriculum was traditional. The purpose of the school is to help the child make these necessary adjustments. On the whole, Rousseau believed that society's influence is evil. Therefore, he prescribed that the child be educated apart from society: from birth to four years his activities should be largely physical to develop the body; the period from five to twelve should be spent in acquiring knowledge of the world through sensory impressions; from thirteen to fifteen is the period to begin intellectual training through books and the time to learn a trade. This ends the period of his natural education apart from society. During the last period of formal education, from fifteen to twenty, the youth should come into contact with his fellow men so he can learn the great moral and spiritual principles of sympathy, goodness, and service.

As can be readily seen, Rousseau revolted against his precarious education by constructing a romantic picture of what it might have been under ideal circumstances.

Rousseau was one of the greatest creative geniuses of modern times. His thoughts were often paradoxical and extreme. Taken together they made little "common sense"; they were absurd, but never ridiculous. He fought for unity as well as diversity among men and for individual freedom as well as for the authority of an absolute general will. His influence on modern thought has been considerable. Kant, who was so methodical that the people of Koenigsberg could set their watches by his movements, failed to take his customary walk on receiving his copy of *Emile.* His *categorical imperative* was derived from Rousseau's dictum that the only absolute good in the universe is the human will governed by a respect for the moral law and a sense of duty. Fichte, Hegel, and others distorted his notion that man could fulfill himself only as part of an absolute state into a philosophy that ended in totalitarianism.

Rousseau believed that man was neither a machine to be conditioned nor a scientific mind, but a feeling heart. Educationally, he influenced Pestalozzi, Basedow, and Froebel, and the whole modern trend toward naturalism and the child-centered school.

He was a transitional thinker. He lived at the opening of new worlds: at the beginnings of the rise of the common man. His works were a protest against what had been and a call to what might be. He was the first of the moderns.

Emile*

In Emile, *which has been called the greatest book in the Western world next to* The Bible, *Rousseau advances the idea that if the earliest years of childhood are lived in accordance with the laws of nature, the child will be able to withstand the temptations and foibles of the world and will endeavor to bring about the reconstruction of society. In* Emile *the tutor uses nature as a tool for education, and does not advocate that nature take its course as some "progressive" educators do. The last part of the selection gives some idea of Rousseau's deistic religion.*

God makes all things good; man meddles with them and they become evil. He forces one soil to yield the products of another, one tree to bear another's fruit. He confuses and confounds time, place, and natural conditions. He mutilates his dog, his horse, and his slave. He destroys and defaces all things; he loves all that is deformed and monstrous; he will have nothing as nature made it, not even man himself, who

*Source: Jean Jacques Rousseau, *Emile on Education,* trans. Barbara Foxley (London: Dent, 1930).

must learn his paces like a saddlehorse, and be shaped to his master's taste like the trees in his garden.

Yet things would be worse without this education, and mankind cannot be made by halves. Under existing conditions a man left to himself from birth would be more of a monster than the rest. Prejudice, authority, necessity, example, all the social conditions into which we are plunged, would stifle nature in him and put nothing in her place. She would be like a sapling chance sown in the midst of the highway, bent hither and thither and soon crushed by the passers-by.

Plants are fashioned by cultivation, man by education. If a man were born tall and strong, his size and strength would be of no good to him till he learnt to use them; they would even harm him by preventing others from coming to his aid; (1) left to himself he would die of want before he knew his needs. We lament the helplessness of infancy; we fail to perceive that the race would have perished had not man begun by being a child.

This education comes to us from nature, from men, or from things. The inner growth of our organs and faculties is the education of nature, the use we learn to make of this growth is the education of men, what we gain by our experience of our surroundings is the education of things.

Now of these three factors in education nature is wholly beyond our control, things are only partly in our power; the education of men is the only one controlled by us; and even here our power is largely illusory, for who can hope to direct every word and deed of all with whom the child has to do.

Viewed as an art, the success of education is almost impossible, since the essential conditions of success are beyond our control. Our efforts may bring us within sight of the goal, but fortune must favour us if we are to reach it.

In the natural order men are all equal and their common calling is that of manhood, so that a well-educated man cannot fail to do well in that calling and those related to it. It matters little to me whether my pupil is intended for the army, the church, or the law. Before his parents chose a calling for him nature called him to be a man. Life is the trade I would teach him. When he leaves me, I grant you, he will be neither a magistrate, a soldier, nor a priest; he will be a man. All that becomes a man he will learn as quickly as another. In vain will fate change his station, he will always be in his right place. "Occupavi te, fortuna, atque cepi; omnes-que aditus tuos interclusi, ut ad me aspirare non posses." The real object of our study is man and his environment. To my mind those of us who can best endure the good and evil of life are the best educated; hence it follows that true education consists less in precept than in practice. We begin to learn when we begin to live; our education begins with ourselves, our first teacher is our nurse.

People think only of preserving their child's life; this is not enough, he must be taught to preserve his own life when he is a man, to bear the buffets of fortune, to brave wealth and poverty, to live at need among the snows of Iceland or on the scorching rocks of Malta. In vain you guard against death; he must needs die; and even if you do not kill him with your precautions they are mistaken. Teach him to live rather than to avoid death: life is not breath, but action, the use of our senses, our mind, our faculties, every part of ourselves which makes us conscious of our being. Life consists less in length of days than in the keen sense of living. A man may be buried at a hundred and may never have lived at all. He would have fared better had he died young.

• • • • •

The only habit the child should be allowed to contract is that of having no habits. . . .

If Emile must get used to the sound of a gun, I first fire a pistol with a small charge. He is delighted with this sudden flash, this sort of lightning; I repeat the process with more powder; gradually I add a small charge without a wad, then a larger; in the end I accustom him to the sound of a gun, to fireworks, cannon, and the most terrible explosions.

As the child grows it gains strength and becomes less restless and unquiet and more independent. Soul and body become better balanced and nature no longer asks for more movement than is required for self-preservation. But the love of power does not die with the need that aroused it; power arouses and flatters self-love, and habit strengthens it; thus caprice follows upon need, and the first seeds of prejudice and obstinacy are sown.

First Maxim. Far from being too strong, children are not strong enough for all the claims of nature. Give them full use of such strength as they have; they will not abuse it.

Second Maxim. Help them and supply the experience and strength they lack whenever the need is of the body.

Third Maxim. In the help you give them confine yourself to what is really needful, without granting anything to caprice or unreason; for they will not be tormented by caprice if you do not call it into existence, seeing it is no part of nature.

Fourth Maxim. Study carefully their speech and gestures, so that at an age when they are incapable of deceit you may discriminate between those desires which come from nature and those which spring from perversity.

The best way of learning to reason aright is that which tends to simplify our experiences, or to enable us to dispense with them altogether without falling into error. Hence it follows that we must learn to confirm the experiences of each sense by itself, without recourse to any other, though we have been in the habit of verifying the experience of one sense by that of another. Then each of our sensations will become an idea, and this idea will always correspond to the truth. This is the sort of knowledge I have tried to accumulate during this third phase of man's life.

Self-love is always good, always in accordance with the order of nature. The preservation of our own life is specially entrusted to each one of us, and our first care is, and must be, to watch over our own life; and how can we continually watch over it, if we do not take the greatest interest in it?

Self-preservation requires, therefore, that we shall love ourselves; we must love ourselves above everything, and it follows directly from this that we love what contributes to our preservation. Every child becomes fond of its nurse, Romulus must have loved the she-wolf who suckled him. At first this attachment is quite unconscious; the individual is attracted to that which contributes to his welfare and repelled by that which is harmful; this is merely blind instinct. What transforms this instinct into feeling, the liking into love, the aversion into hatred, is the evident intention of helping or hurting us.

The child's first sentiment is self-love, his second, which is derived from it, is love of those about him; for his present state of weakness he is only aware of people through the help and attention received from them.

Man's proper study is that of his relation to his environment. So long as he only knows that environment through his physical nature, he should study himself in relation to things; this is the business of his childhood; when he begins to be aware of his moral nature, he should study himself in relation to his fellow-men; this is the business of his whole life, and we have now reached the time when that study should be begun.

Do you desire to stimulate and nourish the first stirrings of awakening sensibility in the heart of a young man, do you desire to incline his disposition towards kindly deed and thought, do not cause the seeds of pride, vanity, and envy to spring up in him through the misleading picture of the happiness of mankind; do not show him to begin with the pomp of courts, the pride of palaces, the delights of pageants; do not take him into society and into brilliant assemblies; do not show him the outside of society till you have made him capable of estimating it at its true worth. To show him the world before he is acquainted with men, is not to train him, but to corrupt him; not to teach, but to mislead.

What then is required for the proper study of men? A great wish to know men, great impartiality of judgment, a heart sufficiently sensitive to understand every human passion, and calm enough to be free from passion. If there is any time in our life when this study is likely to be appreciated, it is this that I have chosen for Emile, before this time men would have been strangers to him; later on he would have been like them. Convention, the effects of which he already perceives, has not yet made him its slave, the passions, whose consequences he realises, have not yet stirred his heart. He is a man; he takes an interest in his brethren; he is a just man and he judges his peers. Now it is certain that if he judges them rightly he will not want to change places with any one of them, for the goal of all their anxious efforts is the result of prejudices which he does not share, and that goal seems to him a mere dream. For his own part, he has all he wants within his reach.

I am never weary of repeating: let all the lessons of young people take the form of doing rather than talking; let them learn nothing from books which they can learn from experience.

But remember, in the first place, that when I want to train a natural man, I do not want to make him a savage and to send him back to the woods, but that living in the whirl of social life it is enough that he should not let himself be carried away by the passions and prejudices of men; let him see with his eyes and feel with his heart, let him own no sway but that of reason. Under these conditions it is plain that many things will strike him; the oft-recurring feelings which affect him, the different ways of satisfying his real needs, must give him many ideas he would not otherwise have acquired or would only have acquired much later. The natural progress of the mind is quickened but not reversed. The same man who would remain stupid in the forests should become wise and reasonable in towns, if he were merely a spectator in them. Nothing is better fitted to make one wise than the sight of follies we do not share, and even if we share them, we still learn, provided we are not the dupe of our follies and provided we do not bring to them the same mistakes as the others.

·   ·   ·   ·   ·

I have transcribed this document not as a rule for the sentiments we should adopt in matters of religion, but as an example of the way in which we may reason with our pupil without forsaking the method I have tried to establish. So long as we yield nothing to human authority, nor to the prejudices of our native land, the light of reason alone, in a state of nature, can lead us no further than to natural religion; and this is as far as I should go with Emile. If he must have any other religion, I have no right to be his guide; he must choose for himself.

We are working in agreement with nature, and while she is shaping the physical man, we are striving to shape his moral being, but we do not make the same progress. The body is already strong and vigorous, the soul is still frail and delicate, and whatever can be done by human art, the body is always ahead of the mind. Hitherto all our care has been devoted to restrain the one and stimulate the other, so that the man might be as far as possible at one with himself. By developing his individuality, we have kept his growing susceptibilities in check; we have controlled it by cultivating his reason. Objects of thought moderate the influence of objects of sense. By going back to the causes of things, we have withdrawn him from the sway of the senses; it is an easy thing to raise him from the study of nature to the search for the author of nature.

So a young man when he enters society must be preserved from vanity rather than from sensibility; he succumbs rather to the tastes of others than to his own, and self-love is responsible for more libertines than love.

We have reached the last act of youth's drama; we are approaching its closing scene.

It is not good that man should be alone. Emile is now a man, and we must give him his promised helpmeet. That helpmeet is Sophy. Where is her dwelling-place, where shall she be found? We must know beforehand what she is, and then we can decide where to look for her. And when she is found, our task is not ended. "Since our young gentlemen," says Locke,

"is about to marry, it is time to leave him with his mistress."
And with these words he ends his book. As I have not the
honour of educating "a young gentlemen," I shall take care
not to follow his example.

THOMAS JEFFERSON

Notable among early American educational theorists are Benjamin
Franklin (1706-1790) and Thomas Jefferson (1743-1826). Franklin's interest in education was almost entirely practical and utilitarian. He advocated the teaching of the vernacular, and with
others proposed the establishment of a charity school to teach
English to the German population of Pennsylvania as a means of
unifying the colony. His proposals for the establishment of a
public academy in Philadelphia led to the founding of the University of Pennsylvania.

Jefferson, on the other hand, though imbued with the democratic and utilitarian spirit, was steeped in the classical tradition.
He was born at Shadwell, on the Virginia frontier, of a frontier
colonel and a daughter of the famous Randolph family. Although
he often referred to himself as a child of the wilderness, he lived in
an aristocratic tradition. He studied the classics at the College of
William and Mary, and graduated with highest honors in 1762. He
entered the law office of George Wythe and was admitted to the
Bar in 1767, after when he began his political career, which was to
take him from the House of Burgesses to the Second Continental
Congress, the ministry to France, and the presidency of the United
States. His tombstone records what he considered to be his three
greatest achievements: writing the Declaration of Independence
and the Statute of Virginia for Religious Freedom, and founding
the University of Virginia.

Metaphysically Jefferson might be called a materialist. However, he rejected the hypothesis of chance and blind necessity as a
cosmological first principle. He is sometimes called a deist because
he believed that a creator endowed the material cerebrum with the
activity of thought. He tried to reconcile "essential" Christianity
with the scientific findings of his day. Epistemologically he believed in specific faculties of the brain. He followed the empiricism
of Locke, rejecting the immaterialism of Plato, Descartes, and
Berkeley in favor of direct experience, both individual and social.
He believed that matter exercised the faculty of thought, and
accepted as valid evidence within the limits of human under-

standing. Ethically, he accepted the morals of Jesus, but rejected all dogmatic theology, agreeing with Locke that one must trust one's own reason rather than mystical revelation. He combined Epicurean search for happiness through contemplation with stoic resignation to the Divine Will and attempted to obtain tranquility of soul through self-discipline. He championed freedom in speech and religion with complete confidence in the democratic process. In his first inaugural address he said: "If there be any among us who would wish to dissolve the Union or to change its republican form, let them stand undisturbed as monuments of the safety with which error of opinion may be tolerated where reason is left free to combat it."[16]

Concerning freedom of religion, he wrote: "I contemplated with sovereign reverence that act of the whole American people which declares that their legislature should make no law respecting the establishment of religion, or prohibiting the free exercise thereof, thus building a wall of separation between Church and State."[17]

He believed that the clergy should confine their preaching to religious instruction. "In choosing our pastor we should look to his religious qualifications, without inquiring into his physical or political dogmas with which we mean to have nothing to do."[18]

He feared the domination of higher education by religious groups, because most colonial colleges, the College of Philadelphia excepted, owed their origins to religious foundations. He asserted that faculty and students at the University of Virginia should be free to exercise their own religious preferences. He wrote: "Freedom of religion [is] the most inalienable and sacred of all human rights, over which the people of this state, individually and publicly, have ever manifested the most watchful jealousy."[19]

Public education for Jefferson was concerned with the preparation of citizens and leaders for American democracy. During the early days of the republic he wrote to James Madison: "Above all things I hope the education of the common people will be attended to; convinced that on their good sense we may rely with

---

[16] First Inaugural Address, March 4, 1801, in Gordon C. Lee, ed., *Crusade Against Ignorance* (New York: Teachers College, Columbia University Press, 1961), p. 51.

[17] To Messers Nehemiah Dodge, Ephraim Robbins, and Stephen Nelson, A Committee of the Danbury Baptist Association, in the State of Connecticut, January 1, 1802, in *ibid.*, p. 69.

[18] Letter to P. H. Wendover, March 13, 1815, in *ibid.*, p. 73.

[19] Annual Report of the Board of Visitors of the University of Virginia, October 7, 1822, in *ibid.*, p. 77.

the most security for the preservation of a due sense of liberty."[20]

To George Washington he wrote: "It is an axiom in my mind that our liberty can never be safe but in the hands of the people with a certain degree of instruction. This is the business of the state to effect and on a general plan."[21]

It was his opinion that "If a nation expects to be ignorant and free in a state of civilization, it expects what never was and never will be."[22]

Therefore he could maintain: "I know no safe depository of the ultimate power of society but in the people themselves; and if we think them not enlightened enough to exercise their control with a wholesome discretion, the remedy is not to take it from them, but to inform their discretion by education."[23]

In his "Bill for the General Diffusion of Knowledge" he proposed that each county should be divided into hundreds and that a committee of citizens should pick a site for a schoolhouse within convenient reach of its students. These schools were to teach reading, writing, and common arithmetic. Ancient, English, and American history were to be taught indirectly through reading. All students, both boys and girls, were to receive free instruction for a period of three years, and as long after that as their parents were able to pay for it. The overseers of each county were to pick a suitable place for a grammar school. These boarding schools were to teach the standard English grammar school subjects. From each lower school the school visitors were to choose "one promising scholar," whose parents were too poor to afford further education, to receive one or two years of grammar school education gratis, after which the "best genius" in each grammar school was to be chosen to receive six more years of education at public expense. Then half the free students would be chosen to continue their education on scholarships at the College of William and Mary. Thus Jefferson assured Virginia a literate citizenry and a select group of well-educated leaders.

Bill for the More General Diffusion of Knowledge

The Bill for the More General Diffusion of Knowledge, written by Jefferson in 1779 for the State of Virginia, was not adopted in

[20] Letter to James Madison, December 20, 1787, in *ibid.*, p. 38.
[21] Letter to George Washington, January 4, 1786, in *ibid.*, p. 19.
[22] Letter to Colonel Charles Yancey, January 6, 1816, *ibid.*, pp. 18-19.
[23] Letter to William C. Jarvis, September 28, 1820, in *ibid.*, p. 17.

its original form, but it gives a clear statement of Jefferson's ideas on education.

Whereas it appeareth that however certain forms of government are better calculated than others to protect individuals in the free exercise of their natural rights, and are at the same time themselves better guarded against degeneracy, yet experience hath shewn, that even under the best forms, those entrusted with power have, in time, and by slow operations, perverted it into tyranny; and it is believed that the most effectual means of preventing this would be, to illuminate, as far as practicable, the minds of the people at large, and more especially to give them knowledge of those facts, which history exhibiteth, that, possessed thereby of the experience of other ages and countries, they may be enabled to know ambition under all its shapes, and prompt to exert their natural powers to defeat its purposes; And whereas it is generally true that that people will be happiest whose laws are best, and are best administered, and that laws will be wisely formed, and honestly administered, in proportion as those who form and administer them are wise and honest; whence it becomes expedient for promoting the public happiness that those persons, whom nature hath endowed with genius and virtue, should be rendered by liberal education worthy to receive, and able to guard the sacred deposit of the rights and liberties of their fellow citizens, and that they should be called to that charge without regard to wealth, birth or other accidental condition or circumstance; but the indigence of the greater number disabling them from so educating, at their own expence, those of their children whom nature hath fitly formed and disposed to become useful instruments for the public, it is better that such should be sought for and educated at the common expence of all, than that the happiness of all should be confided to the weak or wicked.

Be it therefore enacted by the General Assembly, that in every county within this commonwealth, there shall be chosen annually, by the electors qualified to vote for Delegates, three of the most honest and able men of their county, to be called the Aldermen of the county; and that the election of the said

Source: Gordon C. Lee (ed.), *Crusade Against Ignorance* (New York: Teacher's College, Columbia University Press, 1961). pp. 83-92. Reprinted with permission.

Aldermen shall be held at the same time and place, before the same persons, and notified and conducted in the same manner as by law is directed for the annual election of Delegates for the county.

The electors aforesaid residing within every hundred shall meet on the third Monday in October after the first election of Aldermen, at such place, within their hundred, as the said Aldermen shall direct, notice thereof being previously given to them by such person residing within the hundred as the said Aldermen shall require who is hereby enjoined to obey such requisition, on pain of being punished by amercement and imprisonment. The electors being so assembled shall choose the most convenient place within their hundred for building a school-house.

At every of these schools shall be taught reading, writing, and common arithmetick, and the books which shall be used therein for instructing the children to read shall be such as will at the same time make them acquainted with Grecian, Roman, English, and American history. At these schools all the free children, male and female, resident within the respective hundred, shall be entitled to receive tuition gratis, for the term of three years, and as much longer, at their private expence, as their parents, guardians or friends, shall think proper.

Over every ten of these schools (or such other number nearest thereto, as the number of hundreds in the county will admit, without fractional divisions) an overseer shall be appointed annually by the Aldermen at their first meeting, eminent for his learning, integrity, and fidelity to the commonwealth, whose business and duty it shall be, from time to time, to appoint a teacher to each school, who shall give assurance of fidelity to the commonwealth, and to remove him as he shall see cause; to visit every school once in every half year at the least; to examine the schollars; see that any general plan of reading and instruction recommended by the visitors of William and Mary College shall be observed; and to superintend the conduct of the teacher in every thing relative to his school.

Every teacher shall receive a salary of ＿＿ by the year, which, with the expences of building and repairing the schoolhouses, shall be provided in such manner as other county expences are by law directed to be provided and shall also have his diet, lodging, and washing found him, to be levied in like manner, save only that such levy shall be on the inhabitants of each hundred for the board of their own teacher only.

The said overseers shall forthwith proceed to have a house of brick or stone, for the said grammar school, with necessary offices, built on the said lands, which grammar school-house shall contain a room for the school, a hall to dine in, four rooms for a master and usher, and ten or twelve lodging rooms for the scholars.

To each of the said grammar schools shall be allowed out of the public treasury, the sum of _____ pounds, out of which shall be paid by the Treasurer, on warrant from the Auditors, to the proprietors or tenants of the lands located, the value of their several interests as fixed by the jury, and the balance thereof shall be delivered to the said overseers to defray the expence of the said buildings.

In these grammar schools shall be taught the Latin and Greek languages, English grammar, geography, and the higher part of numerical arithmetick, to wit, vulgar and decimal fractions, and the extraction of the square and cube roots.

• • • • •

Every overseer of the hundred schools shall, in the month of September annually, after the most diligent and impartial examination and enquiry, appoint from among the boys who shall have been two years at the least at some one of the schools under his superintendance, and whose parents are too poor to give them farther education, some one of the best and most promising genius and disposition, to proceed to the grammar school of his district; which appointment shall be made in the court-house of the county, on the court day for that month if fair, and if not, then on the next fair day, excluding Sunday, in the presence of the Aldermen, or two of them at the least, assembled on the bench for that purpose, the said overseer being previously sworn by them to make such appointment, without favor or affection, according to the best of his skill and judgment, and being interrogated by the said Alderman, either on their own motion, or on suggestions from the parents, guardians, friends, or teachers of the children, competitors for such appointment; which teachers shall attend for the information of the Aldermen. On which interrogatories the said Aldermen, if they be not satisfied with the appointment proposed, shall have right to negative it; whereupon the said visiter may proceed to make a new appointment, and the said Aldermen again to interrogate and negative, and so toties quoties [just as many times] until an appointment be approved.

Every boy so appointed shall be authorised to proceed to the grammar school of his district, there to be educated and boarded during such time as is hereafter limited; and his quota of the expences of the house together with a compensation to the master or usher for his tuition, at the rate of twenty dollars by the year, shall be paid by the Treasurer quarterly on warrant from the Auditors.

A visitation shall be held, for the purpose of probation, annually at the said grammar school on the last Monday in September, if fair, and if not, then on the next fair day, excluding Sunday, at which one third of the boys sent thither by appointment of the said overseers, and who shall have been there one year only, shall be discontinued as public foundationers, being those who, on the most diligent examination and enquiry, shall be thought to be of the least promising genius and disposition; and of those who shall have been there two years, all shall be discontinued, save one only the best in genius and disposition, who shall be at liberty to continue there four years longer on the public foundation, and shall thence forward be deemed a senior.

The visiters for the districts which, or any part of which, be southward and westward of James river, as known by that name, or by the names of Fluvanna and Jackson's river, in every other year, to wit, at the probation meetings held in the years, distinguished in the Christian computation by odd numbers, and the visiters for all the other districts at their said meetings to be held in those years, distinguished by even numbers, after diligent examination and enquiry as before directed, shall chuse one among the said seniors, of the best learning and most hopeful genius and disposition, who shall be authorised by them to proceed to William and Mary College, there to be educated, boarded, and clothed, three years; the expence of which annually shall be paid by the Treasurer on warrant from the Auditors.

BIBLIOGRAPHY

COMENIUS
Butler, N. M., *Place of Comenius in the History of Education* (Syracuse: Barden, 1892).
Comenius, John Amos, *Analytical Didactic*, trans. and with an introduction and notes by Vladimir Jelinek (Chicago: University of Chicago Press, *ca.* 1953).

——, *Orbis Sensualium Pictus* (Sydney: Sydney University Press, 1967).
——, *School of Infancy,* ed. with an introduction and notes by William S. Monroe (New York: Heath, 1893).
——, *Selections,* with an introduction by Jean Piaget (Paris: UNESCO, 1957).
——, *The Great Didactic,* trans. and with an introduction by M. W. Keatinge (New York: Russell and Russell, 1967).
Needham, Joseph, *The Teacher of Nations* (Cambridge, Eng.: Cambridge University Press, 1942).
Sadler, John Edward, *J. A. Comenius and the Concept of Universal Education* (New York: Barnes and Noble, 1966).
Spinka, Matthew, *John Amos Comenius: That Incomparable Moravian* (Chicago: University of Chicago Press, 1943).

   LOCKE
*Locke, John, *Essay Concerning Human Understanding,* ed. A. D. Woozley (New York: Meridian Books, World, 1964).
*——, *John Locke on Education,* ed. P. Gay (New York: Teachers College Press, 1964).
*——, *Locke on Politics, Religion and Education,* ed. M. Cranston (New York: Collier Books, Macmillan, 1965).
*——, *Of Civil Government,* (Chicago: Gateway Edit'ons, Regnery, 1960).
*——, *Of Civil Government* (Chicago: Gateway Editions, Regnery, 1960). Teachers College Press, 1966).
*——, *On the Reasonableness of Christianity* (Chicago: Gateway Editions, Regnery, 1965).
*——, *Second Treatise of Government,* ed. T. P. Peardon (Indianapolis: Liberal Arts Press, Bobbs-Merrill, 1952).
*——, *Some Thoughts Concerning Education,* ed. F. W. Garforth (Woodbury, N.Y.: Barron, 1965).
*——, *Treatise of Civil Government: Letter Concerning Toleration* (New York: Appleton-Century-Crofts, 1959).

   ROUSSEAU
*Rousseau, Jean Jacques, *Confessions,* trans. J. M. Cohen (Baltimore: Penguin).
*——, *Emile, Julie, and Other Writings,* ed. R. L. Archer, trans. S. E. Frost, Jr. (Woodbury, N.Y.: Barron, 1964).
*——, *Minor Educational Writings of Jean Jacques Rousseau,* ed. W. H. Boyd (New York: Teachers College Press, 1962).
*——, *Rousseau's First and Second Discourses,* trans. R. D. Masters (New York: St. Martin's Press, 1911).
*——, *Social Contract,* trans. W. Kendall (Chicago: Gateway Editions, Regnery, 1960).

   JEFFERSON
*Jefferson, Thomas, *Autobiography of Thomas Jefferson,* with an introduction by D. Malone (New York: Capricorn Books, Putnam, 1959).
*——, *Crusade Against Ignorance: Thomas Jefferson on Education,* ed. G. C. Lee (New York: Teachers College Press, 1961).
*——, *Notes on the State of Virginia,* ed. B. Wishy and W. E. Leuchtenburg,

with an introduction by T. P. Abernathy (New York: Torchbooks, Harper & Row, 1964).

*———, *Political Writings of Thomas Jefferson*, ed. E. Dumbauld (Indianapolis: Liberal Arts Press, Bobbs-Merrill, 1955).

*———, *Thomas Jefferson on Democracy*, ed. S. Padover (New York: Mentor Books, New American Library, 1939).

*———, *Thomas Jefferson Papers*, ed. F. Donovan (New York: Apollo Editions, T.Y. Crowell, 1964).

Koch, Adrienne, *The Philosophy of Thomas Jefferson* (New York: Columbia University Press, 1943).

Malone, Dumas, *An Outline of the Life of Thomas Jefferson 1743-1826*, University of Virginia Record Extension Series, Vol. VIII, No. 7, (Charlottesville: University of Virginia, March 1924).

*Paperback editions.

Chapter Six
Ninteenth-Century Innovators: Pestalozzi, Hegel, Herbart, and Froebel

WHEN THE ENLIGHTENMENT came to Germany under the influence of Frederick the Great, King of Prussia (1740-1786), the influence of Rousseau was brought to new philosophical heights by the writings of Kant (1724-1804) and was applied to education in both theory and practice. All the thinkers of this period were interested in promoting the good life: Hegel by conformity to the Absolute, Pestalozzi and Froebel by a mystical interpretation of the child's experience, and Herbart by pedagogical methods based on psychological principles.

JOHANN HEINRICH PESTALOZZI

Pestalozzi's (1746-1827) writing and work were concerned with the fundamental problem of control: the individual vs. the group, social control vs. natural forces. He believed that the individual was superior to the group, although all should work together for the common good, and that control by the ways of nature took precedence over control by men. His thought was influenced by Rousseau's *Emile* and the works of Immanuel Kant with which he became acquainted through his friend, Johann Gottlieb Ficthe (1762-1814), who in turn formulated a plan for the Prussian system

of education based on the principles of Pestalozzi. He was born at
Zurich, Switzerland. When he was five years old, his father, a competent physician, died, leaving him to be brought up by a devoted
mother. His early contacts with poverty through visiting his grandfather's parishioners during his summer vacation made him determined to raise the level of the poor from a state of abject poverty to
humanity, and to secure a happier and more virtuous life for every
individual. After unsuccessful attempts at the ministry and the law
he came into possession of a property of considerable size at Neuhof,
where he decided to become a farmer and to establish an industrial
boarding school in 1774. This venture failed in 1780. He had a
school at Stanz in 1798, at Burgdorf from 1799 to 1804, and at
Yverdon from 1805 to 1825. During much of his life he lived on the
edge of poverty. He wrote: "Long years I lived surrounded by more
than fifty beggar children. In poverty I shared my bread with them. I
lived like a beggar in order to learn how to make beggars live like
men."[1]

In his two principal works, *Leonard and Gertrude* (1782) and
How Gertrude Teaches Her Children (1801), he tells how a proper
education reforms a Swiss village and how education according to
nature mingled with human affection is practical. Man is a natural
(not a supernatural) being; he is the same whether on the throne
or in the hut. All must follow the road of nature, but it is not the
same road for everybody. He constantly worked against the
ignorance, poverty, and injustice of his day. "Man," he wrote,
"creates organizations, laws, customs, even religion, but uses them
for his own personal and selfish ends rather than for the good of
all. We live in a state of institutionalized injustice."[2] He believed
that reform begins with the individual and not with the group. The
individual must be given the chance and the power to help himself
to a harmonious functioning of head, heart, and hand. Pestalozzi
was among the first to view education as organic development. He
inveighed against the traditional education with its overemphasis
on mental discipline and memorization. In "The Swan Song" he
wrote, "only that which affects man as an indissoluble unit is
educative in our sense of the word."[3] By organic development he
implied that general education must precede vocational education,
that education should be concerned with growth in knowledge and

[1] J. H. Pestalozzi, *How Gertrude Teaches Her Children*, trans. L. E. Holland and
F. C. Turner (Syracuse: Bardeen, 1894), p. 9.
[2] From *The Evening Hour of an Hermit*, quoted in Robert Ulich, *History of
Educational Thought* (New York: American Book, 1945), p. 258.
[3] Quoted in Frederick Eby and Charles Arrowood, *The Development of Modern
Education* (New York: Prentice-Hall, 1947), p. 638.

power rather than with the acquisition of knowledge, that the child's innate capacities should be awakened by a series of experiences arranged according to his maturation, and that method should follow the order of nature.

It is like the art of the gardener under whose care a thousand trees blossom and grow. He contributes nothing to their actual growth; the principle of growth lies in the trees themselves. He plants and waters, but God gives the increase. . . . So with the educator; he imparts no single power to men. He only watches lest external force should injure or disturb. He takes care that development runs its course in accordance with its own law. . . . The moral, the intellectual and practical powers of our nature must, as it were, spring out of themselves for themselves.[4]

Pestalozzi recommended that the curriculum correspond with the three constituents of human nature which he listed as intellectual, practical power, morality, and religion. He stressed the cultivation of the emotions and the need for religious experiences, which he said are to be experienced by the example of the teacher and the activity of the learner. Faith, not reason, is the faculty by which man apprehends his Maker.

Basing all learning on sense perception and activity, Pestalozzi developed a curriculum made up of object lessons, development of language skills, arithmetic, geography, music (especially singing), drawing, modeling, geometry, gymnastics, and manual training. He rejected, as did Rousseau, the study of history, myth, and literature because they had no direct connection with sense perception.

His views on education were not clearly stated because he was not always sure of them himself. Eby and Arrowood[5] list his influence as follows:

1. He had an unshakable faith in the power of education.
2. He showed the importance of psychology in education.
3. He demonstrated the organic character of education.
4. He believed that intellectual life begins with sense impressions.
5. He taught that the concrete must always precede the abstract.
6. He believed that human development is a gradual building of power.
7. He considered religion to be a matter of faith and action.
8. He introduced new teaching devices.

[4] J. H. Pestalozzi, "The Swan Song," in *Pestalozzi's Educational Writings,* ed. J. A. Green (London: Edward Arnold, 1916), p. 195.
[5] Eby and Arrowood, *op. cit.,* pp. 662-666.

Twenty-five Centuries of Educational Thought   CHART 5: MODELS OF 19th CENTURY HUMANITARIANISM

1700	1800	1900		

JOHANN B. BASEDOW 1723-1790 — Vocational education

IMMANUEL KANT 1724-1804 — Critical idealism; Categorical Imperative

THOMAS JEFFERSON 1743-1826 — Followed Locke; founded University of Virginia

JOHANN HERDER 1744-1803 — Followed Spinoza; unity of mind and matter

JOHANN HEINRICH PESTALOZZI 1746-1827 — Followed Rousseau; combined naturalism and religious mysticism

COUNT DE SIMON 1760-1825 — Utopian socialism

JOHANN G. FICHTE 1762-1814 — Absolute idealism; Prussian educational system

FRIEDRICH SCHLEIERMACHER 1768-1834 — Emotions the fundamental seat of human behavior

GEORG W. F. HEGEL 1770-1831 — Absolute idealism; dialectic

FRIEDRICH SCHLEGEL 1772-1839 — Romantic school of literature

SAMUEL TAYLOR COLERIDGE 1772-1834 — Introduced Kant to England

JAMES MILL 1773-1836 — Followed Hume; utilitarianism; friend of Bentham

FRIEDRICH W. J. SCHELLING 1775-1854 — Absolute idealism

JOHANN FRIEDRICH HERBART 1776-1841 — Realist; educational psychology

FRIEDRICH FROEBEL 1782-1852 — Kindergarten

JEREMY BENTHAM 1784-1832 — Ethics based on regard for consequences (pleasure-pain)

ARTHUR SCHOPENHAUER 1788-1860 — Pessimism

THOMAS CARLYLE 1795-1881 — Studied German philosophy, especially Fichte

AUGUSTE COMTE 1798-1857 — Positivist; father of sociology

CARDINAL JOHN HENRY NEWMAN 1801-1890 — Oxford movement; Roman Catholicism

RALPH WALDO EMERSON 1803-1882 — Transcendentalism

LUDWIG A. FEUERBACH 1804-1872 — Religious humanism

JOHN S. MILL 1806-1873 — Utilitarianism; happiness is the pleasure of enlightened minds

9. He based discipline on mutual empathy and understanding between teacher and pupil.
10. He advocated a new system of teacher training.

Pestalozzi has been called "education's most successful failure." He died, revered by all who knew him, but without a full realization of how widespread his influence was to be. He gave impetus to the manual-labor movement in education in Europe and America through his friend and associate, Philipp E. von Fellenberg (1771-1844). After the Swiss reforms of 1830 his principles were introduced into the educational practice of many cantonal schools. Although there was not much interest in his theories in England and France because of the weight of tradition, the influence of a small group made his ideas known in America, where his methods were introduced as early as 1806. The great interest in his method and the growth in its application, however, occurred after 1860.

Leonard and Gertrude*

In this selection from the delightful romantic novel, Leonard and Gertrude, *Pestalozzi describes the introduction of the new schoolmaster and his method of instruction and discipline.*

GERTRUDE'S METHOD OF INSTRUCTION

It was quite early in the morning when Arner, Glülphi and the pastor went to the mason's cottage. The room was not in order when they entered, for the family had just finished breakfast, and the dirty plates and spoons still lay upon the table. Gertrude was at first somewhat disconcerted, but the visitors reassured her, saying kindly: "This is as it should be; it is impossible to clear the table before breakfast is eaten!"

Chart 5 shows the diversity of thought of the late eighteenth and the nineteenth centuries. German idealism developed through Kant, Fichte, Hegel, Schelling, Coleridge, Carlisle, and Emerson. The spirit of Locke was alive in Jefferson. Rousseau's emphasis of emotions and the natural man was carried forward by Pestalozzi and Froebel. Romanticism flourished in Schleierman and Schlegel. Positivism developed under Comte. Utilitarianism and a teleological ethic were advocated by James Mill, Jeremy Bentham, and John Stuart Mill. There was a Catholic revival in England in which Cardinal Newman was involved. The whole century was alive with intellectual activity.

*Source: Johann Heinrich Pestalozzi, *Leonard and Gertrude,* trans. and abr. Eva Channing (New York: Heath, 1885), pp. 129-131, 152-156.

The children all helped wash the dishes, and then seated themselves in their customary places before their work. The gentlemen begged Gertrude to let everything go on as usual, and after the first half hour, during which she was a little embarrassed, all proceeded as if no stranger were present. First the children sang their morning hymns, and then Gertrude read a chapter of the Bible aloud, which they repeated after her while they were spinning, rehearsing the most instructive passages until they knew them by heart. In the mean time, the oldest girl had been making the children's beds in the adjoining room, and the visitors noticed through the open door that she silently repeated what the others were reciting. When this task was completed, she went into the garden and returned with vegetables for dinner, which she cleaned while repeating Bible-verses with the rest.

It was something new for the children to see three gentlemen in the room, and they often looked up from their spinning toward the corner where the strangers sat. Gertrude noticed this, and said to them: "Seems to me you look more at these gentlemen than at your yarn." But Harry answered: "No, indeed! We are working hard, and you'll have finer yarn to-day than usual."

Whenever Gertrude saw that anything was amiss with the wheels or cotton, she rose from her work, and put it in order. The smallest children, who were not old enough to spin, picked over the cotton for carding, with a skill which excited the admiration of the visitors.

Although Gertrude thus exerted herself to develop very early the manual dexterity of her children, she was in no haste for them to learn to read and write. But she took pains to teach them early how to speak; for, as she said, "of what use is it for a person to be able to read and write, if he cannot speak?—since reading and writing are only an artificial sort of speech." To this end she used to make the children pronounce syllables after her in regular succession, taking them from an old A-B-C book she had. This exercise in correct and distinct articulation was, however, only a subordinate object in her whole scheme of education, which embraced a true comprehension of life itself. Yet she never adopted the tone of instructor toward her children; she did not say to them: "Child, this is your head, your nose, your hand, your finger;" or: "Where is your eye, your ear?"—but instead, she would say: "Come here child, I will wash your little hands," "I will comb your hair," or: "I will cut your finger-nails." Her verbal instruction seemed to vanish in the spirit of her real activity, in which it always had its source. The result of her system was that each child was skilful, intelligent and active to the full extent that its age and development allowed.

The instruction she gave them in the rudiments of arithmetic was intimately connected with the realities of life. She taught them to count the number of steps from one end of the room to the other, and two of the rows of five panes each, in one of the windows, gave her an opportunity to unfold the decimal relations of numbers. She also made them count their threads while spinning, and the number of turns on the reel, when they wound the yarn into skeins. Above all, in every occupation of life she taught them an accurate and intelligent observation of common objects and the forces of nature.

All that Gertrude's children knew, they knew so thoroughly that they were able to teach it to the younger ones; and this they often begged permission to do. On this day, while the visitors were present, Jonas sat with each arm around the neck of a smaller child, and made the little ones pronounce the syllables of the A-B-C book after him; while Lizzie placed herself with her wheel between two of the others, and while all three spun, taught them the words of a hymn with the utmost patience.

When the guests took their departure, they told Gertrude they would come again on the morrow. "Why?" she returned, "You will only see the same thing over again." But Glülphi said: "That is the best praise you could possibly give yourself." Gertrude blushed at this compliment and stood confused when the gentleman kindly pressed her hand in taking leave.

The three could not sufficiently admire what they had seen at the mason's house, and Glülphi was so overcome by the powerful impression made upon him, that he longed to be alone and seek counsel of his own thoughts. He hurried to his room and as he crossed the threshold the words broke from his lips: "I must be schoolmaster in Bonnal!" All night visions of Gertrude's schoolroom floated through his mind, and he only fell asleep toward morning. Before his eyes were fairly open, he murmured: "I will be schoolmaster!"—and hastened to Arner to acquaint him with his resolution.

•   •   •   •   •

THE ORGANIZATION OF A NEW SCHOOL

Glülphi was full of the idea of his school, and could speak of nothing else with Arner and the pastor. He used all his spare time in visiting Gertrude, in order to talk it over with her; but she seemed quite unable to explain her method in words, and usually deprecated the idea of her advice being necessary. Occasionally, however, she would let drop some significant remark which the lieutenant felt went to the root of the whole matter of education. For example, she said to him one day: "You should do for your children what their parents fail to do for them. The reading, writing and arithmetic are not, after all, what they most need; it is all well and good for them to learn something, but the really important thing is for them to *be* something,—for them to become what they are meant to be, and in becoming which they so often have no guidance or help at home."

Finally, the day arrived on which the new schoolmaster was to be formally presented to the village. Arner and the pastor led him solemnly between them to the church, which was crowded with the inhabitants of Bonnal. The good clergyman preached a sermon on the ideal function of the school in its relation to the home, and to the moral development of the community; after which Arner led Glülphi forward to the railing of the choir, and introducing him to the people, made a short but earnest plea in his behalf. The lieutenant was much affected, but mastered his emotion sufficiently to express in a few words his sense of the responsibility conferred upon him, and his hope that the parents would cooperate with him in his undertaking. . . .

On the following morning the lieutenant began his school, and Gertrude helped him in the arrangement of it. They examined the children with regard to their previous studies, and seated those together who were equally advanced. First there were those who had not learned their letters, then those who could read separate words, and finally, those who already knew how to read. Besides reading, all were to learn writing and arithmetic, which previously had only been taught to the more wealthy, in private lessons.

At first Glülphi found it harder than he had expected; but every day, as he gained in experience, his task became easier and more delightful. A good and capable woman, named Margaret, who came to take charge of the sewing, spinning etc., proved a most valuable and conscientious helper in the work. Whenever a child's hand or wheel stopped, she would step up and restore things to their former condition. If the children's hair was in disorder, she would braid it up while they studied and worked; if there was a hole in their clothes, she would take a needle and thread, and mend it; and she showed them how to fasten their shoes and stockings properly, besides many other things they did not understand.

The new master was anxious, above all, to accustom his charges to strict order, and thus lead them to the true wisdom of life. He began school punctually on the stroke of the clock, and did not allow any one to come in late. He also laid great stress on good habits and behavior. The children were obliged to come to school clean in person and apparel, and with their hair combed. While standing, sitting, writing and working, they always were taught to keep the body erect as a candle. Glülphi's schoolroom must be clean as a church, and he would not suffer a pane of glass to be missing from the window, or a nail to be driven crooked in the floor. Still less did he allow the children to throw the smallest thing upon the floor, or to eat while they were studying; and it was even arranged that in getting up and sitting down they should not hit against each other.

Before school began, the children came up to their teacher one by one, and said: "God be with you!" He looked them over from head to foot, so that they knew by his eye if anything was wrong. If this glance was not sufficient, he spoke to them, or sent a message to their parents. A child would not infrequently come home with the word: "The schoolmaster sends greeting, and wants to know whether you have no needles and thread," or "whether water is dear," etc. At the close of school, those who had done well went up to him first, and said: "God be with you!" He held out his hand to each one, replying: "God be with you, my dear child!" Then came those who had only done partly well, and to these he merely said: "God be with you!" without giving them his hand. Finally, those who had not done well at all had to leave the room without even going to him.

The lieutenant's punishments were designed to remedy the faults for which they were inflicted. An idle scholar was made to cut fire-wood, or to carry stones for the wall which some of the older boys were constructing under the master's charge; a forgetful child was made school-messenger, and for several days was obliged to take charge of all the teacher's business in the village. Disobedience and impertinence he punished by not speaking publicly to the child in question for a number of days, talking with him only in private, after school. Wickedness and lying were punished with the rod, and any child thus chastised was not allowed to play with the others for a whole week; his name was registered in a special record-book of offences, from which it was not erased until plain evidence of improvement was given. The schoolmaster was kind to the children while punishing them, talking with them more then than at any other time, and trying to help them correct their faults.

GEORG WILHELM FRIEDRICH HEGEL

G.W.F. Hegel (1770-1831) was born of well-to-do parents in Stuttgart. He was a fellow student of Schelling at Tübingen and in 1805 attained to a professorship at Jena, a position he held for one year until the defeat by Napoleon in 1806. He was employed as a newspaper editor and as headmaster of a boy's school until he became a professor at Heidelberg in 1816. Two years later he went to Berlin, where he remained until his death. He was everywhere regarded as the greatest philosopher of Germany, and many Americans went to study with him.

His philosophy stemmed from Neoplatonism and derived from Leibnitz (1648-1716). He studied Kant, whom he considered too subjective. Fichte had reinterpreted Kant's "thing-in-itself" as an "ego-in-itself," an absolute reason manifesting itself from generation to generation in a superior race. Hegel accepted the idea of universal Will, but concluded that it operated through relationships and that each individual must be considered in relation to this all-inclusive "ground-of-the-universe." Universal reason is the "Absolute" moving through eternity in a logical process of evolution and embodying itself in the active universe, creating and realizing itself in objects and institutions.

The all-inclusive "ground-of-the-universe" takes many diverse and even opposing forms, and in the course of history these opposites become reconciled. Reality is thus *process,* moving from the unclear to the more clear. Thinking is an inductive process, new content being assimilated into the old. The true is the whole, a totality that is never reached, but that drives thought on in an endless process. Its method of reconciling contradictions is called "dialectic." In the process of thought man arrives at a concept: for example, "idea." This is called the "thesis." He must now search for its exact opposite, the "antithesis," which in this case Hegel declared to be "nature." We have then "idea" or "spirit" on the one hand and "nature" or "matter" on the other. These opposites can be brought together in a synthesis called "mind." Another example takes as its thesis, "evil." The antithesis is "innocence," that which is non-evil. To possess a knowledge of evil and yet to will to do what is good gives us the synthesis, "virtue."

Other examples are: thesis, "War is evil"; antithesis, "War is good"; synthesis, "Despite the evils of war good comes of it." Thus, Hegel argued that war is justified because it is the way progress is made. The Prussians believed that their state was the instrument for the realization of universal reason which would eventually conquer the world.

Similarly, Hegel argued, man is a microcosm of the macrocosm, God, or Absolute Mind, one of whose attributes is freedom. Man is therefore free to realize himself to the fullest in the development from the primitive toward Absolute Mind. Since an individual can only be considered in relation to others, it follows that the highest freedom is attained when free individuals subordinate individual reason to universal reason. By substituting a materialistic metaphysic for Hegel's idealism, as did Karl Marx, it is easy to follow the Soviet argument that the individual attains his greatest freedom through the state.

Hegel's educational theories grew directly out of his absolute idealism. He considered education to be a life process, a mental discipline that makes man religious, moral, cultured, and rational. Education should be compulsory through the state and for the state because only through education is the Will of God transmitted.

The aim of education is utilitarian in the sense that it is necessary to bring about an understanding of the unity of man with the universal spirit. Education must lead man to break from the natural order to be at home in the intellect. "With the schools begins the life of universal regulation, according to a rule applicable to all alike. For the individual spirit or mind must be brought to the putting away of its own peculiarities, must be brought to the knowing and willing of what is universal, must be brought to the acceptance of that general culture which is immediately at hand."[6]

[6] Georg Wilhelm Friedrich Hegel, *Werke* (Berlin: Duncker, 1832), VIII, 82. Quoted in William M. Bryant, *Hegel's Educational Ideas* (Chicago: Werner School Book, 1896), p. 38.

While others in his day were writing about elementary education, Hegel championed the secondary school. He believed that the aim of the school should determine its curriculum. Languages, literature, history, philosophy, and logic were recommended as the best subjects, the latter especially for its mental discipline. Latin and Greek he considered to be especially good, because as dead languages they impose a barrier between the natural self and the developing mind.

Method, he taught, should be through the child's self-activity, and should be rational, because the child is naturally a rational being, although only potentially so. Learning should be vital and spontaneous and should achieve a synthesis of the child's self-motivation and his respect for the discipline of the school. In the classroom the mind of the teacher and the mind of the pupil are bound together by a principle of knowledge to be taught and learned which constitutes the spiritual mind, the synthesis of the other two minds.

Hegel believed that he had brought about a perfect synthesis of the philosophies of Kant and Fichte and all those who had preceded them. He has been compared to Aquinas for his powers of systematization. His influence has been felt in the thought of the modern world until today. After a temporary eclipse at the beginning of the present century his ideas are experiencing a revival in neo-Hegelianism. In France, Henri Bergson (1859-1941) developed a theory of "creative evolution" and of the *elan vital* (vital force) that derives from Hegel's evolutionism. In Italy, Giovanni Gentile (1875-1944), the fascist, and Benedetto Croce (1866-1952), the aesthetician and anti-fascist, presented opposite interpretations of Hegel's idealism. His most famous German disciple, Karl Marx (1818-1885), developed what has been called Hegelianism of the left in *Das Kapital.* Among his most ardent followers in Great Britain were Samuel Taylor Coleridge (1772-1834), the philosopher and poet, Thomas Carlyle (1795-1881), the historian and essayist, Benjamin Jowett (1817-1898), the classicist, and the philosophers Edward Caird (1875-1908), Edward Herbert Bradley (1864-1924), and George Sylvester Morris (1840-1889).

In America, Ralph Waldo Emerson (1803-1882) expanded and modified Hegel's idealism into New England transcendentalism in accordance with the American intellectual climate. Among professional philosophers who wore the tag of Hegelianism were Josiah Royce (1855-1916), Mary W. Calkins (1863-1930), and Henry Harrell Horne (1874-1946). Among American educators who incorporated Hegel's thoughts into American educational theory and practice were Horace Mann (1796-1859), Henry Barnard (1811-1900), and William T. Harris (1835-1909). John Dewey (1859-1952) incorporated Hegel's social evolution into his instrumentalism.

General Notion of Education*

In his discussion of the nature and purposes of education, Hegel stresses the universal nature of man and insists that education must lead him to break with the merely temporal to live in the realm of the universal mind as it evolves through history. After stating that the purpose of education is to make men moral, that is, to live in accordance with the aims of a great and good people, Hegel continues that only through such culture can a man become what he should be. That is, man develops an unselfish sharing of intellectual interests with others, differentiates the essential from the non-essential, reserves his judgment, absorbs the culture of the race, transcends his physical self, and becomes a positive and Universal being.

1. DEFINITION OF EDUCATION

Education is the art of making men moral. It regards man as natural, and points out how he may be born anew—how his first nature may be changed to a second, spiritual nature.

Education may be defined as the visible, progressive transcending of the negative or subjective. For, the child, as the form of the potentiality of a moral individual, is a subjective or negative. His becoming a man is the outgrowing this form; and his education is the discipline or process by which this is done. To gain his positive and essential character, he must be nourished at the breast of the universally moral; he first must live as a stranger in the absolute intuition of that morality; he must make more and more of it his own, and finally pass over into the universal spirit. It is evident from this that the effort to be virtuous, to obtain absolute morality through education, is not at all a striving after an individual and separate morality. Indeed, such an effort after a positive morality peculiarly one's own, would be vain and in itself impossible. Regarding moral-

*Source: Frederick Ludlow Luqueer, *Hegel as Educator* (New York: Macmillan, 1896), pp. 107-109, 111-114.

ity, the wisest men of old said truly: To be moral, is to live in accord with one's country—and in regard to education, the answer of a Pythagorean to the question, What is the best education for my son?—That which makes him a citizen amid a great and good people.

The spirit must be brought to lay aside its separateness, it must be brought to know and to will the universal. It must learn to live and have its being in the world-culture. This reforming of the soul—this alone is education.

2. EDUCATION SHOULD LEAD TO REFLECTIVE SELF-CONSCIOUSNESS

The child, as man in general, is a reasonable being. But the reason of the child as such is at first only an inner, that is, is present only as potency, faculty, etc.; and this inner at the same time has for the child the form only of an outer, apparent in the will of his parents, in the knowledge of his teachers, and in the surrounding world. The education and culture of the child consists then in this: what he is at first *in himself* and so, *for others* (the adults), he must become *for himself.*

3. EDUCATION SHOULD MAKE FREE

Man becomes what a man should be only through culture.

Culture in its absolute signification is freedom, and the work of attaining the higher freedom. It is the absolute transition to the unlimited subjective substantiality of morality, raised to the form of the universal. It is no longer immediate, natural; but is spiritual. This freedom is won for the subject through the stern strife against the naive subjectivity of life, against the immediateness of arbitrary desire and passion. This stern strife makes many turn back. But it is only through this battle that culture is attained. It is through this that the subjective will wins in itself its objectivity, by which alone it becomes worthy and fitted to be the realization of the Idea.

This form of universality, to which the individual has been transformed, has this significance, that the individual becomes a true being-for-himself. While recognizing the content and the unlimited self-determination of the universal, yet, in the moral realm, the individual knows himself to be a free subject, infinitely existent for himself. This is the standpoint from which culture is seen to be the absolute's essential mode of progress, and to be of infinite worth.

4. EDUCATION SHOULD LEAD TO UNSELFISH INTEREST IN WHAT IS ACTUAL AND TRUE

To theoretic culture belongs the sense for objects in themselves, independently of any subjective interest. This is born of a many-sided knowledge. It possesses universality of standpoint from which things may be judged. Thereby man rises from a particular knowledge of insignificant things to a general knowledge. Sharing in general interests, he meets other men in a community of knowledge. In going beyond his immediate knowledge and experience, a man learns that there are better ways than his own. He transcends himself, and can discriminate the essential from the non-essential.

·   ·   ·   ·   ·

The things of nature are immediate and singular. But man, as spirit, duplicates himself; since at first he is but one of the things of nature; and then, just as truly, exists for himself, beholds himself, pictures himself, thinks, and is a spirit only through this active being-for-himself.

This consciousness of self is attained in two ways. First introspectively, insofar as he himself, looking within, must bring himself to consciousness—must be conscious of what moves in his breast, of his impulses and passions. Secondly, through practical activity a man becomes an object for himself, since he has the impulse himself to produce what is given him as present and immediate, and so to know himself, to measure himself by his achievement. He does this by altering outer things; he puts upon them the stamp of the inner, finding in them again his own character. The first impulses of the child have this tendency to alter outer things. The boy throws a stone in the stream and is pleased with the circles made in the water. Thereby he becomes aware of his own activity. This tendency expresses itself most variously. And it is not only with outer things that man acts in this way, but also with himself. He does not leave his own nature as he found it, but alters it to his purpose. Forms, manners, every kind of outer expression, may be changed by spiritual culture.

The culture of the race must be absorbed by the individual.

The individual must traverse the stages of culture already traversed by the universal spirit. Doing this, he must yet be aware that the spirit has outgrown these older forms. He must pass through them as over a well-traveled and even way. Thus we see knowledges which in early times taxed the maturest minds of men, now become the property, or means for exercise and even play, of school children. This past existence now belongs to the universal spirit, which, constituting as it does the substance of the individual and his non-organic nature, appears to him as something outer. In this aspect, the education of the individual consists in his acquiring this which is already at hand, in his absorbing his non-organic nature and winning it as a possession for himself. Regarded from the side of the universal spirit, it is nothing else than this spirit's growth to self-consciousness. It is its becoming, and its reflection thereupon.

7. MANKIND A UNITY IN THEIR RATIONALITY; BUT THIS DOES NOT MEAN UNATTACHED COSMOPOLITANISM FOR THE INDIVIDUAL

It belongs to culture, to thought as consciousness of the individual in the form of universality, that the ego should be conceived as the universal person, wherein all persons are identical. So a man counts wherever he is found, not because he is Jew, Catholic, Protestant, German, Italian—but is man. This consciousness is of infinite importance. It is at fault, however, if it becomes a certain cosmopolitanism—too broad visioned to enter into the concerns of one's own country.

Man is essentially reasonable. Herein lies the possibility of equality of rights of all men.

8. THE INDIVIDUAL WILL OF THE PUPIL TO BE BROUGHT INTO ACCORD WITH THE SOCIAL GOOD

The peculiarities of men must not be rated too highly. The assertion, that a teacher must carefully adjust himself to the individuality of his pupils so as to develop it—this assertion is empty. The teacher has no time for that. The individuality of the children is met in the family. But with the school begins a life in accord with a general order, after general rules for all. In school the spirit must be brought to lay aside its particularities, it must know and will the universal.

JOHANN FRIEDRICH HERBART

Johann Friedrich Herbart (1776-1841) was born in Aldenberg in northwestern Germany. After attending the University of Jena (1794-1797), he became tutor to the three sons of the governor of Interlocken, Switzerland. While there he visited Pestalozzi and was much impressed by the great Swiss educator, especially by his views of psychology. The two men, however, offer considerable contrast. Pestalozzi was active, impulsive, and developed his psychology in actual practice; Herbart, on the other hand, was thoughtful, scholarly, systematic, and developed his theory of psychology in connection with his teaching of philosophy. While Pestalozzi was interested in the education of childhood and youth through sense perception, Herbart was interested in the intellectual development of the secondary school pupil and the university student. Herbart taught at Göttingen from 1802 to 1809, when he became successor to Kant in the chair of philosophy at Koenigsberg, where he remained until 1833. Returning to Göttingen in 1833, he remained there until his death in 1841. His careful and systematic mind caused him to avoid the subjective and romantic interpretation of many of his contemporary German philosophers and to combine the rigorous method of Kant and the observational techniques of the English to the sense impressions, which he believed, with Pestalozzi, to be at the basis of all human experience.

The whole work of education, he taught, was to produce the man of culture whose actions would be constantly motivated by the highest ethical values of life. With Rousseau he believed that youth wills the good constantly and consistently, but he believed that youth did not know the good until the teacher had represented it to him and made him aware of it. The purpose of education, therefore, is to develop insights, to instill the proper interests and desires, to give a complete experience of life in its many phases, to mature the judgment, and to impart inner control. The teacher must prepare the learner to accept these aims and help him to realize them through a scientific method of procedure. Then youth will do good because it is his very nature to do so and morality which is the end of education, will be achieved.

Herbart's idea of "conditioning" the learner to "right action" according to absolute moral principles led him to criticize the "soft pedagogy" of Locke, Montaigne, and Rousseau.

With regard to the curriculum, Herbart maintained that there were two sources of knowledge—experience with things and social intercourse. From things one gained empirical knowledge and learned the laws of nature; from people one learned the nature of man and man's achievements as recorded in history and geography. He accepted the traditional curriculum of the early nineteenth-century gymnasium: mathematics, history, languages, literature, and religion. Through these subjects the learner's mind was to be lifted from the sensory and concrete level to concepts and judgments. Education was to proceed from the particular to the general. From sympathy for the individual the pupil should learn sympathy for mankind; from relationships with a few, to relationships with society and with God.

Much knowledge, he declared, was acquired before the child came to school and much of this was inaccurate, incomplete, and unsystematic. The amount, kind, and quality of knowledge would vary with each individual. The teacher, therefore, must take individual differences into account when selecting subject matter to correct and supplement the learner's experiences. Herbart gave support to the then popular "cultural epochs theory" that the child's education should recapitulate the history of the race. Accordingly the sequence in history and literature included Homer, the Greek and Roman period, the stories of the Old and New Testaments, the medieval romances, and modern history and literature.

Although Herbart held chairs of philosophy at two distinguished German universities and wrote a number of treatises on the nature and method of philosophy, he is chiefly known for his works on psychology and education. Two views of psychology were current in the early nineteenth century. One held that the soul or mind had certain capacities, functions or activities, instincts, and impulses that gave rise to sensations, perceptions, and intellectual processes. Among those who maintained this position were Rousseau, Pestalozzi, and Froebel. The other viewpoint, held by the English and French associationists and derived from Locke, considered the soul or mind to be empty and devoid of content, nothing being present until the first sensation. Herbart held the latter point of view, although he differed from the strict materialistic interpretation. He carried on his analyses in great detail, agreeing with Locke on the indispensability of sense perceptions. To pure psychology he made four significant contributions: He turned from speculative philosophy to empirical observation and rejected faculty psychology. He demonstrated the physiological basis for psychology, and applied mathematical procedures to the analysis and description of psychological phenomena. His psychology recognized three basic states: feeling, knowing, and willing.

Herbart's theory of mind admitted two states, the conscious and the unconscious. Between the two, Herbart described a threshold that he called the "limen." An object presented to the mind does not remain long in consciousness, but drops into the unconscious which is always active and contains all past experiences, for no object once presented to consciousness is ever forgotten.

Interest is basic to Herbart's principles of learning because it is the inner force that determines what ideas and experiences will be brought into consciousness and how long they will be retained there. For example, a person is reading a historical novel. His past experiences that bear a relationship to the events about which he reads are brought into consciousness and form a cluster of ideas around the center of interest. The doorbell rings and a stranger asks directions to a nearby address. Historical incidents are put aside and the new center of interest brings forth known facts about the distance, the direction of turns, familiar landmarks, and perhaps incidents and acquaintances along the way. When the stranger leaves and the reader returns to his book, the historical associations again come to the fore, but the experiences of the stranger persist in consciousness for a time, perhaps with mental queries as to whether the information given was accurate and easy to follow, before they slip into the unconscious. Thus each center of interest draws from the unconscious whatever past experiences bear a relation to it. This unconscious state has come to be known as the "apperceptive mass" and is related to Herbart's steps of learning: clearness, association, system, and method.[7]

The teacher should frequently bring into consciousness ideas he wishes to be cultivated and learned. He should present new material in terms of former experiences so that associations can be formed, and concepts can be clearly formulated. Perceptions in the unconscious are in a highly disorganized state. It is the function of education to systematize them and to derive generalizations for easy recall and action. Thus a right method of instruction will develop readily available systems of thought and action in the stream of consciousness. Herbart, foreshadowing John Dewey, made no distinction between content and process. He held that the mind developed by expanding percepts into concepts. Perceptions are primary. Feeling and willing are secondary or derived

[7] See Robert Ulich, *History of Educational Thought* (New York: American Book, 1945), pp. 279-280.

mental states springing from objects known and the relationship between them. "The circle of thought contains the store of that which by degrees can mount by the steps of interest to desire, and then by means of action to volition."[8]

Herbart is often called the father of the modern science of education and of modern psychology. His method of learning was expanded into the five "formal steps" of teaching and learning: preparation, presentation, association, generalization, and application, which became the basis for teaching methods in teacher-training institutions. Eduard Zeller and Wilhelm Rein developed a system of Herbartian pedagogy for the elementary school in Germany, and Frank and Charles McMurry popularized and somewhat distorted the method in the United States. William James's psychology, especially the theory of the stream of consciousness, owes much to Herbart. A lot of Dewey's early writing in the fields of educational philosophy and psychology also owes much to Herbart, although with Colonel Parker Dewey was skeptical of applying the Herbartian pattern strictly to American education. Herbart's influence on American pedagogical thought and practice has been profound. One may say that all essentialists are in his debt and that all who follow the unit method of teaching as developed by H.C. Morrison are modern Herbartians.

The Science of Education*

In this selection Herbart sets forth his theory of learning based on his psychological theory of association. Out of this theory grew the formal steps that had such vogue at the beginning of the present century.

Concentration, above all, ought to precede reflection, but at what distance? This question remains generally undetermined. Both certainly must be kept as near as possible together, for we desire no concentrations to the detriment of personal unity, which is preserved by means of reflection. Their long and unbroken succession would create a tension, incompatible with the existence of the healthy mind in the healthy body. In order then always to maintain the mind's coherence, instruc-

[8] Johann Friedrich Herbart, *The Science of Education* (Boston: Heath, 1902), p. 213.

Source: Johann Friedrich Herbart, *The Science of Education*, trans. Henry M. Felkin and Emmie Felkin (Boston: Heath, 1908), pp. 144-147.

tion must follow the rule of giving equal weight in every smallest possible group of its objects to concentration and reflection; that is to say, it must care equally and in regular succession for clearness of every particular, for association of the manifold, for coherent ordering of what is associated, and for a certain practice in progression through this order. Upon this depends the distinctness which must rule in all that is taught. The teacher's greatest difficulty here, perhaps, is to find real particulars—to analyse his own thoughts into their elements. Text books can in this case partly prepare the ground.

If however, instruction handles each little group of objects in this manner, many groups arise in the mind, and each one is grasped by a relative concentration until all are united in a higher reflection. But the union of the groups presupposes the perfect unity of each group. So long, therefore, as it is still possible for the last particular in the content of each group to fall apart from the rest, higher reflection cannot be thought of. But there is above this higher reflection a still higher, and so on indefinitely upwards, to the all-embracing highest, which we seek through the system of systems, but never reach. In earlier years nothing of this can be attempted; youth is always in an intermediate state between concentration and distraction. We must be contented in earlier years with not attempting to give what we call system in the higher sense, but must on the other hand so much the more create clearness in every group; we must associate the groups the more sedulously and variously, and be careful that *the approach to the all-embracing reflection is made equally from all sides.*

Upon this depends the articulation of instruction. The larger members are composed of smaller, as are the lesser of the least. In each of the smallest members, four stages of instruction are to be distinguished; it must provide for Clearness, Association, Arrangement, and the Course of this order. These grades, which with the smallest members quickly succeed each other, follow one another more slowly, when those next in comprehensiveness are formed from the smallest members, and with ever-increasing spaces of time, as higher steps of reflection have to be climbed.

If we now look back on the analysis of the concept of interest, we find therein also, certain steps differentiated—Observation, Expectation, Demand and Action.

Observation depends on the relative power of a presentation to that of others which must yield to it—depends therefore partly on the intrinsic strength of the one, partly on the ease with which the remainder yield. The latter leads to the idea of a discipline of thought, which we preferred to treat of specially in the *A B C of Anschauung*. The strength of a presentation can be partly attained through the power of the sensuous impression (as, for example, through the simultaneous speaking of several children, also by the display of the same object in different ways with drawings, instruments, models, etc.), partly through the vividness of descriptions, especially if already connected presentations rest in the depths of the mind, which will unite with the one to be given. To effect this union generally, there is need of great skill and thought, which aims at anticipating furture efforts by giving something to prepare the ground for them, as for instance the *A B C of Anschauung* does for mathematics, as the play of combinations does for grammar, and as narratives from antiquity do for a classical author.

Through observation the singular becomes distinct, but association, order, and progress according to order, must also be observed.

In the same way we get clearness of the expectations and association of them; in fact, systematic and methodical expectation.

Nevertheless these complications do not now claim our chief interest. We know that when the expected appears, only a new observation is produced. This is generally the case in the sphere of knowledge. Where some store of knowledge is already accumulated, it is not easy to observe anything to which expectations were not attached, yet the expectation dies out or becomes satisfied with new knowledge. If vehement desires arise therefrom, they would fall under the rule of temperance and consequently of discipline. But there is a species of observation which is not so easily satisfied or forgotten; there is a demand which is intended to be transformed into action; this is the *demand for sympathy*. Whatever rights then temperance exercises in this case, that education would nevertheless be a failure which did not leave behind resolutions to work for the good of humanity and society, as well as a certain energy of the religious postulate. Accordingly, in the cultivation of sympathy, the higher steps to which interest may pass come much into consideration. And it is quite clear that these steps correspond with those of human life. In the child a *sympathis-*

ing observation is appropriate, in the boy *expectation,* in the youth the *demand for sympathy,* that the man may *act* for it. The articulation of instruction, however, here permits again, even in the smallest subjects which belong to early years, demand (for sympathy) to be so stimulated that it would pass into action. Out of such stimulations there grows in later years, assisted at the same time by the formation of character, that powerful demand which begets actions.

Allow me briefly to define the results in few words, which can easily be understood.

Instruction must universally
        point out,
        connect,
        teach,
        philosophise.
In matters appertaining to sympathy it should be
observing,   observing,
        continuous,
        elevating,
        active in the sphere of reality.

FRIEDRICH WILHELM AUGUST FROEBEL

Friedrich Froebel (1782-1852) was born in Oberwiesbach in the Thuringian mountains of southern Germany. His mother died when he was nine months old and his father, the pastor of a large parish, paid little attention to the boy or his education. His stepmother treated him with noticeable contempt after her own children were born. This early unfortunate childhood probably shaped the whole course of his life and was influential in centering his interest on early childhood education, making him sympathetic to and understanding of the problems of the very young. He received his only formal education during the four happy years he lived with his uncle, Pastor Hoffman, from whom he received his religious training and his profound spiritual convictions. After some years of study at Jena he successively taught drawing at the normal school at Frankfort and served as tutor for three boys while he lived and studied with Pestalozzi at Yverdon. In 1817, after having studied at Göttingen and Berlin where he began his attempt to form a synthesis of existing philosophies, he established a school for boys at Keilhaus in Thuringia. He founded the first kindergarten at Blankenburg in 1837 and devoted the rest of his life to early childhood education and the preparation of teachers.

His idealism was in accord with Plato and Goethe, and he absorbed the romantic pantheism of Schelling, which identified man and nature. He was a Christian mystic in the primitive sense of that term and revived the early Christian interest in the very young. Although he differed in many respects from Rousseau and his teacher Pestalozzi, he shared with them a concern for the continuous development of the individual from infancy. He aimed to rear free-thinking, independent men through developing the inner nature of the child, and believed that all learning should be oriented in the direction of the child's interest and capacities. "Education" for him "consisted in leading man, as a thinking, intelligent being, growing into self-consciousness, to a pure and unsullied, conscious and free representation of the inner law of Divine Unity, and in teaching him the means thereto."[9]

Central to his philosophy of life and education was the unity of all things. In order that the child experience this organic unity of man and nature and learn their interrelationships, he must have experience with things. He must study man in nature, learn the art of cooperation rather than competition, and develop mind and hand simultaneously. For him childhood was an essential phase of human development, a recapitulation of the childhood of the race, and was therefore to be studied and lived for its own sake rather than as a prelude to maturity.

Believing that education must give man free play to develop his creative powers and that "in the development of the inner life of the individual man, the history of the spiritual development of the race is repeated,"[10] Froebel selected materials and activities to this end. Natural science was included in his curriculum because it revealed the workings of God's law; mathematics and languages linked the mind and the natural world; and the arts, drawing, and music, were a means for the soul to express itself. All these he approached with religious mysticism. He refused to believe that the child possessed evil tendencies at birth, for God and man were one. Therefore education was an epigenetic unfoldment of the spirit of God within man. He likened education to a garden and believed that the school should cultivate and develop the potential in each child as a horticulturist tends each tender plant. To this

[9] Friedrich Froebel, *The Education of Man,* trans. William Hailmann (New York: D. Appleton, 1892), pp. 1-2.

[10] *Ibid.,* p. 160.

end he used color, motion, spheres, cubes, and other geometric forms and figures for their symbolic meaning. For example, a sphere taught the child the unity of mankind in God.

The idea of growth in a garden was incorporated into the name "kindergarten," which he gave to the institution with which his name is most frequently associated. In fact he recommended that a garden of living things be a part of every kindergarten. Trades were also given a prominent place in his school at Keilhau to show the unity and equality of mental and physical occupations among men.

Possibly Froebel's greatest contribution to educational method was the doctrine that play was itself educational. He believed that play and free self-activity were nature's way of developing the child and that the child's activities should be prompted by the development of his own nature. The parent-teacher role was to keep the child from the possible evil effects of the environment; it was protective rather than prescriptive. With Comenius and Pestalozzi he recognized the importance of the mother in the child's early training. Froebel wrote a songbook for mother and child to sing together, and he showed the value of women as teachers, especially in the early grades. All learning, he believed, should take place in a social setting and in harmony with the society to which man belongs, for every act of man has social implications.

Rusk[11] calls Froebel "one of the most idealistic of educational philosophers," and Brubacher[12] writes that the *"Education of Man* is idealism's most notable innovation in education." A comparison with the educational philosophy of Hegel, generally acknowledged to be the greatest idealist philosopher of his day, however, shows interesting points of difference.

HEGEL	FROEBEL
Education helps man break away from his natural self, from the world of nature. (Hegel limited "nature" to the world of sense experiences, the antithesis of the spirit.)	Education promotes the harmonious development of the child according to the laws of nature. (Froebel understood nature to cover all the phenomena of the unfolding life of the individual mind.)
The teacher should not study the individual child but seek to bring him out of himself, to seek a new birth through obedience.	The teacher studies the individual following the laws of nature, thus warding off evil. He helps the child's nature unfold to mental and moral maturity.

Latin and Greek are especially good subjects, because, being dead languages, they impose an effectual barrier between the natural self and the developing mind.	The harmonious study of nature, of man in nature, and of man in society is stressed.
Emphasized antagonisms.	Emphasized reconciliation.
The child is to learn the seriousness of work as opposed to play. The two should never be combined.	A child's play is his serious attempt to understand life. His natural expression is a guide to the teacher's methods.
Education for the few. (He knew only boys from 14 to 18).	Chiefly concerned with universal education for young children.
Uncertain about the education of women.	Advocated the education of girls. Recommended the training of young women for teaching.
Hegel's intellect was logical and scientific.	Froebel's method was more intuitive.

Both aimed at giving the young man to himself so that he might attain "true freedom" by realizing his oneness with the universe.

In the same manner it will be interesting to show the points of difference between the idealistic philosophy of Froebel and the realism of Herbart.

HERBART	FROEBEL
Directed the education of adolescents of superior mentality.	Developed (unfolded) the life and powers of the preschool child.
Herbart's realistic education placed emphasis on factors external to the individual. His psychology suggested the connectionism of the twentieth century.	Froebel's idealism emphasized the unfolding of the inner potential of the individual. His psychology was the forerunner of present-day gestalt psychology.
Herbart's method manipulated the reals (externals) with which the mind comes into contact.	Froebel's method was a mystical becoming or unfolding of the inner reality and unity of the individual, an unfolding of what was already enfolded in the germ.

Whereas Herbart influenced the essentialist educators of the twentieth century, Froebel gave considerable impetus to the progressive education movement. His principles of trade training inspired a similar development in Sweden, and in America Felix

---

[11] Robert R. Rusk, *The Philosophical Bases of Education* (Boston: Houghton Mifflin, 1956), p. 8

[12] John S. Brubacher, *A History of the Problems of Education* (New York: McGraw-Hill, 1947), p. 124.

Adler's Workingman's School introduced the Swedish method, by which individuals could shape objects to serve human purposes.

Froebel's work at Blankenburg inspired the development of early childhood education in America. The first American kindergarten was established in 1855 in Watertown, Wisconsin by Mrs. Karl Schurz, who came from Germany with her husband after the abortive Stuttgart revolution of 1848. Five years later, Elizabeth P. Peabody established the first English-speaking kindergarten in Boston.

He inspired Dewey's faith in the importance of play and the creative possibility of activity. However, Dewey did not use objects to develop mystical meanings, nor did he believe that facts must be understood before they could be used, but rather he maintained that facts could be understood through their use.

Froebel, together with Comenius, Pestalozzi, Locke, and Herbart helped to lay the psychological and sociological foundations of education.

The Education of Man*

In The Education of Man, *Froebel sets forth the mystical relation of the individual to God, and his theory of the unfolding of the human potential through education. He goes on to discuss the nature of man and his education in the earliest period of childhood, in boyhood, and as a scholar or pupil. He ends with a discussion of the content and method of various school subjects.*

GROUNDWORK OF THE WHOLE

In all things there lives and reigns an eternal law. To him whose mind, through disposition and faith, is filled, penetrated, and quickened with the necessity that this can not possibly be otherwise, as well as to him whose clear, calm mental vision beholds the inner in the outer and through the outer, and sees the outer proceeding with logical necessity from the essence of the inner, this law has been and is enounced with equal clearness and distinctness in nature (the external), in the spirit (the internal), and in life which unites the two. This all-controlling law is necessarily based on an

Source: Friedrich Froebel, *The Education of Man*, trans. W. N. Hailman (New York: D. Appleton, 1887), pp. 1-7, 137-139.

all-pervading, energetic, living, self-conscious, and hence eternal Unity. This fact, as well as the Unity itself, is again vividly recognized, either through faith or through insight, with equal clearness and comprehensiveness; therefore, a quietly observant human mind, a thoughtful, clear human intellect, has never failed, and will never fail, to recognize this Unity.

This Unity is God. All things have come from the Divine Unity, from God, and have their origin in the Divine Unity, in God alone. God is the sole source of all things. In all things there lives and reigns the Divine Unity, God. All things live and have their being in and through the Divine Unity, in and through God. All things are only through the divine effluence that lives in them. The divine effluence that lives in each thing is the essence of each thing.

It is the destiny and life-work of all things to unfold their essence, hence their divine being, and, therefore, the Divine Unity itself—to reveal God in their external and transient being. It is the special destiny and life-work; and to accomplish this, to render it (his essence) active, to reveal it in his own life with self-determination and freedom.

Education consists in leading man, as a thinking, intelligent being, growing into self-consciousness, to a pure and unsullied, conscious and free representation of the inner law of Divine Unity, and in teaching him ways and means thereto.

The knowledge of that eternal law, the insight into its origin, into its essence, into the totality, the connection, and intensity of its effects, the knowledge of life in its totality, constitute *science, the science of life!* and, referred by the self-conscious, thinking, intelligent being to representation and practice through and in himself, this becomes *science of education.*

To educate one's self and others, with consciousness, freedom, and self-determination, is a twofold achievement of wisdom: it began with the first appearance of man upon the earth; it was manifest with the first appearance of full self-consciousness in man; it begins now to proclaim itself as a necessary, universal requirement of humanity, and to be heard and heeded as such. With this achievement man enters upon the path which alone leads to life; which surely tends to the fulfillment of the inner, and thereby also to the fulfillment of the outer, requirement of humanity; which, through a faithful, pure, holy life, attains beatitude.

By education, then, the divine essence of man should be unfolded, brought out, lifted into consciousness, and man himself raised into free, conscious obedience to the divine principle that lives in him, and to a free representation of this principle in his life.

Education, in instruction, should lead man to see and know the divine, spiritual, and eternal principle which animates surrounding nature, constitutes the essence of nature, and is permanently manifested in nature; and, in living reciprocity and united with training, it should express and demonstrate the fact that the same law rules both (the divine principle and nature) as it does nature and man.

Education as a whole, by means of instruction and training, should bring to man's consciousness, and render efficient in his life, the fact that man and nature proceed from God and are conditioned by him—that both have their being in God.

Education should lead and guide man to clearness concerning himself and in himself, to peace with nature, and to unity with God; hence, it should lift him to a knowledge of himself and of mankind, to a knowledge of God and of nature, and to the pure and holy life to which such knowledge leads.

In all these requirements, however, education is based on considerations of the innermost.

The inner essence of things is recognized by the innermost spirit (of man) in the outer and through outward manifestations. The inner being, the spirit, the divine essence of things and of man, is known by its outward manifestations. In accordance with this, all education, all instruction and training, all life as a free growth, start from the outer manifestations of man and things, and proceeding from the outer, act upon the inner and form its judgments concerning the inner. Nevertheless, education should not draw its inferences concerning the inner from the outer directly, for it lies in the nature of things that always in some relation inferences should be drawn inversely. Thus, the diversity and multiplicity in nature do not warrant the inference of multiplicity in the ultimate cause—a multiplicity of gods—nor does the unity of God warrant the inference of finality in nature; but, in both cases, the inference lies conversely from the diversity in nature to the oneness of its ultimate cause, and from the unity of God to an eternally progressing diversity in natural developments.

The failure to apply this truth, or rather the continual sinning against it, the drawing of direct inferences concerning the inner life of childhood and youth from certain external manifestations of life, is the chief cause of antagonism and contention, of the frequent mistakes in life and education. This furnishes constant occasion for innumerable false judgments concerning the motives of the young, for numberless failures in the education of children, for endless misunderstanding between parent and child, for so much needless complaint and unseemly arraignment of children, for so many unreasonable demands made upon them. Therefore, this truth, in its application to parents, educators, and teachers, is of such great importance that they should strive to render themselves familiar with its application in its smallest details. This would bring into the relations between parents and children, pupils and educators, teacher and taught, a clearness, a constancy, a serenity which are now sought in vain: for the child that seems good outwardly often is not good inwardly, i.e., does not desire the good spontaneously or from love, respect, and appreciation; similarly, the outwardly rough, stubborn, self-willed child that seems outwardly not good, frequently is filled with the liveliest, most eager, strongest desire for spontaneous goodness in his actions; and the apparently inattentive boy frequently follows a certain fixed line of thought that withholds his attention from all external things.

Therefore, education in instruction and training, originally and in its first principles, should necessarily be passive, following (only guarding and protecting), not prescriptive, categorical, interfering.

•　　•　　•　　•　　•

What, now, shall the school teach? In what shall the human being, the boy as scholar, be instructed?

Only the consideration of the nature and requirements of human development at the stage of boyhood will enable us to answer this question. But the knowledge of this nature and these requirements can be derived only from the observation of the character of man in his boyhood.

Now, in accordance with this character, this manner of being, in what things is the boy to be instructed?

The life and outward being of man in the beginning of boyhood show him, in the first place, to be animated by a spiritual self of his own; they show, too, the existence of a vague feeling that this spiritual self has its being and origin in a higher and Supreme Being, and depends on this Being in which, indeed, all things have their being and origin, and on which all things depend. The life and outward being of man in boyhood show the presence of an intense feeling and anticipation of the existence of a living, quickening Spirit, in which and by which all things live, by which all things are invisibly surrounded, as a fish is surrounded by water and man and all creatures by the clear, pure atmosphere.

In his boyhood, in the beginning of his school-life, man seems to feel the power of his spiritual nature, to anticipate vaguely God and the spiritual nature of all things. He shows, at the same time, a desire to attain ever more clearness in that feeling, and to confirm his anticipation.

Man, in boyhood, approaches the outer world, placed over against him, with the feeling and hope and belief that it, too, is animated and ruled by a spirit, like that which animates and rules him; and he is filled by an intense, irresistible longing—which returns with every new spring and every new fall, with every new, fresh morning and calm evening, with every peaceful festive day—a longing to know this all-ruling spirit, to make it his own, as it were.

The outer world confronts man in boyhood in a two-fold character—first, as the product of human requirements and human power, and, secondly, as the outcome of the requirements of the power that works in nature.

Between this outer world (the world of form and matter) and the inner world (the world of mind and spirit), language appears—originally united with both, but gradually freeing itself from both, and thereby uniting the two.

Thus the *mind* and the *outer world* (first as *nature*), and *language* which unites the two, are the poles of boy-life, as they also were the poles of mankind as a whole in the first stage of approaching maturity (as the sacred books show). Through them the school and instruction are to lead the boy to the threefold, yet in itself one, knowledge—to the knowledge of himself in all his relations, and thus to the knowledge of man as such; to the knowledge of God, the eternal condition, cause, and source of his being and of the being of all things; and to the knowledge of nature and the outer world as proceeding from the Eternal Spirit, and depending thereon.

Instruction and the school are to lead man to a life in full harmony with that threefold, yet in itself one, knowledge. By this knowledge they are to lead man from desire to will, from will to firmness of will, and thus in continuous progression to the attainment of his destiny, to the attainment of his earthly perfection.

BIBLIOGRAPHY

PESTALOZZI

Green, J. A., *The Educational Ideas of Pestalozzi* (Baltimore: Warwick and York, 1907).

*Gutek, Gerald Lee, *Pestalozzi and Education* (New York: Random House, 1968).

Pestalozzi, Johann Heinrich, *How Gertrude Teaches Her Children,* trans. Lucy E. Holland and Francis C. Turner, ed. Ebenezer Cooke (London: George Allen and Unwin, 1915).

————, *Leonard and Gertrude,* trans. and abr. Eva Channing (Boston: Heath, 1885).

————, *The Education of Man, Aphorisms,* trans. Heinz and Ruth Norden (New York: Philosophical Library, 1951).

HEGEL

Bryant, William M., *Hegel's Educational Ideas* (Chicago: Werner, 1896).

*Hegel, G. W., *Philosophy of Hegel,* ed. C. J. Friedrich (New York: Modern Library College Editions, Random House, 1954).

*————, *Reason in History: A General Introduction to the Philosophy of History,* trans. R. S. Hartman (Indianapolis: Liberal Arts Press, Bobbs-Merrill, 1953).

*————, *Selections,* ed. J. Loewenberg (New York: Scribner, 1957).

Luquier, Frederic Ludlow, *Hegel as Educator* (New York: Macmillan, 1896).

Mackenzie, Millicent, *Hegel's Educational Theory and Practice* (London: Sonnenschein, 1909).

HERBART

Chalke, Richard David, *A Synthesis of Froebel and Herbart* (London: W. B. Clive, 1912).

DeGarmo, Charles, *Herbart and the Herbartians* (New York: Scribner, 1896).

*Dunkel, Harold Baker, *Herbart and Education* (New York: Random House, 1969).

Herbart, Johann Friedrich, *Herbart's A.B.C. of Sense-Perception and Minor Pedagogical Works,* trans. and with an introduction by William J. Eckoff (New York: D. Appleton, 1896).

————, *The Science of Education,* trans. Henry M. and Emmie Felkin, with a preface by Oscar Browning (Boston: Heath, 1895).

McMurray, Charles Alexander, *The Elements of General Method Based on the Principles of Herbart* (New York: Macmillan, 1903).

FROEBEL

Froebel, Frederick, *Pedagogics of the Kindergarten,* trans. Josephine Jarvis (New York: D. Appleton, 1917).

————, *The Education of Man,* trans. William Hailmann (New York: D. Appleton, 1892).

Kilpatrick, William Heard, *Froebel's Kindergarten Principles Critically Examined* (New York: Macmillan, 1916).

*Paperback editions.

Chapter Seven
Idealism and Naturalism: Emerson and Spencer

AMONG THE DOMINANT IDEAS affecting education in the nineteenth century were idealism and naturalism.

Ralph Waldo Emerson was a leader among New England transcendentalists who adapted German idealism to American life and thought.

As important as the Copernican revolution that had dislodged the earth from the center of the universe, was the joint statement regarding biological evolution by Alfred R. Wallace and Charles Darwin in July, 1858, and the publication of the *Origin of Species* in 1859, the year in which John Dewey was born.

Biological evolution further dislodged man from his unique place as lord of creation by positing that he was the latest, not necessarily the ultimate, in a long line of descent from the single cell, that he was closely related biologically to the other primates, and that he was part and parcel of one inscrutable struggle through "the survival of the fittest."[1]

American education seized upon Herbert Spencer's social Darwinism to state the aims of education in terms of individual and social welfare.

---

[1] Spencer's phrase. Although Spencer's "social Darwinism" seemed to emphasize "the law of tooth and nail," and to justify racism and imperialism, later biologists and anthropologists have given the phrase a more altruistic interpretation.

RALPH WALDO EMERSON

Ralph Waldo Emerson (1803-1882), born in Concord, Massachusetts, achieved fame as a poet, essayist, lecturer, and minister of the Old North Church in Boston. Although he studied briefly in Göttingen in 1824, his best contact with German thought was through English sources. As an idealist, he believed that man lives in an innately moral and friendly world. As a Protestant, he believed that only the most personal contacts between man and God were religious. His philosophy descended in a direct line from Plato, through Plotinus, Eckhart, Bruno, and Leibnitz, to Goethe and Coleridge. He had a great regard for the poetic and symbolic works of Plato. For the philosopher-king he substituted the scholar, whom he called the guide to mankind because he lived the examined life.

He was acquainted with oriental philosophy through the *Upanishads* and based many of his moral utterances upon the stoicism of Marcus Aurelius and the *categorical imperative* of Kant. He was a great admirer of the educational theories and humanity of Pestalozzi and of the poetry and thought of Goethe. As a leader among the New England transcendentalists he did for America what Carlyle and Coleridge had done for English thought.

He held that reason is greater than empirical science. In "Worship"[2] he wrote: "It is a short sight to limit our faith in laws to those of gravity, of chemistry, of botany, and so forth. Those laws do not stop where our eyes lose them, but push the same geometry and chemistry up into the invisible plan of social and rational life." He maintained that truth, reason, and virtue are lodged in the *over-soul* of which all men are a part. Nature is purposive, and all men are innately moral. Each individual aspires to realize, through insight, the moral perfection within himself, for to be good is also to be wise.

Chart 6 shows the great diversity of ideas flourishing now that are outgrowths of the philosophies of earlier times. For example, Darwin's biological evolution is alive in Spencer, Huxley, Fiske, and Bergson; Pope Leo XIII's return to scholasticism has its counterpart in Maritain; the influence of German idealism is seen in Porter, Harris, Ladd, Vaihinger, Royce, McTaggart, Croce, and Gentile; adaptations and revolt against Hegel's absolute idealism are found in Kierkegaard, Marx, and Nietzsche; pragmatism can be traced from Peirce through James and Dewey, and the science of psychology through Wundt, James, McDougal, and Watson. Finally, the influence of Plato can be seen in the works of Herman Cohen and especially in the writings of Alfred North Whitehead.

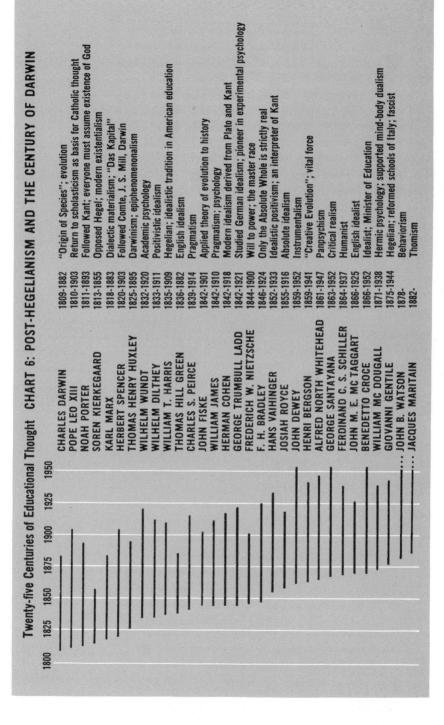

Since man's destiny does not lie in the material but in the spiritual world, education, he believed, is a sort of spiritual dedication. Therefore it should teach moral and spiritual self-reliance. It should be as broad as man. The schoolroom is only an insignificant part of education. After describing the eager curiosity, the initiative, and activity of boys in the community in his essay on "Education," he concludes: "They are there only for fun, and not knowing that they are at school, in the courthouse, or the cattle show, quite as much and more than they were, an hour ago, in the arithmetic class."[3] Emerson believed that all subjects in the school should be taught to give insight into the symbolic character of life, for education is a communication of a spiritual attitude or way of looking at life rather than a communication of knowledge. Facts, therefore, are to be subordinated to values, all knowledge should be applied, and correct habits should be formed as the basis for genuine freedom.

The true teacher should realize the greatness of children. He should believe that even the most perverted human being can be raised up to the society of men. His chief duty is to direct the child toward the Eternal Truth, to which every individual aspires, to give him a standard of moral judgment, and to strengthen the power of his will.

Emerson's advice to the teacher can be stated briefly as follows:

1. Possess a great ideal.
2. Respect your pupil as you respect yourself.
3. Develop an enthusiasm derived from inspiring values.
4. Combine drill and discipline with initiative and self-expression for accuracy and inspiration complement each other.
5. Have high standards and do not compromise with the vulgar.
6. Relate all things to the divine plan of the universe.
7. Relate school work to all of community living.[4]

Emerson was a poet and essayist rather than a philosopher in the technical sense. His many lecture tours and his published works gave his ideas great currency, so that his influence, while indirect, was widespread. The idealistic tradition in American education has been carried on by such men as Henry Harrell

---

[2] Ralph Waldo Emerson, "Worship," in *Conduct of Life,* Vol. VI of the Centenary Ed., *Complete Works,* ed. Edward Waldo Emerson (Boston, 1903), pp. 218-219. Quoted in Robert Ulich, *History of Educational Thought* (New York: American Book, 1945), p. 303.

[3] Ulich, *op. cit.,* p. 305

[4] *Ibid.,* pp. 312-313, provides an excellent treatment of these points.

Horne, Edgar S. Brightman, William E. Hocking, and J. Donald Butler.

Education*

In "Education" Emerson makes a plea for broad human education, stating that basic training comes through direct contact with things and men and that such experiences make books meaningful. He condemns the teacher who would hastily put a thin veneer of knowledge over children's minds because children should be regarded with respect for their individual personalities. He concludes that the teacher's life influences his teaching. In this essay as well as in "The American Scholar" and "Self Reliance" we find Emerson the true advocate of the spirit of American democracy when he urges scholars to develop their own ideas as an outgrowth of the intellectual climate of America without looking to the past and to Europe, and when he urges the individual to "do his own thing" (Emerson's phrase). "Education" was pieced together by Emerson's literary representatives and appeared in Letters and Social Aims *in 1876.*

The great object of Education should be commensurate with the object of life. It should be a moral one; to teach self-trust; to inspire the youthful man with an interest in himself; with a curiosity touching his own nature; to acquaint him with the resources of his mind, and to teach him that there is all his strength, and to inflame him with a piety towards the Grand Mind in which he lives. Thus would Education conspire with the Divine Providence. A man is a little thing whilst he works by and for himself, but, when he gives voice to the rules of love and justice, is godlike, his word is current in all countries; and all men, though his enemies, are made his friends and obey it as their own.

In affirming that the moral nature of man is the predominant element and should therefore be mainly consulted in the arrangements of a school, I am very far from wishing that it should swallow up all the other instincts and faculties of man. It should be enthroned in his mind, but if it monopolize the man he is not yet sound, he does not yet know his wealth. He is in danger of becoming merely devout, and wearisome through the monotony of his thought. It is not less necessary

*Source: Ralph Waldo Emerson, *Education and Other Selections*, ed. Henry Suzzallo (Boston: Houghton Mifflin, 1909), pp. 11-14, 19-20, 22-24.

that the intellectual and the active faculties should be nourished and matured. Let us apply to this subject the light of the same torch by which we have looked at all the phenomena of the time; the infinitude, namely, of every man. Everything teaches that.

One fact constitutes all my satisfaction, inspires all my trust, viz., this perpetual youth, which, as long as there is any good in us, we cannot get rid of. It is very certain that the coming age and the departing age seldom understand each other. The old man thinks the young man has no distinct purpose, for he could never get anything intelligible and earnest out of him. Perhaps the young man does not think it worth his while to explain himself to so hard and inapprehensive a confessor. Let him be led up with a long-sighted forbearance, and let not the sallies of his petulance or folly be checked with digust or indignation or despair.

•   •   •   •   •

. . . A low self-love in the parent desires that his child should repeat his character and fortune; an expectation which the child, if justice is done him, will nobly disappoint. By working on the theory that this resemblance exists, we shall do what in us lies to defeat his proper promise and produce the ordinary and mediocre. I suffer whenever I see that common sight of a parent or senior imposing his opinion and way of thinking and being on a young soul to which they are totally unfit. Cannot we let people be themselves, and enjoy life in their own way? You are trying to make that man another *you*. One's enough.

Or we sacrifice the genius of the pupil, the unknown possibilities of his nature, to a neat and safe uniformity, as the Turks whitewash the costly mosaics of ancient art which the Greeks left on their temple walls. Rather let us have men whose manhood is only the continuation of their boyhood, natural characters still; such are able and fertile for heroic action; and not that sad spectacle with which we are too familiar, educated eyes in uneducated bodies.

•   •   •   •   •

I believe that our own experience instructs us that the secret of Education lies in respecting the pupil. It is not for you to choose what he shall know, what he shall do. It is chosen and foreordained, and he only holds the key to his own secret. By your tampering and thwarting and too much governing he may be hindered from his end and kept out of his own.

Respect the child. Wait and see the new product of Nature. Nature loves analogies, but not repetitions. Respect the child. Be not too much his parent. Trespass not on his solitude.

But I hear the outcry which replies to this suggestion:— Would you verily throw up the reins of public and private discipline; would you leave the young child to the mad career of his own passions and whimsies, and call this anarchy a respect for the child's nature? I answer,—Respect the child, respect him to the end, but also respect yourself. Be the companion of his thought, the friend of his friendship, the lover of his virtue,—but no kinsman of his sin. Let him find you so true to yourself that you are the irreconcilable hater of his vice and the imperturbable slighter of his trifling.

The two points in a boy's training are, to keep his *nature* and train off all but that:—to keep his *nature,* but stop off his uproar, fooling and horse-play;—keep his nature and arm it with knowledge in the very direction in which it points. Here are the two capital facts, Genius and Drill.

•   •   •   •   •

Nor are the two elements, enthusiasm and drill, incompatible. Accuracy is essential to beauty. The very definition of the intellect is Aristotle's "that by which we know terms or boundaries." Give a boy accurate perceptions. Teach him the differences between the similar and the same. Make him call things by their right names. Pardon in him no blunder. Then he will give you solid satisfaction as long as he lives. It is better to teach the child arithmetic and Latin grammar than rhetoric or moral philosophy, because they require exactitude of performance; it is made certain that the lesson is mastered, and that power of performance is worth more than the knowledge. He can learn anything which is important to him now that the power to learn is secured: as mechanics say, when one has learned the use of tools, it is easy to work at a new craft. . . .

It is curious how perverse and intermeddling we are, and what vast pains and cost we incur to do wrong. Whilst we all know in our own experience and apply natural methods in our business,—in Education our common sense fails us, and we are continually trying costly machinery against nature, in patent schools and academies, and in great colleges and universities.

The natural method forever confutes our experiments, and we must still come back to it. The whole theory of the school is on the nurse's or mother's knee. The child is as hot to learn as the mother is to impart. There is mutual delight. The joy of our childhood in hearing beautiful stories from some skilful aunt who loves to tell them, must be repeated in youth. The boy wishes to learn to skate, to coast, to catch a fish in the brook, to hit a mark with a snowball or a stone; and a boy a little older is just as well pleased to teach him these sciences. Not less delightful is the mutual pleasure of teaching and learning the secret of algebra, or of chemistry, or of good reading and good recitation of poetry or of prose, or of chosen facts in history or in biography.

Nature provided for the communication of thought, by planting with it in the receiving mind a fury to impart it. 'T is so in every art, in every science. One burns to tell the new fact, the other burns to hear it.

•   •   •   •   •

I confess myself utterly at a loss in suggesting particular reforms in our ways of teaching. No discretion that can be lodged with a school-committee, with the overseers or visitors of an academy, of a college, can at all avail to reach these difficulties and perplexities, but they solve themselves when we leave institutions and address individuals. The will, the male power, organizes, imposes its own thought and wish on others, and makes that military eye which controls boys as it controls men; admirable in its results, a fortune to him who has it, and only dangerous when it leads the workman to overvalue and overuse it and precludes him from finer means. Sympathy, the female force,—which they must use who have not the first,—deficient in instant control and the breaking down of resistance, is more subtle and lasting and creative. I advise teachers to cherish mother-wit. I assume that you will keep the grammar, reading, writing, and arithmetic in order; 't is easy and of course you will. But smuggle in a little contraband wit, fancy, imagination, thought.

•   •   •   •   •

Of course you will insist on modesty in the children, and respect to their teachers, but if the boy stops you in your speech, cries out that you are wrong and sets you right, hug him!

To whatsoever upright mind, to whatsoever beating heart I speak, to you it is committed to educate men. By simple living, by an illimitable soul, you inspire, you correct, you instruct, you raise, you embellish all. By your own act you teach the beholder how to do the practicable. According to the depth from which you draw your life, such is the depth not only of your strenuous effort, but of your manners and presence.

The beautiful nature of the world has here blended your happiness with your power. Work straight on in absolute duty, and you lend an arm and an encouragement to all the youth of the universe. Consent yourself to be an organ of your highest thought, and lo! suddenly you put all men in your debt, and are the fountain of an energy that goes pulsing on with waves of benefit to the borders of society, to the circumference of things.

HERBERT SPENCER

Herbert Spencer (1820-1903) was born in Derby, England, the son of a nonconformist schoolmaster. He was educated at home and had few contacts with other boys. At seventeen he became a civil engineer for a railway company, but soon turned to journalism. In 1850 he published his *Social Statics* and shortly thereafter conceived his idea of developing a synthetic philosophy to which he devoted forty years of his life, publishing the entire work complete in ten volumes in 1896. In 1861 he published *Education, Intellectual, Moral, and Physical* upon which his fame as an educational theorist rests.

He was largely self-taught. Reading Kant he regarded as a waste of time, and he was bored by Plato, Locke, and John Stuart Mill. He was greatly influenced by the works of Bacon, the positivism of Comte, and the evolutionary and biological writings of Lamarck and Darwin. He adopted a naturalistic metaphysic similar in many respects to that of Democritus and Epicurus, and is known as the chief exponent of the philosophy of evolution, which he applied to biology, psychology, sociology, and ethics. Philosophy, he said, arranges the material of the sciences systematically.

He maintained that human knowledge deals with phenomena that can be divided into *outer*, explained in terms of time, space, matter, motion, and force, and *inner* explained in terms of sensation and states of consciousness. Both are aspects of an absolute reality that we cannot know, but in which we are constantly involved and in which we have an indestructible belief. Religion is an affirmation of this inscrutable power, which is beyond the range of human knowledge and cannot, therefore, be displaced by science. Accordingly, science and religion complement each other in peaceful harmony.

In his classification of the sciences, physics deals with the basic laws of nature; biology, with the relations between the organism and the environment; and sociology, with society as an evolving organism from uniformity to multiformity. Politics is the balance between the ideal and the state.

In his consideration of ethics he regarded "good" as the type of conduct that is relatively more involved in society, and "bad" as what is relatively less involved. That is, a good act would be concerned with the welfare of the social group, whereas a bad act would be motivated solely by selfish interests. Evolution, he contended, furnishes the major criterion for moral judgment, because it guarantees that life will become fuller, more complete, and more harmonious. Egoism is the original or primitive nature of man, but as society evolves and becomes more complex, egoism must give way to altruism.

He divided all of reality into science (which deals with the knowable) and religion (which deals with the unknowable). For Spencer there were three levels of knowledge: the lowest, common sense, unorganized knowledge; second, the sciences; and third, philosophy, which organizes all knowledge into a single comprehensive system.

Although he interpreted "the survival of the fittest" to mean the dependence of the individual on the life of the group, he would not accept the socialism of Mill. He wished to restrict the powers of the state, and defended the economic doctrine of *laissez faire*.

In *Education, Intellectual, Moral, and Physical,* Spencer introduced naturalism into education and was among the first to develop its scientific study. As an advocate of the phylogenetic theory he wrote: "The education of the child must accord both in mode and in arrangement with the education of mankind considered historically. In other words, the genesis of knowledge in the individual must follow the same course as the genesis of knowledge in the race."[5]

Believing that science surpasses languages as an intellectual discipline, and that practical subjects are of greater value than cultural subjects, he attacked the traditional curriculum. He replaced the Latin of the classicists and history of the Herbartians

---

[5] Herbert Spencer, *Education, Intellectual, Moral, and Physical* (London: Williams and Norgatte, 1906), p. 90.

with science as the core of the curriculum which was to provide a liberal education.

He believed that the most valuable education is centered in human welfare and prepares the child for complete living, for education should aim to enable a person to perform his function in society as efficiently as his social and economic position demands. These activities include: self-preservation, securing the necessities of life, rearing and disciplining offspring, maintaining proper social and political relations, and performing a miscellany of leisure-time activities.

In method he followed Pestalozzi, but he proposed that the object lesson should be continued throughout education until it merged into the methods of science. Children, he thought, should be told as little as possible, and should discover much by themselves. In discipline he followed Rousseau's theory of natural consequences, but where Rousseau would supplement this by direct moral training in adolescence, Spencer believed that it should provide complete moral training. As a hedonist, he held that the student would refrain from whatever produced pain and would repeat experiences that gave him pleasure.

Spencer enunciated eight principles of education, which may be listed as follows:

1. Education must conform to the natural processes of growth and mental development.
2. Education should be pleasurable.
3. Education should engage the spontaneous activity of the child.
4. Education should be concerned with the acquisition of knowledge.
5. Education is for the body as well as the mind.
6. Education should practice the art of delay.
7. Education should use an inductive method of instruction.
8. Education should develop moral conduct through natural consequences, tempered with sympathy.[6]

Spencer's influence was widespread. Bergson was partly his disciple, and James taught a course about his philosophy and psychology at Harvard. Santayana remarked, "I belong to Herbert Spencer's camp," and traces of his philosophy can be found in the writings of George Edward Woodbridge and F. J. E. Caird. His educational writings began a complete reorganization of educational thought, especially with regard to the curriculum and the

[6] See J. Donald Butler, *Four Philosophies* (New York: Harper, 1957), pp. 110-113, upon which this list is based.

aims of education. The now famous "Cardinal Principles of Secondary Education," presented by The Commission on the Reorganization of Secondary Education in 1918, clearly shows the influence of Spencer's thought, as indeed do most restatements of aims of education since his time.

What Knowledge is of Most Worth*

In "What Knowledge is of Most Worth," the first of four essays from Herbert Spencer's Education, *the author states the five topics of knowledge necessary for the preservation of the individual and society. He claims the supremacy of the biological, physical, and social sciences as curricular material and shows the relationship between the sciences and aesthetics and religion.*

The idea of ornament predominates over that of use . . . the like relations hold with the mind. Among mental as among bodily acquisitions, the ornamental comes before the useful.

•   •   •   •   •

If we were to inquire what is the real motive for giving boys a classical education, we find it to be simply conformity to public opinion. Men dress their children's minds as they do their bodies, in the prevailing fashion. As the Orinoco Indian puts on his paint before leaving his hut, not with a view to any direct benefit, but because he would be ashamed to be seen without it; so, a boy's drilling in Latin and Greek is insisted on, not because of their intrinsic value, but that he may not be disgraced by being found ignorant of them—that he may have "the education of a gentlemen"—the badge marking a certain social position, and bringing a consequent respect.

This parallel is still more clearly displayed in the case of the other sex. In the treatment of both mind and body, the decorative element has continued to predominate in a greater degree among women than among men.

We are none of us content with quietly unfolding our own individualities to the full in all directions, but have a restless craving to impress our individualities upon others, and in the same way subordinate them. And this it is which determines the character of our education. Not what knowledge is of most real worth, is the consideration; but what will bring most applause, honor, respect—what will most conduce to social

*Source: Herbert Spencer, *Education, Intellectual, Moral, and Physical* (New York: A. L. Burt, n.d.), pp. 6-93.

position and influence—what will be most imposing. As, throughout life, not what we are, but what we shall be thought, is the question; so in education, the question is, not the intrinsic value of knowledge, so much as its extrinsic effects on others. And this being our dominant idea, direct utility is scarcely more regarded than by the barbarian when filing his teeth and staining his nails.

But we that have but span-long lives must ever bear in mind our limited time for acquisition ... we ought to be especially solicitous to employ what time we have to the greatest advantage.

The first in importance, though the last to be considered is the problem—how to decide among the conflicting claims of various subjects on our attention.

How to live?—that is the essential question for us. Not how to live in the mere material sense only, but in the widest sense. The general problem which comprehends every special problem is—the right ruling of conduct in all directions under all circumstances. In what way to treat the body; in what way to treat the mind; in what way to manage our affairs; in what way to bring up a family; in what way to behave as a citizen; in what way to utilize all the sources of happiness which nature supplies—how to use all our facilities to the greatest advantage of ourselves and others—how to live completely? And this being the great thing needful for us to learn, is, by consequence, the great thing which education has to teach. To prepare us for complete living is the function which education has to discharge; and the only rational mode of judging of any educational course is, to judge in what degree it discharges such function.

Our first step must obviously be to classify in the order of their importance, the leading kinds of activity which constitute human life. They must be naturally arranged into: 1. Those activities which directly minister to self-preservation; 2. Those activities which by securing the necessaries of life, indirectly minister to self-preservation; 3. Those activities which have for their end the rearing and disciplining of offspring; 4. Those activities which are involved in the maintenance of proper social and political relations; 5. Those miscellaneous activities which make up the leisure part of life, devoted to the gratification of the tastes and feelings.

That these stand in something like their true order of subordination, it needs no long consideration to show there can be no training for any that is not in some measure a training for all. ... The ideal of education is—complete preparation in all these divisions.

•   •   •   •   •

In a rational estimate, knowledge of intrinsic worth must, other things equal, take precedence of knowledge that is of quasi-intrinsic or conventional worth.

Happily, that all-important part of education which goes to secure direct self-preservation, is in great part already provided for. Too momentous to be left to our blundering, Nature takes it into her own hands.

•   •   •   •   •

What we are chiefly called upon to see, is, that there shall be free scope, for gaining this experience, and receiving this discipline.

•   •   •   •   •

Though Nature has provided efficient safeguards to health, lack of knowledge makes them in a great measure useless.

•   •   •   •   •

They [men] are employed in the production, preparation, and distribution of commodities ... efficiency ... depends on the use of methods fitted to the respective natures of these commodities; it depends on an adequate knowledge of their physical, chemical, or vital properties, as the case may be; that is, it depends on Science.

•   •   •   •   •

For all the higher arts of construction, some acquaintance with Mathematics is indispensable.

•   •   •   •   •

Joined with mathematics it (physics) has given us the steam-engine which does the work of millions of laborers.

•   •   •   •   •

Still more numerous are the bearing of Chemistry on those activities by which men obtain the means of living.

•   •   •   •   •

And then the science of life—Biology: does not this, too, bear fundamentally upon these processes of indirect self-preservation?

Yet one more science have we to note as bearing directly on industrial success—the Science of Society. Without knowing it men ... are students of social science, empirical and blundering students it may be.

•   •   •   •   •

Thus, to all such as are occupied in the production,

exchange, or distribution of commodities, acquaintance with science in some of its departments, is of fundamental importance.

• • • • •

Had there been no teaching but such as is given in our public schools, England would now be what it was in feudal times. ... The vital knowledge ... has gotten itself taught in nooks and corners; while the ordained agencies of teaching have been mumbling little else but dead formulas ... not one word of instruction on the treatment of offspring is ever given to those who will hereafter be parents.

• • • • •

Deeds which she (the mother) thinks it desirable to encourage, she gets performed by threats and bribes; ... and thus cultivating hypocrisy and fear and selfishness instead of good feeling.

The words contained in books can be rightly interpreted by ideas, only in proportion to antecedent experience of things. ... Intellectual progress is of necessity from the concrete to the abstract.

• • • • •

Some acquaintance with the first principles of physiology and the elementary truths of psychology is indispensable for the right bringing up of children.

• • • • •

We must test their [historical facts] worth as we test the worth of other facts, by asking to what use they are applicable.

We yield to none in the value we attach to aesthetic culture and its pleasures. Without painting, sculpture, music, poetry, and the emotions produced by ritual of beauty of every kind, life would lose half its charm. We believe the time will come when they will occupy a much larger share of human life than now.

• • • • •

Accomplishments, the fine arts, belles-lettres and all those things which we say, constitute the efflorescence of civilization should be, wholly subordinate to that knowledge and discipline in which civilization rests, as they occupy the leisure part of education.

• • • • •

We do not for a moment believe that science will make an artist. While we contend that the leading laws both of objective and subjective phenomena must be understood by him, we by no means contend that knowledge of such laws will serve in place of natural perception. Not only the poet, but also the artist of every type, is born, not made. What we assert is, that innate faculty alone will not suffice; but must have the aid of organized knowledge.

• • • • •

And now let us not overlook the further great fact that not only does science underlie sculpture, painting, music, poetry, but that science is itself poetic. The current opinion that science and poetry are opposed is a delusion. ... On the contrary science opens up realms of poetry where to the unscientific all is blank.

• • • • •

And whoever will contemplate the life of Goethe will see that the poet and the man of science can co-exist in equal activity. ... And we not only find that science is the handmaid to all forms of art and poetry, but that, rightly regarded, science is itself poetical.

• • • • •

The education of most value for guidance, must at the same time be the education most valuable for discipline.

While for the training of mere memory, science is as good as, if not better than, language; it has immense superiority in the kind of memory it cultivates. A great superiority of science over language, as a means of discipline, is, that it cultivates the judgment. ... Not only however, for intellectual discipline is science the best, but also for *moral* discipline. ... By science, constant appeal is made to individual reason. Its truths are not accepted upon authority alone, but all are at liberty to test them.

Lastly we have to assert ... that the discipline of science is superior to that of our ordinary education because of the *religious* culture that it gives. Not science, but the neglect of science, is irreligious. Devotion to science is a tacit worship—a tacit recognition of worth in the things studied; and by implication in their cause.

It is religious, too, inasmuch as it generates a profound respect for, and an implicit faith in, those uniform laws which underlie all things.

We conclude, then, that for discipline, as well as for guidance, science is of chiefest value. In all its effects learning the meaning of things, is better than learning the meanings of words, whether for intellectual, moral, or religious training, the study of surrounding phenomena is immensely superior to the study of grammar and lexicons.

What knowledge is of most worth?—the uniform reply is—Science. Science, proclaimed as highest alike in worth and beauty, will reign supreme.

BIBLIOGRAPHY

RALPH WALDO EMERSON

Emerson, Ralph Waldo, *Complete Works,* with a biographical introduction and notes by Edward Waldo Emerson. New Centenary Edition (Boston: Houghton Mifflin, 1903-1904).

——, *Education* (Boston: Houghton Mifflin, 1883).

Frothingham, Octavius Brooks, *Transcendentalism in New England* (Boston: Beacon, n.d.).

*Jones, Howard Mumford, *Emerson on Education* (New York: Teachers College Press, 1966).

Perry, Bliss, *Emerson Today* (Princeton: Princeton University Press, 1931).

HERBERT SPENCER

*Hofstadter, Richard, *Social Darwinism in American Thought* (Boston: Beacon, 1964).

*Kazamias, A. M., *Herbert Spencer on Education* (New York: Teachers College Press, 1966).

*Rumney, Jay, *Herbert Spencer's Sociology* (New York: Atherton, 1966).

*Spencer, H., *Education, Intellectual, Moral, and Physical* (Totowa, N.J.: Littlefield, Adams, 1963).

*——, *Study of Sociology* (Ann Arbor: Ann Arbor Books, University of Michigan Press, 1961).

*Paperback editions.

Chapter Eight
The Post-Darwinians: James, Dewey, and Whitehead

DURING THE CLOSING YEARS of the nineteenth century and the beginning of the twentieth century, American philosophy and educational thought began to shake off the shackles of German idealism. The scientific method began to be applied rigorously in the study of educational problems and in other behavioral sciences.

William James explored new paths of interrelationships between philosophy, psychology, medicine, religion, and education and made his theories about the psychology of learning available to the classroom teacher.

Dewey showed the relevance of philosophy to education in terms of an ongoing society and is perhaps the most influential American educational philosopher. However, his views have by no means been universally understood or accepted.

Finally, Alfred North Whitehead developed a philosophy of organism, of process, and of interreaction between man and his environment.

WILLIAM JAMES

William James (1842-1910) was born in New York City of wealthy and cultured parents. He traveled widely and lived and studied both in England and America. He had many interests, notably art, biology, medicine, psychology, and philosophy. His thought was influenced by the materialism of John Stuart Mill, the biology of Louis Agassiz, the positivism of Auguste Comte, the psychology of Wilhelm Wundt, and the philosophy of Charles S. Peirce. He accepted Darwinian evolution but insisted on provision for individual initiative. He dubbed Spencer's theory of automatic progress an "obsolete anachronism" and broke with Hegel's block universe, calling his dialectic a "mousetrap" in which those who enter "may be lost forever." He was a prophet of individualism and of voluntarism. He never accepted a scientific conclusion as final truth, but always insisted on leaving room for exceptions.

Philosophy for James is connected with the solution of social problems and of social issues; it is our more or less dumb sense of what life honestly and deeply means. The real world is the world of human experiences beyond which the human mind cannot go. It is an unfinished lot of things, and man is in the center of it because what he experiences is real. This world of our knowledge lies within a larger unseen world. Belief in God is necessary for the satisfaction of man's nature. The will to believe is man's greatest companion and helper. Man wants to believe in a certain way because these beliefs seem to satisfy him. If this will to believe is fundamental, man cannot be bound by immutable laws, but must be free to build his own ideas, and to risk everything on their fulfillment.

Truth, in the long run, he believes, is the overall expediency in ways of believing as goodness is in ways of behaving. The good is that which serves the ends of the group and the individual in the group, for the individual is an end in himself and not a means to an end. The ultimate measure of the good is the human individual as a social unit.

With regard to cherished formulas, James holds that they are often obstacles rather than aids to thinking. Theories and ideas should be instruments and plans for action. Beliefs are not pictures of the past but factors we can rely on for the future. To think is to be prepared to do. We must have confidence in the future. Absolute truth is a distant vanishing point to which our contemporary truths converge.

James's psychology, published in 1890, was written in his usual vivid, concrete, and pragmatic style. Mind, he said, is a kind of behavior, and is a latecomer in the evolutionary series. It aids man to make better practical adjustments to his environment. He showed the neurological, physiological, and organic bases for psychology and maintained that there was "no psychosis without neurosis," that is, that mental life was grounded in experience. A famous example of this is the James-Lange theory of the emotions with its sequence, "I see a bear; I run; I am afraid," by which he attempted to illustrate his hypothesis that emotional states were the result of mental and organic activity arising from an external stimulus.

Although he held that there was no reception of external stimuli without reaction, and no impression without expression, he rejected the "tabula rasa" theory of Locke and the environmental theory of Herbart for the theory of unlearned native endowments or instincts of Aristotle. He listed these instincts as: fear, love, curiosity, imitation, pride, ambition, pugnacity, ownership, and constructiveness. His belief that every acquired action supplements or supplants a native one anticipated present day theories of conditioning and associative shifting. To develop habits he recommended beginning with strong initiative, permitting no exceptions, and seizing upon every opportunity for practice.

Among his most important contributions to psychology was his description of consciousness as awareness of experience and as experience in a medium in which objects and organisms are related. He did not believe that consciousness could be described in terms of individual sensations, but that it was a continuous stream, always flowing, always changing, appearing in new concepts, always impulsive, affective and personal, and only sometimes intellectual. It is much more than the brain, which consciousness uses as an instrument to localize our purposes and to act efficaciously upon the world. With Kant, he believed that mind contributes to the structure of experience.

"We think for a purpose," wrote James. Thought was process, and the business of the psychologist and educator was to discover how thinking could be done more efficiently, for it is no better than the service it can render in a situation.

James is a universal genius, and therefore defies classification. His many works show the variety of his interests. Beginning with his *Psychology* in 1890, he forged new paths by bringing his medical knowledge to bear on this new science. He popularized his psychology and applied it directly to teaching situations in his popular *Talks to Teachers on Psychology* published in 1899. These works have not only influenced the development of educational psychology, but have had a profound effect on teaching methods.

His two works on the philosophy of religion, *The Will to Believe* and *The Varieties of Religious Experience,* were published in 1897 and 1902 respectively. Religion, for James, is the cause of the individual's striving for the unknown. On the other hand, for Emerson, it springs from our being embedded in something greater than man. For both there was the universal will to believe.

Possibly his best known work is *Pragmatism* (1907), which he described as a new way to express old ideas, and which he claimed must be constantly redefined or it will become a dogma instead of a "living vision." His *Essays in Radical Empiricism* was published posthumously in 1912. Almost every psychologist and philosopher since G. Stanley Hall who studied with him at Harvard has come under his influence at some time. Through his greatest interpreter, Ralph Barton Perry, he has had a profound influence on the "new-realism" in philosophy. Morton White says of him:

> James . . . was no second-rate imitator or satellite of British or continental philosophy; he was a major philosophical planet who whirled on his own axis and drew all of the other pragmatic luminaries into his powerful field. His pragmatism was anticipated by Peirce and revised by Dewey, but he was unquestionably the central literary figure in the pragmatic movement, an "adorable genius" as Whitehead called him, and the man of whom Russell said: "No degree of democratic feeling and of desire to identify himself with the common herd could make him anything but a natural aristocrat, a man whose personal distinction commanded respect."[1]

The Association of Ideas*

James's Talks to Teachers *is a popular simplification of his monumental* Principles of Psychology *prepared especially for classroom teachers with little or no technical knowledge. Chapter 8, which immediately precedes the chapter quoted here deals with the laws of habit. James writes that pupils can easily understand at an early age that our lives are but a mass of habits. He agrees with Aristotle that habit is man's second nature and with Kant that education is for behavior and habit the stuff of which nature consists. Like many modern psychologists, he advises the person to accumulate all the possible connections that will reinforce the right motives and warns that deferring the establishment of a new habit lessens the chance that it will ever be formed.*

[1] Morton White, *The Age of Analysis* (New York: Mentor Books, New American Library, 1955), p. 154.

*Source: William James, *Talks to Teachers on Psychology and to Students of Life's Ideals* (New York: Norton, 1958). pp. 65-72.

Then he sets forth the following five laws of habit:

1. Launch the new habit or the discontinuation of the old one with as strong and decided initiative as possible.
2. Never suffer an exception to occur until the new habit is securely rooted in your life.
3. Seize every opportunity to act out the new habit.
4. Don't preach too much. The strokes of behavior are what builds the new habit into the organic tissue.
5. Keep the faculty of effort alive in you by a little gratuitous exercise every day.

He concludes that "Nothing we ever do is, in strict scientific literalness, wiped out. . , Let no youth have any anxiety about the upshot of his education, whatever the line of it may be. If he keep faithfully busy each hour of the working day, he may safely leave the final result to itself."

Chapter 9, quoted here, deals with the changing configurations with which ideas can be associated.

In my last talk, in treating of Habit, I chiefly had in mind our *motor* habits,—habits of external conduct. But our thinking and feeling processes are also largely subject to the law of habit, and one result of this is a phenomenon which you all know under the name of 'the association of ideas.' To that phenomenon I ask you now to turn.

You remember that consciousness is an ever-flowing stream of objects, feelings, and impulsive tendencies. We saw already that its phases or pulses are like so many fields or waves, each field or wave having usually its central point of liveliest attention, in the shape of the most prominent object in our thought, while all around this lies a margin of other objects more dimly realized, together with the margin of emotional and active tendencies which the whole entails. Describing the mind thus in fluid terms, we cling as close as possible to nature. At first sight, it might seem as if, in the fluidity of these successive waves, everything is indeterminate. But inspection shows that each wave has a constitution which can be to some degree explained by the constitution of the waves just passed away. And this relation of the wave to its predecessors is expressed by the two fundamental 'laws of association,' so-called, of which the first is named the Law of Contiguity, the second that of Similarity.

The *Law of Contiguity* tells us that objects thought of in the coming wave are such as in some previous experience were *next* to the objects represented in the wave that is passing away. The vanishing objects were once formerly their neighbors in the mind. When you recite the alphabet or your prayers, or when the sight of an object reminds you of its name, or the name reminds you of the object, it is through the law of contiguity that the terms are suggested to the mind.

The *Law of Similarity* says that, when contiguity fails to describe what happens, the coming objects will prove to resemble the going objects, even though the two were never experienced together before. In our 'flights of fancy,' this is frequently the case.

If, arresting ourselves in the flow of reverie, we ask the question, "How came we to be thinking of just this object now?" we can almost always trace its presence to some previous object which has introduced it to the mind, according to one or the other of these laws. The entire routine of our memorized acquisitions, for example, is a consequence of nothing but the Law of Contiguity. The words of a poem, the formulas of trigonometry, the facts of history, the properties of material things, are all known to us as definite systems or groups of objects which cohere in an order fixed by innumerable iterations, and of which any one part reminds us of the others. In dry and prosaic minds, almost all the mental sequences flow along these lines of habitual routine repetition and suggestion.

In witty, imaginative minds, on the other hand, the routine is broken through with ease at any moment; and one field of mental objects will suggest another with which perhaps in the whole history of human thinking it had never once before been coupled. The link here is usually some *analogy* between the objects successively thought of—an analogy often so subtle that, although we feel it, we can with difficulty analyze its ground; as where, for example, we find something masculine in the color red and something feminine in the color pale blue, or where, of three human beings' characters, one will remind us of a cat, another of a dog, the third perhaps of a cow.

Psychologists have of course gone very deeply into the question of what the causes of association may be; and some of them have tried to show that contiguity and similarity are not two radically diverse laws, but that either presupposes the presence of the other. I myself am disposed to think that the phenomena of association depend on our cerebral constitution, and are not immediate consequences of our being rational beings. In other words, when we shall have become disembodied spirits, it may be that our trains of consciousness will follow different laws. These questions are discussed in the books on psychology, and I hope that some of you will be interested in following them there. But I will, on the present occasion, ignore them entirely; for, as teachers, it is the *fact* of association that practically concerns you, let its grounds be spiritual or cerebral, or what they may, and let its laws be reducible, or non-reducible, to one. Your pupils, whatever else they are, are at any rate little pieces of associating machinery. Their education consists in the organizing within them of determinate tendencies to associate one thing with another,— impressions with consequences, these with reactions, those with results, and so on indefinitely. The more copious the associative systems, the completer the individual's adaptations to the world.

The teacher can formulate his function to himself therefore in terms of 'association' as well as in terms of 'native and acquired reaction.' It is mainly that of *building up useful systems of association* in the pupil's mind. This description sounds wider than the one I began by giving. But, when one thinks that our trains of association, whatever they may be, normally issue in acquired reactions or behavior, one sees that in a general way the same mass of facts is covered by both formulas.

It is astonishing how many mental operations we can explain when we have once grasped the principles of association. The great problem which association undertakes to solve is, *Why does just this particular field of consciousness, constituted in this particular way, now appear before my mind?* It may be a field of objects imagined; it may be of objects remembered or of objects perceived; it may include an action resolved on. In either case, when the field is analyzed into its parts, those parts can be shown to have proceeded from parts of fields previously before consciousness, in consequence of one or other of the laws of association just laid down. Those laws *run* the mind: interest, shifting hither and thither, deflects it; and attention, as we shall later see, steers it and keeps it from too zigzag a course.

To grasp these factors clearly gives one a solid and simple understanding of the psychological machinery. The 'nature,' the 'character,' of an individual means really nothing but the habitual form of his associations. To break up bad associations or wrong ones, to build others in, to guide the associative tendencies into the most fruitful channels, is the educator's principal task. But here, as with all other simple principles, the difficulty lies in the application. Psychology can state the laws: concrete tact and talent alone can work them to useful results.

Meanwhile it is a matter of the commonest experience that our minds may pass from one object to another by various intermediary fields of consciousness. The indeterminateness of our paths of association *in concreto* is thus almost as striking a feature of them as the uniformity of their abstract form. Start from any idea whatever, and the entire range of your ideas is potentially at your disposal. If we take as the associative starting-point, or cue, some simple word which I pronounce before you, there is no limit to the possible diversity of suggestions which it may set up in your minds. Suppose I say 'blue,' for example: some of you may think of the blue sky and hot weather from which we now are suffering, then go off on thoughts of summer clothing, or possibly of meteorology at large; others may think of the spectrum and the physiology of color-vision, and glide into X-rays and recent physical speculations; others may think of blue ribbons, or of the blue flowers on a friend's hat, and proceed on lines of personal reminiscence. To others, again, etymology and linguistic thoughts may be suggested; or blue may be 'apperceived' as a synonym for melancholy, and a train of associates connected with morbid psychology may proceed to unroll themselves.

In the same person, the same word heard at different times will provoke, in consequence of the varying marginal preoccupations, either one of a number of diverse possible associative sequences. Professor Münsterberg performed this experiment methodically, using the same words four times over, at three-month intervals, as 'cues' for four different persons who were the subjects of observation. He found almost no constancy in their associations taken at these different times. In short, the entire potential content of one's consciousness is accessible from any one of its points. This is why we can never work the laws of association forward: starting from the present field as a cue, we can never cipher out in advance just what the person will be thinking of five minutes later. The elements which may become prepotent in the process, the parts of each successive field round which the associations shall chiefly turn, the possible bifurcations of suggestion, are so numerous and ambiguous as to be indeterminable before the fact. But, although we cannot work the laws of association forward, we can always work then backwards. We cannot say now what we shall find ourselves thinking of five minutes hence; but, whatever it may be, we shall then be able to trace it through intermediary links of contiguity or similarity to what we are thinking now. What so baffles our prevision is the shifting part played by the margin and focus—in fact, by each element by itself of the margin or focus—in calling up the next ideas.

For example, I am reciting 'Locksley Hall,' in order to divert my mind from a state of suspense that I am in concerning the will of a relative that is dead. The will still remains in the mental background as an extremely marginal or ultra-marginal portion of my field of consciousness; but the poem fairly keeps my attention from it, until I come to the line, "I, the heir of all the ages, in the foremost files of time." The words, 'I, the heir,' immediately make an electric connection with the marginal thought of the will; that, in turn, makes my heart beat with anticipation of my possible legacy, so that I throw down the book and pace the floor excitedly with visions of my future fortune pouring through my mind. Any portion of the field of consciousness that has more potentialities of emotional excitement than another may thus be roused to predominant activity; and the shifting play of interest now in one portion, now in another, deflects the currents in all sorts of zigzag ways, the mental activity running hither and thither as the sparks run in burnt-up paper.

One more point, and I shall have said as much to you as seems necessary about the process of association.

You just saw how a single exciting word may call up its own associates prepotently, and deflect our whole train of thinking from the previous track. The fact is that every portion of the field *tends* to call up its own associates; but, if these associates be severally different, there is rivalry, and as soon as one or a few begin to be effective the others seem to get siphoned out, as it were, and left behind. Seldom, however, as in our example, does the process seem to turn round a single item in the mental field, or even round the entire field that is immediately in the act of passing. It is a matter of *constellation,* into which portions of fields that are already past especially seem to enter and have their say. Thus, to go back to 'Locksley Hall,' each word as I recite it in its due order is suggested not solely by the previous word now expiring on my lips, but it is rather the effect of all the previous words, taken together, of the verse. "Ages," for example, calls up "in the foremost files of time," when preceded by "I, the heir of all the"—; but, when preceded by "for I doubt not through the,"—it calls up "one increasing purpose runs." Similarly, if I write on the blackboard the letters A B C D E F, . . . they probably suggest to you G H I. . . . But if I write A B A D D E F, if they suggest anything, they suggest as their complement E C T or E F I C I E N C Y, the result depending on the total constellation, even though most of the single items be the same.

My practical reason for mentioning this law is this, that it follows from it that, in working associations into your pupils' minds, you must not rely on single cues, but multiply the cues as much as possible. Couple the desired reaction with numerous constellations of antecedents,—don't always ask the question, for example, in the same way; don't use the same kind of data in numerical problems; vary your illustrations, etc., as much as you can. When we come to the subject of memory, we shall learn still more about this.

So much, then, for the general subject of association. In leaving it for other topics (in which, however, we shall abundantly find it involved again), I cannot too strongly urge you to acquire a habit of thinking of your pupils in associative terms. All governors of mankind, from doctors and jail-wardens to demagogues and statesmen, instinctively come so to conceive their charges. If you do the same, thinking of them (however else you may think of them besides) as so many little systems of associating machinery, you will be astonished at the intimacy of insight into their operations and at the practicality of the results which you will gain. We think of our acquaintances, for example, as characterized by certain 'tendencies.' These tendencies will in almost every instance prove to be tendencies to association. Certain ideas in them are always followed by certain other ideas, these by certain feelings and impulses to approve or disapprove, assent or decline. If the topic arouse one of those first ideas, the practical outcome can be pretty well foreseen. 'Types of character' in short are largely types of association.

JOHN DEWEY

John Dewey (1859-1952), born in Burlington, Vermont, was descended from a long line of Vermont farmers who came from Flanders to Massachusetts in 1630. He attended the local schools and the University of Vermont. After three years of high school teaching, he went to Johns Hopkins University, where he studied with George S. Morris and G. Stanley Hall, and took his doctorate in 1884. He taught philosophy at the Universities of Michigan and Minnesota, was professor of philosophy and pedagogy at the University of Chicago from 1894-1904, and was professor of philosophy at Columbia University from 1905 until his retirement in 1931. Edman writes of him:

> It might be said, that if Dewey is recognized as a peculiarly American philosopher, it is because he caught the voice, accent and temper of the American tradition and the nature of the special contingencies and choices before it in his own era. He did not, it may be argued, make the tradition, or, for that matter, remake it. The expanding forces of technology, the intervolvement of public and private affairs, the rising tide of the labor movement, the revolt against authoritarianism in religion and in education—all these play a large part in and color his social philosophy—were, it may be argued, themes he translated into general terms of philosophical analysis; they were *not* consequences of his published ideas.[2]

During all of his life, he retained much of the quiet simplicity and the wholesome regard for facts of the Vermonters among whom he grew up, and the respect for the private dignity of the individual so characteristic of his fellow New Englander, Emerson.

Among Dewey's chief philosophical problems were an analysis of the thinking process and the establishment of a medial position which would show the relation between the great number of dualisms, such as mind and body, interest and effort, change and permanence, with which many of the philosophers who preceded him had been concerned.

To Plato, Kant, and many others, time and change were mere illusions, mere opinions with respect to reality. In ancient Greece, on the other hand, Heraclitus had said that the only certainty was the law of change. Dewey accepted this idea, except that he

---

[2] Irwin Edman, *John Dewey* (New York: Bobbs-Merrill, 1955), pp. 21-22. Copyright © 1955 by The Bobbs-Merrill Company, Inc., and used by special permission.

believed with James in a constant flow or continuity of experience that, while always changing, contained elements from the past as well as for the future. Also, he maintained that man's ability to think can be and should be instrumental in affecting the direction of change. For Dewey, then, reality is *change,* the universe is *process,* and man is coexistent with nature.

Instead of the absolute and universal he wrote in terms of the relative and contingent. Facts became knowledge only through activity in social situations. Knowledge itself was fractional and situational, being true only for one place, at one point of time, under certain circumstances. It was a sort of hypothesis, born in perplexity and proved through experience. Changes cause conflicts between new problems and old patterns, and call for constant reevaluation and reconstruction of experience. The key to life is growth, which is a kind of alertness to the changing patterns of life. Intelligence is man's means of evaluating and of adapting himself to his environment, and his environment to himself. This and man's use of symbols to preserve past experiences are man's distinctive characteristics. Thus history may be said to be the mother of civilizations. But not all of human events are recorded, and Dewey points out that those possessed of the use of symbols select the events which are most favorable to them and which advance their position among those who pursue only manual occupations. In time there arose class distinctions with all their attendant circumstances between the thinker and the doer, and as laws codified and strengthened customs, these distinctions became fixed and similar types of dualisms became accepted modes of thought. Such dualisms as work-play mental-physical, liberal-vocational, are conventions which must be reexamined in the light of the on-going process of change. Intelligence is instrumental to this examination of values.

Thinking arises, says Dewey, in a forked-road situation. It is "in the first instance the up-welling of a suggestion, and imaginative rehearsal, a leap into some envisioned possibility, an enactment in imagination, of what may be done."[3] Or more specifically, the problem, which arises in activity (which may, of course, be entirely mental), calls for the assembling, organization, and comparison of data, the vicarious exploration of the bearings of the situation, and the formulation of a tentative hypothesis which is tested, modified, and probably discarded through experience.

This formula is also the basis for establishing ethical standards.

[3] *Ibid.,* p. 29.

Values are determined not by intention, but by their salutary effect on the social group they concern. This shared life for the good of the individual and the community—and Dewey thought in terms of the world community—is the ideal of democracy, an ideal which was for Dewey at once moral, religious, and esthetic. He wrote:

> The most penetrating definition of philosophy which can be given is that it is the theory of education in its most general phases. . . .
>
> A democracy is more than a form of government: it is primarily a mode of associated living, of conjoint communicated experience. . . .
>
> Men live in a community in virtue of the things which they have in common, and communication is the way in which they come to possess things in common. What they must have in common in order to form a community or a society are aims, beliefs, aspirations, knowledge, a common understanding—likemindedness, as the sociologists say. Persons do not become a society by living in physical proximity. . . . Individuals do not even compose a social group because they all work together for a common end. . . . If however, they were all cognizant of the common end, and all interested in it so that they regulated their specific activity in view of it, then they would form a community. . . . Consensus demands communication. . . . To be a recipient of a communication is to have an enlarged and changed experience. Except in dealing with commonplaces and catch phrases one has to assimilate, imaginatively, something of another's experiences in order to tell him of his own experience. . . . Not only does social life demand teaching and learning for its own permanence, but the very process of living together educates.[4]

Dewey stigmatizes the type of interest that is an attempt to secure effort and attention by offering a bribe as "soft pedagogy, soup-kitchen theory of education. . . ." In learning, interest is necessary to sustain effort during the period between the acceptance of an objective and its realization. The teacher challenges the active interest of the learner by presenting old material in new settings, or new material to challenge old ideas. In the same vein Dewey continues:

In learning, the present powers of the pupil are the initial

[4] John Dewey, *Democracy and Education* (New York: Macmillan, 1916), pp. 386, 101, 5-7. Copyright 1916 by the Macmillan Company and reprinted by their permission.

stage; the aim of the teacher represents the remote limit. Between the two lies *means*—that is middle conditions—acts to be performed; difficulties to be overcome; appliances to be used. Only *through* them, in the literal sense, will the initial activities reach a satisfactory consummation. To be means for the achieving of present tendencies, to be "between" the agent and his end, to be of interest are different names for the same things. When material has to be made interesting, it signifies that, as presented, it lacks connection with purposes and present power; or that if the connection be there, it is not perceived. To make it interesting by extraneous and artificial inducements deserves all the bad names which have been applied to the doctrine of interest in education.[5]

Thus, Dewey explains the intimate relationship between interest and means in education. These means move toward further ends—ends that must be personal and more or less immediate, and the motivation to these ends must arise from within the individual who governs his course of action in accordance with his goals. This Dewey describes as discipline, saying, "discipline means power at command."[6]

With regard to the relation between work and play Dewey remarks:

When fairly remote results of a definite character are foreseen and enlist persistent effort for their accomplishment, play passes into work. Like play, it signifies purposeful activity and differs *not* in that activity is subordinated to an external result, but in the fact that a longer course of activity is occasioned by the idea of a result. The demand for continuous attention is greater, and more intelligence must be shown in selecting and shaping means. ... Activity carried on under conditions of external pressure or coercion (namely drudgery) is not carried on for any significance attached to the doing. ... What is inherently repulsive is endured for the sake of averting something still more repulsive or of securing a gain hitched on by others. ... Only the hold which the completion of the work has upon a person will keep him going. But the end should be intrinsic to the action; it should be its end—a part of its own course.[7]

[5] *Ibid.,* pp. 149-150.
[6] *Ibid.,* p. 151.
[7] *Ibid.,* pp. 240-289.

Such a reorientation of aims will have a decided effect on the curriculum. In *The Child and the Curriculum* Dewey writes:

> Abandon the notion of subject-matter as something fixed and ready-made in itself, outside the child's experience; cease thinking of the child's experience also as something hard and fast; see it as something fluent, embryonic, vital; and we realize that the child and the curriculum are simply two limits which define a single process.[8]

Dewey stresses the importance of the cultural heritage, but warns: "A knowledge of the past and its heritage is of great significance when it enters into the present, but not otherwise."[9] He continues:

> An experimental school is under the temptation to improvise its subject-matter. It must take advantage of unexpected events and turn to account unexpected questions and interests. Yet if it permits improvisation to dictate its course, the result is a jerky, discontinuous movement which works against the possibility of making any important contribution to educational subject-matter. Incidents are momentary, but the use made of them should not be momentary or short-lived. They are to be brought within the scope of a developing whole of content and purpose, which is a whole because it has continuity and consecutiveness in its parts. There is no single subject matter which all schools must adopt, but in every school there should be some significant subject-matters undergoing growth and formulation.[10]

Dewey was a great moral philosopher but not a religionist in the accepted sense of the term. He had great faith in democracy and to that end he thought the public schools should dedicate themselves, directing all studies and activities thereto.

Just because the studies of the curriculum represent standard factors in social life they are organs of initiation into social values. As mere school studies, their acquisition has only a technical worth. Acquired under conditions where their social significance is realized, they feed moral interest and develop moral insight.[11]

[8] John Dewey, *The Child and the Curriculum* (Chicago: University of Chicago Press, 1902), p. 14.

[9] Dewey, *Democracy and Education*, p. 88.

[10] John Dewey, "Progressive Education and the Science of Education," *Progressive Education*, V (July-September, 1928), 201.

[11] Dewey, *Democracy and Education*, p. 414.

He points out further that studies are pursued not only for practical ends but for values inherent in them.

Appreciation ... denotes an enlarged, an *intensified* prizing. ... Certain conclusions follow with respect to educational values. We cannot establish a hierarchy of values among studies. ... In so far as any study has a unique or irreplaceable function in experience, in so far as it marks a characteristic enrichment of life, its worth is intrinsic or incomparable. ... And what has been said about appreciation means that every study in one of its aspects ought to have just such ultimate significance. It is as true of arithmetic as it is of poetry that in some place and at some time it ought to be a good to be appreciated on its own account—just as an enjoyable experience. In short, if it is not, then when the time and place come for it to be used as a means or instrumentality, it will be just that much handicapped. Never having been realized or appreciated for itself, one will miss something of its capacity as a resource for other ends.[12]

With regard to deferred values in education, he observed:

Who can reckon up the loss of moral power that arises from the constant impression that nothing is worth doing in itself, but only as a preparation for something else, which in turn is only a getting ready for some genuinely serious end beyond?[13]

Of the teaching of religion in the public schools he says:

Already the spirit of our schooling is permeated with the feeling that every topic, every fact, every professed truth must submit to a certain publicity and impartiality. ... It is the essence of all dogmatic faiths to hold that any such "show-down" is sacrilegious and perverse. ... Our schools, in bringing together those of different nationalities, languages, traditions, and creeds, in assimilating them together upon the basis of what is common and public in endeavor and achievement, are performing an infinitely significant religious work. They are promoting the social unity out of which in the end genuine religious unity must grow.[14]

[12] *Ibid.*, pp. 278, 281.

[13] John Dewey, *Moral Principle in Education* (Boston: Houghton Mifflin, 1909), p. 26.

[14] John Dewey, "Religion and Our Schools," *Hibbert Journal,* VI (July, 1908), 804, 807.

John Dewey's influence in American education has been considerable, not only in the mainstream of public education, but among the traditionalists and essentialists who opposed him, and among the ultra-progressives who grossly misinterpreted him. The impact of his writings can be traced in the fields of law and art as well as in the social sciences. As a philosopher's philosopher he added considerably to the technical development of this discipline. He was not as analytic as Peirce nor as fluent a writer as James, but his often difficult style has gotten through to the minds of his countrymen and has influenced every department of American thought.

The Way Out of Educational Confusion*

In the following selection, Dewey suggests the "project," "problem," or "situation" method as a way of gathering, assimilating and evaluating new subject matter. He maintains that the current confusion and lack of interest of students in the traditional curriculum is due to the fragmentation and segregation of subject matter into "disciplines" and courses. The article originally was published as a pamphlet in 1931 by the Harvard University Press.

I recur now to the main theme of which this particular problem supplies one instance. It is fair for an objector to ask what is the substitute, the alternative, to organization of courses on the basis of adherence to traditional divisions and classifications of knowledge. The reply which goes furthest to the left is found in reference to the so-called "project," "problem," or "situation" method, now adopted for trial in many elementary schools. I shall indicate later that I do not believe that this is the only alternative. But the method has certain characteristics which are significant for any plan for change that may be adopted, and accordingly I shall call attention to these features. The method mentioned is called a method; it might be taken, therefore, to be *only* a method. In fact, like anything that *is* a method other than in name, it has definite implications for subject-matter. There cannot be a problem that is not a problem of *something*, nor a project that does not involve doing something in a way which demands inquiry into fresh fields of subject-matter. Many so-called projects are of

Source: Reginald D. Archambault, *John Dewey on Education* (New York: Modern Library, Random House, 1964), pp. 422-426.

such a short-time span and are entered upon for such casual reasons, that extension of acquaintance with facts and principles is at a minimum. In short, they are too trivial to be educative. But the defect is not inherent. It only indicates the need that educators should assume their educational responsibility. It is possible to find problems and projects that come within the scope and capacities of the experience of the learner and which have a sufficiently long span so that they raise new questions, introduce new and related undertakings, and create a demand for fresh knowledge. The difference between this procedure and the traditional one is not that the latter involves acquisition of new knowledge and the former does not. It is that in one a relatively fixed and isolated body of knowledge is assumed in advance; while in the other, material is drawn from any field as it is needed to carry on an intellectual enterprise.

Nor is the difference that in one procedure organization exists and in the other it does not. It is a difference in the type of organization effected. Material may be drawn from a variety of fields, number and measure from mathematics when they are needed, from historical, geographical, biological facts when they carry forward the undertaking, and so on. But the central question acts as a magnet to draw them together. Organization in one case consists in formal relations within a particular field as they present themselves to an expert who has mastered the subject. In the other case, it consists in noting the bearing and function of things acquired. The latter course has at least the advantage of being of the kind followed in study and learning outside of school walls, where data and principles do not offer themselves in isolated segments with labels already affixed.

Another feature of the problem method is that activity is exacted. I suppose that if there is one principle which is not a monopoly of any school of educational thought, it is the need of intellectual activity on the part of teacher and student, the condemnation of passive receptivity. But in practice there persist methods in which the pupil is a recording phonograph, or one who stands at the end of a pipe line receiving material conducted from a distant reservoir of learning. How is this split between theory and practice to be explained? Does not the presentation in doses and chunks of a ready made subject-matter inevitably conduce to passivity? The mentally active scholar will acknowledge, I think, that his mind roams far and wide. All is grist that comes to his mill, and he does not limit his supply of grain to any one fenced-off field. Yet the mind does not merely roam abroad. It returns with what is found, and there is constant exercise of judgment to detect relations, relevancies, bearings upon the central theme. The outcome is a continuously growing intellectual integration. There is absorption; but it is eager and willing, not reluctant and forced. There is digestion, assimilation, not merely the carrying of a load by memory, a load to be cast off as soon as the day comes when it is safe to throw it off. Within the limits set by capacity and experience this kind of seeking and using, of amassing and organizing, is the process of learning everywhere and at any age.

In the third place, while the student with a proper "project" is intellectually active, he is also overtly active; he applies, he constructs, he expresses himself in new ways. He puts his knowledge to the test of operation. Naturally, he does something with what he learns. Because of this feature the separation between the practical and the liberal does not even arise. It does not have to be done away with, because it is not there. In practical subjects, this doing exists in laboratories and shops. But too often it is of a merely technical sort, not a genuine carrying forward of theoretical knowledge. It aims at mere manual facility, at an immediate external product, or a driving home into memory of something already learned as a matter of mere information.

I have referred, as already indicated, to the "project" method because of these traits, which seem to me proper and indispensable aims in all study by whatever name it be called, not because this method seems to be the only alternative to that usually followed. I do not urge it as the sole way out of educational confusion, not even in the elementary school, though I think experimentation with it is desirable in college and secondary school. But it is possible to retain traditional titles and still reorganize the subject-matter under them, so as to take account of interdependencies of knowledge and connection of knowledge with use and application. As the time grows to a close let me mention one illustration, Julian Huxley's and H.G. Wells' recent volumes on Life. They cut across all conventional divisions in the field: yet not at the expense of scientific accuracy but in a way which increases both intellectual curiosity and understanding, while disclosing the world about us as a perennial source of esthetic delight.

I have referred to intellectual interest. It is only too

common to hear students (in name) say in reference to some subject that they "have *had* it." The use of the past tense is only too significant. The subject is over and done with; it is very much in the past. Every intelligent observer of the subsequent career of those who come from our schools deplores the fact that they do not carry away from school into later life abiding intellectual interests in what they have studied. After all, the period from, say, fourteen to twenty-two is a comparatively short portion of a normal life time. The best that education can do during these years is to arouse intellectual interests which carry over and onwards. The worst condemnation that can be passed is that these years are an interlude, a passing interval. If a student does not take into subsequent life an enduring concern for some field of knowledge and art, lying outside his immediate profession preoccupations, schooling for him has been a failure, no matter how good a "student" he was.

The failure is again due, I believe, to segregation of subjects. A pupil can say he has "had" a subject, because the subject has been treated as if it were complete in itself, beginning and terminating within limits fixed in advance. A reorganization of subject-matter which takes account of outleadings into the wide world of nature and man, of knowledge and of social interests and uses, cannot fail save in the most callous and intellectually obdurate to awaken some permanent interest and curiosity. Theoretical subjects will become more practical, because more related to the scope of life; practical subjects will become more charged with theory and intelligent insight. Both will be vitally and not just formally unified.

I see no other way out of our educational confusion. The obvious objection is that this way takes too abrupt a turn. But what alternative is there save a further cluttering up of the curriculum and a steeper dividing wall between the cultural and liberal? The change is in many respects revolutionary. Yet the intelligence needed to bring it about is not lacking, but rather a long-time patience and a will to cooperation and coordination. I can see schools of education leading in the movement. They will hardly do much to reduce the existing confusion if they merely move in the direction of refining existing practices, striving to bring them under the protective shield of "scientific method." That course is more likely to increase confusion. But they can undertake consecutive study of the interrelation of subjects with one another and with social bearing and application; they can contribute to a re-organization that will give direction to an aimless and divided situation.

For confusion is due ultimately to aimlessness, as much of the conflict is due to the attempt to follow tradition and yet introduce radically new material and interests into it—the attempt to superimpose the new on the old. The simile of new wines in old bottles is trite. Yet no other is so apt. We use leathern bottles in an age of steel and glass. The bottles leak and sag. The new wine spills and sours. No prohibitory holds against the attempt to make a new wine of culture and to provide new containers. Only new aims can inspire educational effort for clarity and unity. They alone can reduce confusion; if they do not terminate conflict they will at least render it intelligent and profitable.

ALFRED NORTH WHITEHEAD

Alfred North Whitehead (1861-1947) was born at Ramsgate in Kent, England, of a long line of schoolmasters and Anglican clergymen. He entered Trinity College, Cambridge in 1880 to read mathematics and remained there as a scholar and fellow until 1910. He taught in London till 1924, when he came to Harvard, and in 1937 became emeritus professor. As a mathematician and logician he gained fame through his collaboration with Bertrand Russell on *Principia Mathematica* (1910). While in London he devoted himself to the philosophy of science, but his most famous period was at Harvard, where he published such notable meta-physical studies as *Process and Reality* (1929) and *Adventures of Ideas* (1933). The *Aims of Education* was published in 1929.

Whitehead's philosophy has been called Aristotelianism, realism, panpsychism, and idealism. Actually it is a philosophy of organism, an active philosophy of process, in which he tries to show interrelationships between man and his environment,— natural, social, and spiritual. Maintaining that modern physics has identified matter with energy in a field of force, he claims that matter is alive and in process. Knowledge, he says, is a blend of primary qualities "out there," and of secondary qualities "in here" and adds, "the pain is in us and not in the knife with which we cut ourselves." A dead nature cannot answer "why" for all ultimate reasons are in terms of aim or value.[15]

In *Nature and Life*,[15] Whitehead assigns himself the task of examining the basis for his philosophy. The following paragraphs are a précis of this essay.

The doctrine I am maintaining is that neither physical nature nor life can be understood unless we fuse them together as essential factors in the composition of "really real" things whose interconnection and individual characters constitute the universe. ... Thus there is a unity ... of the body and soul into one person. ... There is a continuity of the soul [through all states of consciousness]. ... The weakness of the epistemology of the eighteenth and nineteenth centuries was that it based itself purely upon a narrow formulation of sense perception.

The experienced world is one complex factor in the composition of many factors constituting the essence of the soul ... in one sense the world is the soul ... an experience of the world involves the exhibition of the soul itself as one of the components within the world. ... The world is included within the occasion in one sense, and the occassion is included in the world in another sense. ... The soul is nothing else than the succession of my occasions of experience, extending from birth to the present moment ... the world for me is nothing else than how the functionings of my body present it for my experience. ... No event can be wholly and solely the cause of another event. ... The only intelligible doctrine of causation is founded on the doctrine of immanence. Each occasion presupposes the antecedent world as active in its own nature. This is the reason why events have a determinate status relatively to each other. ... Descartes' "Cogito, ergo sum" is wrongly translated, "I *think,* therefore I am." It is never bare thought or bare existence that we are aware of. ... My unity—which is Descartes' "I am"—is my process of shaping this welter of material into a constant pattern of feelings.

The most obvious example of conceptual experience is the entertainment of alternatives. Life lies below this grade of mentality. Life is the enjoyment of emotion, derived from the past and aimed at the future. ... The emotion ... is received, it is enjoyed and it is passed along, from moment to moment.

---

[15] Alfred North Whitehead, *Nature and Life* (Chicago: University of Chicago Press, 1934). Quoted in Morton White, *The Age of Analysis,* pp. 86-100 *passim.*

... It is the conjunction of transcendence and immanence. ...
Philosophy begins in wonder, and, at the end, when
philosophic thought has done its best, the wonder remains.
There has been added, however, some grasp of the immensity
of things, some purification of emotion by understanding.

Education is the art of the utilization of knowledge. ... [16]
The essence of education is that it be religious. A religious
education is an education which inculcates duty and reverence.
Duty arises from our potential control over the course of
events. Where attainable knowledge could have changed the
issue, ignorance has the guilt of vice. And the foundation of
reverence is this perception that the present holds within itself
the complete sum of existence, backwards and forwards, that
whole amplitude of time which is eternity. [17]

About the curriculum, he continues: "There is one subject-
matter for education and that is Life in all its manifestations." [18]
He critizes the traditional school for teaching ideas without meaning or application, saying: "Education with inert ideas is not only
useless: it is, above all things, harmful." [19] He continues:

Do not teach too many subjects, and again, what you teach,
teach thoroughly. ... Do not be deceived by the pedantry of
dates ... The communion of saints is a great and inspiring
assemblage, but it has only one possible hall of meeting, and
that is the present. [20]

There is no course of study which merely gives general
culture and another which gives special knowledge. ... You
may not divide the seamless coat of learning. ... Finally there
should grow the most austere of all mental qualities. I mean
the sense of style ... the love of a subject in itself and for
itself. Style is the ultimate morality of the mind. [21]

He believes that each school must develop its own curriculum
and that the sequence of subjects should be determined by readiness, interest, and ability of the learner, and the use he will make
of it.

It is not true that the easier subjects should precede the
harder. On the contrary, some of the hardest must come first

[16] Alfred North Whitehead, *The Aims of Education* (New York: Mentor Books,
New American Library, 1949), p. 16.
[17] *Ibid.*, p. 26.
[18] *Ibid.*, p. 18.
[19] *Ibid.*, p. 13.
[20] *Ibid.*, pp. 14-15.
[21] *Ibid.*, pp. 23-24.

because nature so dictates, and because they are essential to life. . . . The first intellectual task which confronts an infant is the acquirement of spoken language. . . . What an appalling task. . . . We all know that the infant does it and the miracle of his achievement is inexplicable. . . . All I ask is that we should cease to talk nonsense about postponing the harder subjects. . . . The uncritical application of the principle of the necessary antecedent of some subjects to others has, in the hands of dull people with a turn for organization, produced in education the dryness of the Sahara.[22]

"The process of mental development is essentially periodic. . . . I would term them [the stages of development] the stages of romance, the stage of precision, and the stage of generalization."[23] He describes romance as the stage of first apprehension, of vividness, of novelty; precision as the stage of grammar, language, and science, where width of relationships is subordinated to exactness of formulation; and generalization as a synthesis, a return to romance with the advantage of classified ideas and relevant techniques, and as the fruition, the final success of precise training. Education should repeat such cycles. For example, when the study of language has progressed to the stage of precision, the sciences may be introduced on the romantic level. He further warns that although mentality develops in rhythmic cycles, the distinction between the three phases of the cycle should not be exaggerated. "The university course," he concludes, "is the great period of generalization."[24]

About formal discipline, he remarks that the mind never remains passive long enough to be "sharpened." He rejects the idea of deferred values in education and maintains that whatever interest, power, or mental life the teacher wishes to develop in the pupil must be exhibited here and now. This is the golden rule of education.

He is much concerned with liberal, scientific, and technical education, especially on the college level. Of liberal education he observes:

In its essence a liberal education is an education for thought and for aesthetic appreciation. It proceeds by imparting a knowledge of the masterpieces of thought, of imaginative

[22]*Ibid.*, pp. 27-28.
[23]*Ibid.*, pp. 28-29.
[24]*Ibid.*, p. 37.

literature and of art. The action which it contemplates is command. It is aristocratic education implying leisure.[25]

A technical education is not to be conceived as a maimed alternative to the perfect Platonic culture: namely as a defective training unfortunately made necessary by cramped conditions of life. No human being can attain to anything but fragmentary knowledge and a fragmentary training of his capacities. There are, however, three main roads along which we can proceed with good hope of advancing toward the best balance of intellect and character: these are the way of literary culture, the way of scientific culture, the way of technical culture. No one of these methods can be exclusively followed without grave loss of intellectual activity and of character.[26] The antithesis between a technical and a liberal education is fallacious. There can be no adequate technical education which is not liberal, and no liberal education which is not technical: that is no education which does not impart both technique and intellectual vision. In simpler language, education should turn out the pupil with something he knows well and can do well.[27]

With regard to higher education he writes:

During the school period the student has been mentally bending over his desk; at the University he should stand up and look around. . . . Your learning is useless to you till you have forgotten . . . the minutiae which you have learned by heart for the examination. The function of a university is to enable you to shed detail in favor of principles.[28]

The task of a university is to weld together imagination and experience. . . . Prolonged routine work dulls the imagination. . . . Imagination is a contagious disease. It cannot be measured by the yard, or weighed by the pound and then delivered to the students by members of the faculty. It can only be communicated by a faculty whose members themselves wear their learning with imagination.[29]

The ideal of a University is not so much knowledge, as power. Its buisness is to convert the knowledge of the boy into the power of a man.[30]

[25] *Ibid.*, p. 55.
[27] *Ibid.*, p. 58.
[29] *Ibid.*, pp. 98-101.
[26] *Ibid.*, p. 64.
[28] *Ibid.*, pp. 37-38.
[30] *Ibid.*, p. 39.

The Rhythm of Education*

In "The Rhythm of Education," Whitehead suggests that all learning begins in wonder, in delight, in romance. He shows the interdependence of subjects to be learned and declares that the most difficult subjects should be learned first. Whitehead's presentation is never coldly logical, but is filled with aphorisms which are themselves a delight.

By the Rhythm of Education I denote a certain principle which in its practical application is well known to everyone with educational experience. Accordingly, when I remember that I am speaking to an audience of some of the leading educationalists in England, I have no expectation that I shall be saying anything that is new to you. I do think, however, that the principle has not been subjected to an adequate discussion taking account of all the factors which should guide its application.

I first seek for the baldest statement of what I mean by the Rhythm of Education, a statement so bald as to exhibit the point of this address in its utter obviousness. The principle is merely this—that different subjects and modes of study should be undertaken by pupils at fitting times when they have reached the proper stage of mental development. You will agree with me that this is a truism, never doubted and known to all. I am really anxious to emphasise the obvious character of the foundational idea of my address; for one reason, because this audience will certainly find it out for itself. But the other reason, the reason why I choose this subject for discourse, is that I do not think that this obvious truth has been handled in educational practice with due attention to the psychology of the pupils.

THE TASK OF INFANCY

I commence by challenging the adequacy of some principles by which the subjects for study are often classified in order. By this I mean that these principles can only be accepted as correct if they are so explained as to be explained away. Consider first the criterion of difficulty. It is not true that the easier subjects should precede the harder. On the contrary, some of the hardest must come first because nature so dic-

Source: Alfred North Whitehead, *The Aims of Education and Other Essays* (New York: Free Press, 1967) pp. 15-28.

tates, and because they are essential to life. The first intellectual task which confronts an infant is the acquirement of spoken language. What an appalling task, the correlation of meanings with sounds! It requires an analysis of ideas and an analysis of sounds. We all know that the infant does it, and that the miracle of his achievement is explicable. But so are all miracles, and yet to the wise they remain miracles. All I ask is that with this example staring us in the face we should cease talking nonsense about postponing the harder subjects.

What is the next subject in the education of the infant minds? The acquirement of written language; that is to say, the correlation of sounds with shapes. Great heavens! Have our educationists gone mad? They are setting babbling mites of six years old to tasks which might daunt a sage after lifelong toil. Again, the hardest task in mathematics is the study of the elements of algebra, and yet this stage must precede the comparative simplicity of the differential calculus.

I will not elaborate my point further; I merely restate it in the form, that the postponement of difficulty is no safe clue for the maze of educational practice.

The alternative principle of order among subjects is that of necessary antecedence. There we are obviously on firmer ground. It is impossible to read *Hamlet* until you can read; and the study of integers must precede the study of fractions. And yet even this firm principle dissolves under scrutiny. It is certainly true, but it is only true if you give an artificial limitation to the concept of a subject for study. The danger of the principle is that it is accepted in one sense, for which it is almost a necessary truth, and that it is applied in another sense for which it is false. You cannot read Homer before you can read; but many a child, and in ages past many a man, has sailed with Odysseus over the seas of Romance by the help of the spoken word of a mother, or of some wandering bard. The uncritical application of the principle of the necessary antecedence of some subjects to others has, in the hands of dull people with a turn for organisation, produced in education the dryness of the Sahara.

STAGES OF MENTAL GROWTH

The reason for the title which I have chosen for this address, the Rhythm of Education, is derived from yet another criticism of current ideas. The pupil's progress is often conceived as a uniform steady advance undifferentiated by change of type or alteration in pace; for example, a boy may be conceived as starting Latin at ten years of age and by a uniform progression steadily developing into a classical scholar at the age of eighteen or twenty. I hold that this conception of education is based upon a false psychology of the process of mental development which has gravely hindered the effectiveness of our methods. Life is essentially periodic. It comprises daily periods, with their alternations of work and play, of activity and of sleep, and seasonal periods, which dictate our terms and our holidays; and also it is composed of well-marked yearly periods. These are the gross obvious periods which no one can overlook. There are also subtler periods of mental growth, with their cyclic recurrences, yet always different as we pass from cycle to cycle, though the subordinate stages are reproduced in each cycle. That is why I have chosen the term "rhythmic," as meaning essentially the conveyance of difference within a framework of repetition. Lack of attention to the rhythm and character of mental growth is a main source of wooden futility in education. I think that Hegel was right when he analysed progress into three stages, which he called Thesis, Antithesis, and Synthesis; though for the purpose of the application of his idea to educational theory I do not think that the names he gave are very happily suggestive. In relation to intellectual progress I would term them, the stage of romance, the stage of precision, and the stage of generalisation.

The Stage of Romance

The stage of romance is the stage of first apprehension. The subject-matter has the vividness of novelty; it holds within itself unexplored connexions with possibilities half-disclosed by glimpses and half-concealed by the wealth of material. In this stage knowledge is not dominated by systematic procedure. Such system as there must be is created piecemeal *ad hoc.* We are in the presence of immediate cognisance of fact, only intermittently subjecting fact to systematic dissection. Romantic emotion is essentially the excitement consequent on the transition from the bare facts to the first realisations of the import of their unexplored relationships. For example, Crusoe was a mere man, the sand was mere sand, the footprint was a mere footprint, and the island a mere island, and Europe was the busy world of men. But the sudden perception of the half-disclosed and half-hidden possibilities relating Crusoe and the sand and the footprint and the lonely island secluded from Europe constitutes romance. I have had to take an extreme case for illustration in order to make my meaning perfectly plain. But construe it as an allegory representing the first stage in a cycle of progress. Education must essentially be a setting in order of a ferment already stirring in the mind: you cannot educate mind *in vacuo*. In our conception of education we tend to confine it to the second stage of the cycle; namely, to the stage of precision. But we cannot so limit our task without misconceiving the whole problem. We are concerned alike with the ferment, with the acquirement of precision, and with the subsequent fruition.

The Stage of Precision

The stage of precision also represents an addition to knowledge. In this stage, width of relationship is subordinated to exactness of formulation. It is the stage of grammar, the grammar of language and the grammar of science. It proceeds by forcing on the students' acceptance a given way of analysing the facts, bit by bit. New facts are added, but they are the facts which fit into the analysis.

It is evident that a stage of precision is barren without a previous stage of romance: unless there are facts which have already been vaguely apprehended in their broad generality, the previous analysis is an analysis of nothing. It is simply a series of meaningless statements about bare facts, produced artificially and without any further relevance. I repeat that in this stage we do not merely remain within the circle of the facts elicited in the romantic epoch. The facts of romance have disclosed ideas with possibilities of wide significance, and in the stage of precise progress we acquire other facts in a systematic order, which thereby form both a disclosure and an analysis of the general subject-matter of the romance.

The Stage of Generalisation

The final stage of generalisation is Hegel's synthesis. It is a return to romanticism with added advantage of classified ideas and relevant technique. It is the fruition which has been the goal of the precise training. It is the final success. I am afraid that I have had to give a dry analysis of somewhat obvious ideas. It has been necessary to do so because my subsequent remarks presuppose that we have clearly in our minds the essential character of this threefold cycle.

The Cyclic Processes

Education should consist in a continual repetition of such cycles. Each lesson in its minor way should form an eddy cycle issuing in its own subordinate process. Longer periods should issue in definite attainments, which then form the starting grounds for fresh cycles. We should banish the idea of a mythical, far-off end of education. The pupils must be continually enjoying some fruition and starting afresh—if the teacher is stimulating in exact proportion to his success in satisfying the rhythmic cravings of his pupils.

An infant's first romance is its awakening to the apprehension of objects and to the appreciation of their connexions. Its growth in mentality takes the exterior form of occupying itself in the coordination of its perceptions with its bodily activities. Its first stage of precision is mastering spoken language as an instrument for classifying its contemplation of objects and for strengthening its apprehension of emotional relations with other beings. Its first stage of generalisation is the use of language for a classified and enlarged enjoyment of objects.

This first cycle of intellectual progress from the achievement of perception to the acquirement of language, and from the acquirement of language to classified thought and keener perception, will bear more careful study. It is the only cycle of progress which we can observe in its purely natural state. The later cycles are necessarily tinged by the procedure of the current mode of education. There is a characteristic of it which is often sadly lacking in subsequent education; I mean, that it achieves complete success. At the end of it the child *can* speak, its ideas *are* classified, and its perceptions *are* sharpened. The cycle achieves its object. This is a great deal more than can be said for most systems of education as applied to most pupils. But why should this be so? Certainly, a new-born baby looks a most unpromising subject for intellectual progress when we remember the difficulty of the task before it. I suppose it is because nature, in the form of surrounding circumstances, sets it a task for which the normal development of its brain is exactly fitted. I do not think that there is any particular mystery about the fact of a child learning to speak and in consequence thinking all the better; but it does offer food for reflection.

In the subsequent education we have not sought for cyclic processes which in a finite time run their course and within their own limited sphere achieve a complete success. This completion is one outstanding character in the natural cycle for infants. Later on we start a child on some subject, say Latin, at the age of ten, and hope by a uniform system of formal training to achieve success at the age of twenty. The natural result is failure, both in interest and in acquirement. When I speak of failure, I am comparing our results with the brilliant success of the first natural cycle. I do not think that it is because our tasks are intrinsically too hard, when I remember that the infant's cycle is the hardest of all. It is because our tasks are set in an unnatural way, without rhythm and without the stimulus of intermediate successes and without concentration.

I have not yet spoken of this character of concentration which so conspicuously attaches to the infant's progress. The whole being of the infant is absorbed in the practice of its cycle. It has nothing else to divert its mental development. In this respect there is a striking difference between this natural cycle and the subsequent history of the student's development. It is perfectly obvious that life is very various and that the mind and brain naturally develop so as to adapt themselves to the many-hued world in which their lot is cast. Still, after making allowance for this consideration, we will be wise to preserve some measure of concentration for each of the subsequent cycles. In particular, we should avoid a competition of diverse subjects in the same stage of their cycles. The fault of the older education was unrhythmic concentration on a single undifferentiated subject. Our modern system, with its insistence on a preliminary general education, and with its easy toleration of the analysis of knowledge into distinct subjects, is an equally unrhythmic collection of distracting scraps. I am pleading that we shall endeavour to weave in the learner's mind a harmony of patterns, by co-ordinating the various elements of instruction into subordinate cycles each of intrinsic worth for the immediate apprehension of the pupil. We must garner our crops each in its due season.

•   •   •   •   •

The Rhythmic Character of Growth

I will conclude with two remarks which I wish to make by way of caution in the interpretation of my meaning. The point of this address is the rhythmic character of growth. The interior spiritual life of man is a web of many strands. They do not all grow together by uniform extension. I have tried to illustrate this truth by considering the normal unfolding of the capacities of a child in somewhat favourable circumstances but otherwise with fair average capacities. Perhaps I have misconstrued the usual phenomena. It is very likely that I have so failed, for the evidence is complex and difficult. But do not let any failure in this respect prejudice the main point which I am here to enforce. It is that the development of mentality exhibits itself as a rhythm involving an interweaving of cycles, the whole process being dominated by a greater cycle of the same general character as its minor eddies. Furthermore, this rhythm exhibits certain ascertainable general laws which are valid for most pupils, and the quality of our teaching should be so adapted as to suit the stage in the rhythm to which our pupils have advanced. The problem of a curriculum is not so much the succession of subjects; for all subjects should in essence be begun with the dawn of mentality. The truly important order is the order of quality which the educational procedure should assume.

My second caution is to ask you not to exaggerate into sharpness the distinction between the three stages of a cycle. I strongly suspect that many of you, when you heard me detail the three stages in each cycle, said to yourselves—How like a mathematician to make such formal divisions! I assure you that it is not mathematics but literary incompetence that may have led me into the error against which I am warning you. Of course, I mean throughout a distinction of emphasis, of pervasive quality—romance, precision, generalisation, are all present throughout. But there is an alternation of dominance, and it is this alternation which constitutes the cycles.

BIBLIOGRAPHY

WILLIAM JAMES

*James, William, *Pragmatism and Other Essays,* ed. R. B. Perry (New York: Meridian Books, World, 1968).

*——, *Principles of Psychology* (2 Vol., New York: Dover, 1950).

*——, *Psychology: The Briefer Course,* with a foreword by G. Murphy (New York: Collier Books, Macmillan, 1962).

*——, *Talks to Teachers on Psychology and to Students on Some of Life's Ideals,* with an introduction by P. Woodring (New York: Norton, 1958).

*———, *Varieties of Religious Experience,* with an introduction by R. Niebuhr (New York: Collier Books, Macmillan, 1961).

Kallen, Horace M., *The Philosophy of William James* (New York: Modern Library, Random House, 1953).

*Moore, Edward Carter, *William James* (New York: Washington Square, 1965).

*Perry, Ralph Barton, *The Thought and Character of William James* (New York: Torchbooks, Harper and Row, n.d.).

JOHN DEWEY

*Archambault, Reginald D., *Dewey on Education* (New York: Random House, 1968).

*Dewey, John, *Art as Experience* (New York: Capricorn Books, Putnam, 1958).

*———, *Child and the Curriculum: School and Society,* with an introduction by L. Carmichael (Chicago: Phoenix Books, University of Chicago Press, 1915).

*———, *A Common Faith* (New Haven: Yale University Press, 1967).

*———, *Democracy and Education* (New York: Macmillan, 1964).

*———, *Dewey on Education: Selections With an Introduction and Notes,* ed. M. S. Dworkin (New York: Teachers College Press, 1959).

*———, *Experience and Education* (New York: Collier Books, Macmillan, 1963).

*———, *Experience and Nature* (New York: Dover, 1958).

*———, *Philosophy of Education* (Totowa, N.J.: Littlefield, Adams, 1958).

*———, *Reconstruction in Philosophy* (Boston: Beacon, 1957).

ALFRED NORTH WHITEHEAD

Dunkle, Harold B., *Whitehead on Education* (Columbus: Ohio University Press, 1965).

*Johnson, A. H., *Whitehead's American Essays in Social Philosophy* (New York: Harper, 1959).

*———, *Whitehead's Philosophy of Civilization* (New York: Dover, 1962).

*———, *Whitehead's Theory of Reality* (New York: Dover, 1962).

Lowe, Victor, *Understanding Whitehead* (Baltimore: Johns Hopkins Press, 1962).

Wegener, F. C., *The Organic Philosophy of Education* (Dubuque, Iowa: W. C. Brown, 1957).

*Whitehead, Alfred North, *Adventures of Ideas* (New York: Free Press, 1967).

*———, *Aims of Education and Other Essays* (New York: Free Press, 1967).

*———, *Modes of Thought* (New York: Free Press, 1968).

*———, *Process and Reality* (New York: Free Press, 1969).

*———, *Science and the Modern World* (New York: Free Press, 1967)

*Paperback editions.

Chapter Nine
Neo-Thomism, Existentialism, and Logical Empiricism: Maritain, Buber, and Scheffler

NEO-THOMISM

Ever since the encyclical "On Christian Philosophy" of Pope Leo XIII in 1879 and especially since the encyclical "The Christian Education of Youth" of Pope Pius XI in 1936, most Roman Catholic educators have been adapting their philosophies of education to the theology of St. Thomas Aquinas. In the latter encyclical, His Holiness declared that education belongs preeminently to the Church and that it is her inalienable right, as well as her indispensable duty, to watch over the entire education of her children. This mission extends throughout the world both within and without the fold of Roman Catholicism.

Vatican II, under the leadership of Pope Paul VI, expresses other thoughts about the direction of Catholic education and its relation to other types of religious education and public education in general. *The Decree on Ecumenism* asserts that Catholics and Protestants are both responsible for the division of Christianity and that the Church is constantly in need of reformation. Further, the *Decree on the Apostolate of the Laity* places much greater responsibility on parents for the education of their children and for the administration of Catholic schools. In the *Declaration on Christian Education*, Vatican II stresses the importance of freedom in religion and religious education in a pluralistic society and continues:

Parents who have the primary and inalienable right and duty to educate their children must enjoy true liberty in their choice of schools. Consequently, the public power, which has the obligation to protect and defend the right of citizens, must see to it, in its concern for distributive justice, that the public subsidies are paid out in such a way that parents are truly free to choose according to their conscience the schools they want for their children.[1]

Since modern education stresses a philosophy of search rather than a philosophy of statement, Catholic education based upon Thomism and the dogmatism of Pope Pius XI is somewhat out of favor. Yet, the doctrines of St. Thomas, especially the life of love and the life of the mind, are still pertinent to our age.[2] These Jacques Maritain expounds effectively.

JACQUES MARITAIN

Jacques Maritain (1882-   ) was born in Paris of a liberal Protestant family that was devoted to political liberty and the spirit of the republic. At the Sorbonne, he studied skeptical and phenomenalistic philosophy and biological materialistic science. Then he met his future wife and together they determined to work their way out of skepticism and relativism even if suicide were the only solution.

A study of Bergson restored their faith in metaphysics, and under the influence of Léon Bloy they were converted to Catholicism. Maritain studied biology at Heidelberg and at the same time made an intensive study of the *Summa Theologica* of St. Thomas Aquinas. He determined to devote his life to philosophy and to an interpretation of the works of St. Thomas. In 1913 he went to the Institute Catholique in Paris, where he was made professor of philosophy. Although he is not alone in developing the neo-scholastic movement initiated by the encyclical letter "On Christian Philosophy" of Pope Leo XIII, he is possibly the best known Thomist in America, where he has lectured widely, notably at the universities of Toronto, Harvard, Columbia, Chicago, Notre Dame, Yale, and Princeton. He is now living with LePetit Freres de Jesus in Toulouse, France.

In *Man and the State* he distinguishes between a community which he describes as biological and a society, which is more related to the rational and spiritual qualities of man. A community is historical, environmental, and collective and springs from nature. A society springs from individual initiative and imposes patterns derived from law. A nation is a community of people into which one is born. In contradistinction to the nation, both the *body politic* and the *state* pertain to the order of society in its highest or "perfect" form.[3] Since in the political society authority comes through the people, it is normal that the society should be made up of tiers one above the other to the top authority of the state.[4]

The state is not the supreme incarnation of the ideal as Hegel believed: it is but an agency entitled to use power and coercion. But man is by no means for the state. The state is for man.[5] The people have the right to self-government.[6] Neither men nor states are sovereign, and since their rulers are from the people they may be deposed by the people.[7] This is different with the Church where God is sovereign and the Pope rules as his Vicar by divine authority, which cannot be denied or deposed.[8]

The laws and standards made by men can be changed. For example, what might be considered a crime in civilized society can be a heroic virtue in a concentration camp. In the laws of the Church, however, there is but one moral standard. Man-made societies must be pluralistic since they do not derive directly from divine authority, but the Church is supreme and must eventually draw all men to it. When states realize that they are not sovereign (according to Maritain's definition), they will be able to cooperate in world government, and men will then live together in freedom.[9] It is by means of freedom that the peoples of the earth will be brought to a common will to live together.[10] "The cause of freedom and the cause of the Church are one in the defense of man."[11]

In *Education at the Crossroads*,[12] Maritain points out what he

[1] *The Sixteen Documents of Vatican II* (Boston: The Daughters of St Paul, St. Paul Editions, n.d.) p. 240.

[2] See the long but excellent article on Thomism in the *New Catholic Encyclopedia, 1968.* See also John W. Donahue S.J., *St. Thomas Aquinas and Education,* pp. 97-113.

[3] Jacques Maritain, *Man and the State* (Chicago: University of Chicago Press, Phoenix Books, 1955), p. 9.

[4] *Ibid.,* p. 11.

[5] *Ibid.,* p. 13.

[6] *Ibid.,* p. 25.

[7] *Ibid.,* p. 50.

[8] *Ibid.,* pp. 49-50.

[9] *Ibid.,* p. 207.

[10] *Ibid.,* p. 206.

[11] *Ibid.,* p. 187.

[12] Jacques Maritain, *Education at the Crossroads* (New Haven: Yale University Press, 1943).

considers to be the weaknesses of contemporary secular education and explains his theory and system of *true Christian* education according to his interpretation of St. Thomas and the dogma of the Roman Catholic church. The essays were delivered as a part of the Dwight Harrington Terry Foundation Lectures on religion in the light of science and philosophy in 1943.

In the first essay Maritain discusses the "Aims of Education." Education is an ethical art, the chief aim of which is to shape man as man, as an animal of both nature and culture.[13] Present-day secular education suffers from seven fundamental misconceptions:

1. A disregard for ends.
2. Incomplete ideas regarding ends.
3. The pragmatic emphasis on activity.
4. Conditioning for social living.
5. Intellectualism (chiefly an over-emphasis on scientific and technical specialization).
6. Voluntarism (making the intelligence subservient to the will to obey irrational forces).
7. The belief that everything can be learned.

Ends are superior to means and the process of achieving ends is a matter of some indifference. The scientific idea of man has no reference to ultimate reality and distorts the idea of man. The religious-philosophical idea is ontological. "Man is a horizon in which two worlds meet."[14] What is most important is respect for the soul as well as the body of the child.[15] "The man of our civilization is the Christian man. When I state that the education, in order to be completely well grounded, must be based upon the Christian idea of man, it is because I think that this idea of man is the true one."[16] Maritain opposes vocational education[17] and any attempt on the part of the school to impose social or nationalistic patterns,[18] and remarks that "the saints and martyrs are the true educators of mankind."[19] Of the study of educational psychology he says:

> The teacher must be solidly instructed in and deeply aware of the psychology of the child, less in order to form the latter's will and feelings than in order to avoid deforming or wounding them by pedagogical blunders.[20]

[13] *Ibid.*, pp. 1-2.   [14] *Ibid.*, p. 5.   [15] *Ibid.*, p. 9.   [16] *Ibid.*, p. 6.
[17] *Ibid.*, p. 23.   [18] *Ibid.*, pp. 15-22.   [19] *Ibid.*, p. 25.   [20] *Ibid.*, p. 27.

Of the purpose of the school he writes:

> School and school life have to do, in an especially important manner, with "premoral" training, a point which deals not with morality strictly speaking, but with the preparation and first tilling of the soil thereof. The main duty of the school is to enlighten and strengthen reason. . . . Thus the paradox of which I have spoken comes to a solution: what is important in the upbringing of man, that is, the uprightness of the will and the attainment of spiritual freedom, as well as the achievement of a sound relationship with society, is truly the main object of education in its broadest sense.[21]

He begins the second essay, "The Dynamics of Education," by saying that education, like medicine, is an art of ministering, an art subservient to nature. The primary dynamic factor is the internal vital principle in the one to be educated. "Education by the rod is positively bad education. That which reduces the education and progress of man to the mere freeing of the material ego is false."[22]

> Man's perfection consists of the perfection of love. . . . And to advance in this self-perfection is not to copy an ideal. It is to let yourself be led by another where you did not want to go, and to let Divine Love Who calls each being by his own name mold you and make you a person, a true original, not a copy.[23]

The "fundamental norms of education" are:

1. To foster those fundamental dispositions which enable the principal agent to grow in the life of the mind.
2. To lay stress on inwardness and the internalization of the educational influence.
3. To foster internal unity in man.
4. To free the mind through the mastery of reason over the things learned.

He [St. Thomas] knew [that] to raise clever doubts, to prefer searching to finding, and perpetually to pose problems without ever solving them are the great enemies of education.[24]

Thus Maritain would have the pupil free to open his mind to receive the ultimate and eternal truths that the Catholic church has been guarding for centuries, especially those truths that penetrate the here and now.

[21]*Ibid.*, pp. 27-28.   [22]*Ibid.*, pp. 30-32, 35.   [23]*Ibid.*, p. 36.   [24]*Ibid.*, pp. 39-50.

Finally, he would recast the curriculum along the lines of the medieval seven liberal arts. For the elementary school (called rudimentary period in his third essay) there would be the trivium: (1) eloquence, (2) literature and poetry, and (3) music and the fine arts. For the secondary period (called humanities) there would be the quadrivium to each of which he would give a separate year of study: (1) mathematics, (2) physics and the natural sciences, (3) philosophy, and (4) ethical, political, and social philosophy.

In the third essay Maritain adds poetry to the elementary period and in the secondary period he substitutes fine arts for physics.

His third essay, "The Humanities in Education," is a nostalgic recollection of the European system of education for the upper classes. He proposes three layers of education—the rudimentary, the humanities, and advanced studies—which he says correspond to stages of human development. In each the subject matter must be fitted to the learner. College education should be given to all, but to introduce specialization in this sphere is to do violence to the world of youth.[25] All the preceding remarks imply a clear condemnation not only of the many preprofessional undergraduate courses that worm their way into college education, but also of the elective system.[26]

Maritain concludes that the highest aim of liberal education is to give youth the foundations of wisdom. A course in theology would conclude the last undergraduate year.

In "The Trials of Present Day Education" Maritain presents a rhapsodic prophecy of the future.

> Humanism only will counteract the present day threat of slavery and determinism. . . . Bourgeois individualism is done for . . . and must be replaced by a personalistic and communal civilization grounded on human rights and satisfying the social aspirations and needs of man. . . . Education must remove the rift between the social claim and the individual claim within man himself. . . . The problem of leisure . . . will become particularly crucial. . . . The duty of educators is . . . to maintain the essentials of humanistic education and to adapt them to the present requirements of the common good. Pluralism in education demands the right to form private schools and organizations of schools.[27]

The task of moral reeducation is really a matter of public

[25] *Ibid.,* pp. 58-64.   [26] *Ibid.,* p. 65.   [27] *Ibid.,* pp. 88-92.

emergency. Democracy needs "some abiding sense of the reality of original sin.[28] There must not only be teaching of natural morality, but supernatural morality. The greatest education comes through trial and suffering. "The renewal of Christian conscience and a new work of evangelization are the primary and unquestionable conditions for the moral reeducation that the man of our civilization needs."[29] Pragmatism will naturally lead to a "strong positivist or technocratic denial of the objective values of any spiritual need."[30]

Maritain concludes his essay by calling upon American youth to free itself from an instrumentalist and pragmatist philosophy and take refuge in the wisdom of Europe and the truth of the Catholic church.

Dewey and Maritain then represent two contrasting points of view with regard to American education. In order to bring these differences into focus, in the following table we present a number of parallel statements which represent approximately the points of view of these two significant educational theorists.

MARITAIN	DEWEY
Value is found in the thing learned.	Value is found in the process of learning.
The learner is a recipient of the truth.	The learner is a seeker after truth.
Learning comes through precept.	Learning comes through active participation.
Man is the child of the Church.	Man is the child of society.
Truth is absolute and eternal.	Truth is functional, situational, instrumental.
Responsibility for learning lies mainly with the teacher.	Responsibility for learning lies mainly with the pupil.
The pattern for American education is found in Europe and in the Middle Ages.	The pattern for American education is contemporary and indigenous.
Education should fit universal man to live in an ideal community.	Education should fit man for living in present-day society.

Maritain is not an official spokesman for the Roman Catholic church, but he does speak for a large number of Catholics and for a great many perennialist and essentialist educators, in both the scientific and humanistic traditions.

Perhaps it should be said, in conclusion, that, although during most of his life Maritain was considered one of the most liberal of modern Catholic thinkers, since Vatican II he has been classed a

[28] *Ibid.*, p. 94.   [29] *Ibid.*, p. 107.   [30] *Ibid.*, p. 115.

conservative. The student interested in more recent developments in Catholic educational thought should study Walter M. Abbott S.J. (ed.), *The Documents of Vatican II* (Racine, Wis.: American Press, Western Publishing Company, 1966). Numerous commentaries on post-Vatican II thought can be found in such magazines as *America* and *Commonweal*. Also useful is Henry Ehlers, *Crucial Issues in Education*, 4th ed. (New York: Holt, Rinehart and Winston, 1969), pp. 133-145, 172-173.

Education at the Crossroads*

In his discussion of the nature of man, Maritain maintains that the purpose of education is to develop man as man. He talks about the confusion of ends and means and holds up the Christian Idea of man as the model to be achieved.

THE EDUCATION OF MAN

The general title I have chosen is *Education at the Crossroads*. I might also have entitled these chapters *The Education of Man*, though such a title may unintentionally seem provocative: for many of our contemporaries know primitive man, or Western man, or the man of the Renaissance, or the man of the industrial era, or the criminal man, or the bourgeois man, or the working man, but they wonder what is meant when we speak of man.

Of course the job of education is not to shape the Platonist man-in-himself, but to shape a particular child belonging to a given nation, a given social environment, a given historical age. Yet before being a child of the twentieth century, an American-born or European-born child, a gifted or a retarded child, this child is a child of man. Before being a civilized man—at least I hope I am—and a Frenchman nurtured in Parisian intellectual circles, I am a man. If it is true, moreover, that our chief duty consists, according to the profound saying of the Greek poet, Pindar, in *becoming who we are*, nothing is more important for each of us, or more difficult, than to *become a man*. Thus the chief task of education is above all to shape man, or to guide the evolving dynamism through which man forms himself as a man. That is why I might have taken for my title *The Education of Man*.

Source: Jacques Maritain, *Education at the Crossroads* (New Haven: Yale University Press, 1943), pp. 1-10.

We shall not forget that the word education has a triple yet intermingled connotation, and refers either to any process whatsoever by means of which man is shaped and led toward fulfilment (education in its broadest sense), or to the task of formation which adults intentionally undertake with regard to youth, or, in its strictest sense, to the special task of schools and universities.

In the present chapter I shall discuss the aims of education. In the course of this discussion we are to meet and examine, by the way, some significant misconceptions regarding education—seven of them in all.

Man is not merely an animal of nature, like a skylark or a bear. He is also an animal of culture, whose race can subsist only within the development of society and civilization, he is a *historical* animal: hence the multiplicity of cultural or ethico-historical patterns into which man is diversified; hence, too, the essential importance of education. Due to the very fact that he is endowed with a knowing power which is unlimited and which nonetheless only advances step by step, man cannot progress in his own specific life, both intellectually and morally, without being helped by collective experience previously accumulated and preserved, and by a regular transmission of acquired knowledge. In order to reach self-determination, for which he is made, he needs discipline and tradition, which will both weigh heavily on him and strengthen him so as to enable him to struggle against them—which will enrich that very tradition—and the enriched tradition will make possible new struggles, and so forth.

THE FIRST MISCONCEPTION: A DISREGARD OF ENDS

Education is an art, and an especially difficult one. Yet it belongs by its nature to the sphere of ethics and practical wisdom. Education is an *ethical* art (or rather a practical wisdom in which a determinate art is embodied). Now every art is a dynamic trend toward an object to be achieved, which is the aim of this art. There is no art without ends, art's very vitality is the energy with which it tends toward its end, without stopping at any intermediary step.

Here we see from the outset the two most general misconceptions against which education must guard itself. The first misconception is a lack or disregard of ends. If means are liked and cultivated for the sake of their own perfection, and not as means alone, to that very extent they cease to lead to the end, and art loses its practicality; its vital efficiency is replaced by a process of infinite multiplication, each means developing and spreading for its own sake. This supremacy of means over end and the consequent collapse of all sure purpose and real efficiency seem to be the main reproach to contemporary education. The means are not bad. On the contrary, they are generally much better than those of the old pedagogy. The misfortune is precisely that they are so good that we lose sight of the end. Hence the surprising weakness of education today, which proceeds from our attachment to the very perfection of our modern educational means and methods and our failure to bend them toward the end. The child is so well tested and observed, his needs so well detailed, his psychology so clearly cut out, the methods for making it easy for him everywhere so perfected, that the end of all these commendable improvements runs the risk of being forgotten or disregarded. Thus modern medicine is often hampered by the very excellence of its means: for instance, when a doctor makes the examination of the patient's reactions so perfectly and carefully in his laboratory that he forgets the cure; in the meantime the patient may die, for having been too well tended, or rather analyzed. The scientific improvement of the pedagogical means and methods is in itself outstanding progress. But the more it takes on importance, the more it requires a parallel strengthening of practical wisdom and of the dynamic trend toward the goal.

THE SECOND MISCONCEPTION: FALSE IDEAS CONCERNING THE END

The second general error or misconception of education does not consist of an actual dearth of appreciation of the end but false or incomplete ideas concerning the nature of this end. The educational task is both greater and more mysterious and, in a sense, humbler than many imagine. If the aim of education is the helping and guiding of man toward his own human achievement, education cannot escape the problems and entanglements of philosophy, for it supposes by its very nature a philosophy of man, and from the outset it is obliged to answer the question: "What is man?" which the philosophical sphinx is asking.

•   •   •   •   •

THE CHRISTIAN IDEA OF MAN

There are many forms of the philosophical and religious idea of man. When I state that the education of man, in order to be completely well grounded, must be based upon the Christian idea of man, it is because I think that this idea of man is the true one, not because I see our civilization actually permeated with this idea. Yet, for all that, the man of our civilization is the Christian man, more or less secularized. Consequently we may accept this idea as a common basis and imply that it is to be agreed upon by the common consciousness in our civilized countries, except among those who adhere to utterly opposite outlooks, like materialistic metaphysics, positivism, or skepticism—I am not speaking here of Fascist and racist creeds, which do not belong at all in the civilized world.

Now such a kind of agreement is all that any doctrine in moral philosophy can be expected to have, for none can pretend actually to obtain the literal universal assent of all minds—not because of any weakness in objective proof but because of the weakness inherent in human minds.

There does exist, indeed, among the diverse great metaphysical outlooks, if they recognize the dignity of the spirit, and among the diverse forms of Christian creeds, or even of religious creeds in general, if they recognize the divine destiny of man, a community of analogy as concerns practical attitudes and the realm of action, which makes possible a genuine human cooperation. In a Judeo-Greco-Christian civilization like ours, this community of analogy, which extends from the most orthodox religious forms of thought to the mere humanistic ones, makes it possible for a Christian philosophy of education, if it is well founded and rationally developed, to play an inspiring part in the concert, even for those who do not share in the creed of its supporters. Be it added, by the way, that the term concert, which I just used, seems rather euphemistic with regard to our "modern philosophies of education," whose discordant voices have been so valuably studied in Professor Brubacher's book.[31]

In answer to our question, then, "What is man?" we may give the Greek, Jewish, and Christian idea of man: man as an animal endowed with reason, whose supreme dignity is in the intellect; and man as a free individual in personal relation with

[31] Cf. John S. Brubacher, *Modern Philosophies of Education* (New York and London, 1939).

God, whose supreme righteousness consists in voluntarily obeying the law of God; and man as a sinful and wounded creature called to divine life and to the freedom of grace, whose supreme perfection consists of love.

HUMAN PERSONALITY

From the philosophical point of view alone the main concept to be stressed here is the concept of human personality. Man is a person, who holds himself in hand by his intelligence and his will. He does not merely exist as a physical being. There is in him a richer and nobler existence; he has spiritual super-existence through knowledge and love. He is thus, in some way, a whole, not merely a part; he is a universe unto himself, a microcosm in which the great universe in its entirety can be encompassed through knowledge. And through love he can give himself freely to beings who are to him, as it were, other selves; and for this relationship no equivalent can be found in the physical world.

If we seek the prime root of all this, we are led to the acknowledgment of the full philosophical reality of that concept of the soul, so variegated in its connotations, which Aristotle described as the first principle of life in any organism and viewed as endowed with supramaterial intellect in man, and which Christianity revealed as the dwelling place of God and as made for eternal life. In the flesh and bones of man there exists a soul which is a spirit and which has a greater value than the whole physical universe. Dependent though he may be upon the slightest accidents of matter, the human person exists by virtue of the existence of his soul, which dominates time and death. It is the spirit which is the root of personality.

The notion of personality thus involves that of wholeness and independence. To say that a man is a person is to say that in the depth of his being he is more a whole than a part and more independent than servile. It is this mystery of our nature which religious thought designates when it says that the person is the image of God. A person possesses absolute dignity because he is in direct relationship with the realm of being, truth, goodness, and beauty, and with God, and it is only with these that he can arrive at his complete fulfillment. His spiritual fatherland consists of the entire order of things which have absolute value, and which reflect, in some manner, a divine Absolute superior to the world and which have a power of attraction toward this Absolute.

PERSONALITY AND INDIVIDUALITY

Now it should be pointed out that personality is only one aspect or one pole of the human being. The other pole is—to speak the Aristotelian language—individuality, whose prime root is matter. The same man, the same entire man who is, in one sense, a person or a whole made independent by his spiritual soul, is also, in another sense, a material individual, a fragment of a species, a part of the physical universe, a single dot in the immense network of forces and influences, cosmic, ethnic, historic, whose laws we must obey. His very humanity is the humanity of an animal, living by sense and instinct as well as by reason. Thus man is "a horizon in which two worlds meet." Here we face that classical distinction between the *ego* and the *self* which both Hindu and Christian philosophies have emphasized, though with quite diverse connotations. I shall come back to this thought later on.

I should like to observe now that a kind of animal training, which deals with psychophysical habits, conditioned reflexes, sense-memorization, etc., undoubtedly plays its part in education: it refers to material individuality, or to what is not specifically human in man. But education is not animal training. The education of man is a human awakening.

Thus what is of most importance in educators themselves is a respect for the soul as well as for the body of the child, the sense of his innermost essence and his internal resources, and a sort of sacred and loving attention to his mysterious identity, which is a hidden thing that no techniques can reach. And what matters most in the educational enterprise is a perpetual appeal to intelligence and free will in the young. Such an appeal, fittingly proportioned to age and circumstances, can and should begin with the first educational steps. Each field of training, each school activity—physical training as well as elementary reading or the rudiments of childhood etiquette and morals—can be intrinsically improved and can outstrip its own immediate practical value through being *humanized* in this way by understanding. Nothing should be required of the child without an explanation and without making sure that the child has understood.

EXISTENTIALISM

Although existential philosophy has been traced back to Plato and to St. Thomas Aquinas, it is generally agreed that the modern movement arose from the revolt of the Danish theologian Søren Kierkegaard (1813-1855) against the absolute idealism of Hegel and the authoritarianism of church and state, and of the German philosopher Friedrich Nietzsche (1844-1900), who extended Hegel's system into the creation of the superman. This philosophy states that existence precedes essence and attempts to create authentic individuals who are free from the tyranny of the group. Present-day interest in existentialism grew out of the destruction and despair of the concentration camps in Germany and the occupation of France in World War II.

Among those who have written about existentialism in education are Americans Van Cleve Morris of the University of Illinois and George F. Kneller of the University of California at Los Angeles. The English schoolmaster A. S. Neill, who established a school at Summerhill based on his concept of existentialism, has written extensively about his experiences in conducting what was thought at the time of its inception to be a revolutionary educational experiment. The Jewish theologian Martin Buber also has written essays in the field of education.

MARTIN BUBER

Martin Buber (1878-1965) was born in Vienna and until the age of fourteen was brought up in the home of his grandfather, Solomon Buber, one of the last great scholars of the Jewish enlightenment. Martin studied philosophy and the history of art at the Universities of Berlin and Vienna, and took his PhD. in 1904 from the latter institution. In his twenties, he was a leader of those Zionists who advocated a cultural renaissance rather than a political one. As a publisher and editor, he was a spokesman for German-speaking Jewry. From 1923 to 1933 he taught Jewish philosophy of religion and the history of religions at the University of Frankfurt. In 1938 Buber went to Palestine, where he was professor of social philosophy at the Hebrew University in Jerusalem until his retirement in 1951. From 1949 to 1951, he founded and directed the Institute for Adult Education, which trained teachers to help integrate the great influx of immigrants into Israel. He was one of

the foremost Zionist leaders and worked for Jewish-Arab cooperation and friendship.[32]

For Buber, man becomes man only in the life of dialogue, the
act of communion. In his essay "What is Man?" he designates him
as "the eternal meeting of the One with the Other."[33]

His theory of knowledge is based upon an I-thou relationship,
which differs from most subject-object theories. According to
these theories, the child has direct knowledge of things through his
senses and of other persons through the uses he makes of them.
But according to Buber the child becomes aware of himself as a
human being only as he recognizes other human beings and his
relation to them.

Figuratively, therefore, the individual must say "Thou" before
he can say "I." Also, it is only through the mediation of the Other
(Thou) that the individual (the One, the I) can become aware of
"things" and attach names to them. The way in which phenomena
in the external world acquire identity by having names attached to
them is often forgotten and the words are considered as entities
and as designations of entirely empirical realities rather than as
conceptual representations.

This concept of the Thou as the source of identification of the
individual and his world is a social concept and makes it evident
that the Thou is a completely integrated unique being rather than
a sum of concepts or an object of knowledge. He is a substance
experienced in the relationship of giving and receiving.

Buber further contends that it is through our instincts that we
are part of the natural world, through our intellect that we make
use of the world about us, and through our intuition that we get
direct knowledge of the world to which we are bound.[34]

Buber's theory of ethics is built upon the I-Thou relation, the
philosophy of dialogue, with its emphasis on wholeness, decision,
presentness, and uniqueness. Unlike Kant's theory of ethics, it is
not built on a categorical "ought" based on the idea of human
dignity, but on the ontological reality of the life between man and
man. Furthermore, it excludes the loneliness of Kierkegaard.
Unlike the subjective, relativistic ethics of pragmatism, Buber's
ethics is reciprocal because all individuals and groups are cells of
an organic whole. Ethical judgments arise when an individual
confronts himself, "his conscience" as Buber calls it, with his

---

[32] See Maurice S. Friedman, *Martin Buber, The Life of Dialogue* (Chicago: University of Chicago Press, 1953), from which much of the material for this sketch is gleaned.

[33] Martin Buber, *Between Man and Man*, (Boston: Beacon, 1955), p. 205.

[34] See Friedman, *op. cit.*, Ch. 19, for an excellent exposition of this subject.

potentiality and decides what is right and what is wrong in his own situation, taking into consideration the relation of man to man and man to God. This relationship he calls "The Good." Values are discovered in this relationship.[35]

Buber's educational theory is based on a continuing dialogue between pupil and teacher. A good teacher does not impose his personality or will on a student, but rather sets an atmosphere of communication and communion with him. "Action leading to an individual achievement is a one-sided event . . . as an originator man is solitary. . . .What teaches us the saying *Thou* is not the originative instinct, but the instinct for communion."[36] There are three kinds of dialogical relations: that of including the world about us in our own personality, that of friendship—of our influencing the lives of others—and that of inclusion of one another by human souls.[37]

Buber allows the child freedom to venture on his own and then to encounter the real value of the teacher, who avoids tenderness and pampering and is most effective when he is merely there. This meeting of pupil and teacher as two unique individuals is what is educative. The relation of teacher to pupil is the meeting of one who has found direction with one who is finding it. All education is basically character education. The teacher exposes his values to the pupil and allows them to flower in the pupil.[38]

What is important is that by one's intensely experienced action, "something arises that was not there before. . . . [There is] a bursting shower of self-hood."[39]

Buber claims that there is not and never can be a norm and fixed value of education. The teacher must practice experiencing from the other side of the desk, that is, from the pupil's point of view. It is only in this way that he can from time to time learn the needs of the pupil and be led into a closer relationship with him. The pupil must learn not only to be concerned with himself, but must try to discover what he means to the world. "In an age which is losing form . . . the ones who count are those persons who . . . respond to and are responsible for the continuation of the living spirit, each in the active stillness of his sphere of work."[40]

Freedom is essential to education because it is the possibility of communion. However, nothing is accomplished by it: it is the run before the jump, the priming of the pump, the tuning of the violin. It confirms the potential that cannot be realized without it. Discipline and personal responsibility must accompany it.

[35] *Ibid.*, Ch. 22.
[36] Buber, *op. cit.*, p. 88
[37] *Ibid.*, pp. 99-101.
[38] Friedman, *op. cit.*, pp. 178-182.
[39] Buber, *op. cit.*, p. 85.
[40] *Ibid.*, p. 102.

The Education of Character*

Buber wrote two addresses on major problems in education. The first, from which quotations have already been drawn, was first given at the Third International Educational Conference at Heidelberg in 1925. The second, from which excerpts follow, was delivered at the National Conference of Jewish Teachers of Palestine at Tel Aviv in 1939.

Education worthy of the name is essentially education of character. For the genuine educator does not merely consider individual functions of his pupil, as one intending to teach him only to know or be capable of certain definite things; but his concern is always the person as a whole, both in the actuality in which he lives before you now and in his possibilities, what he can become. But in this way, as a whole in reality and potentiality, a man can be conceived either as personality, that is, as a unique spiritual-physical form with all the forces dormant in it, or as character, that is, as the link between what this individual is and the sequence of his actions and attitudes. Between these two modes of conceiving the pupil in his wholeness there is a fundamental difference. Personality is something which in its growth remains essentially outside the influence of the educator; but to assist in the moulding of character is his greatest task. Personality is a completion, only character is a task. One may cultivate and enhance personality, but in education one can and one must aim at character.

However—as I would like to point out straightaway—it is advisable not to over-estimate what the educator can even at best do to develop character. In this more than in any other branch of the science of teaching it is important to realize, at the very beginning of the discussion, the fundamental limits to conscious influence, even before asking what character is and how it is to be brought about.

If I have to teach algebra I can expect to succeed in giving my pupils an idea of quadratic equations with two unknown quantities. Even the slowest-witted child will understand it so well that he will amuse himself by solving equations at night when he cannot fall asleep. And even one with the most sluggish memory will not forget, in his old age, how to play with x and y. But if I am concerned with the education of

Source: Martin Buber, *Between Man and Man* (Boston: Beacon, 1955), pp. 104-105, 112-115, 116-117.

character, everything becomes problematic. I try to explain to my pupils that envy is despicable, and at once I feel the secret resistance of those who are poorer than their comrades. I try to explain that it is wicked to bully the weak, and at once I see a suppressed smile on the lips of the strong. I try to explain that lying destroys life, and something frightful happens: the worst habitual liar of the class produces a brilliant essay on the destructive power of lying. I have made the fatal mistake of *giving instruction* in ethics, and what I said is accepted as current coin of knowledge; nothing of it is transformed into character-building substance.

But the difficulty lies still deeper. In all teaching of a subject I can announce my intention of teaching as openly as I please, and this does not interfere with the results. After all, pupils do want, for the most part, to learn something, even if not overmuch, so that a tacit agreement becomes possible. But as soon as my pupils notice that I want to educate their characters I am resisted precisely by those who show most signs of genuine independent character: they will not let themselves be educated, or rather, they do not like the idea that somebody wants to educate them. And those, too, who are seriously labouring over the question of good and evil, rebel when one dictates to them, as though it were some long established truth, what is good and what is bad; and they rebel just because they have experienced over and over again how hard it is to find the right way. Does it follow that one should keep silent about one's intention of educating character, and act by ruse and subterfuge? No, I have just said that the difficulty lies deeper. It is not enough to see that education of character is not introduced into a lesson in class; neither may one conceal it in cleverly arranged intervals. Education cannot tolerate such politic action. Even if the pupil does not notice the hidden motive it will have its negative effect on the actions of the teacher himself by depriving him of the directness which is his strength. Only in his whole being, in all his spontaneity can the educator truly affect the whole being of his pupil. For educating characters you do not need a moral genius, but you do need a man who is wholly alive and able to communicate himself directly to his fellow beings. His aliveness streams out to them and affects them most strongly and purely when he has no thought of affecting them.

•   •   •   •   •

For the first time a young teacher enters a class independently, no longer sent by the training college to prove his efficiency. The class before him is like a mirror of mankind, so multiform, so full of contradictions, so inaccessible. He feels "These boys—I have not sought them out; I have been put here and have to accept them as they are—but not as they now are in this moment, no, as they *really* are, as they can become. But how can I find out what is in them and what can I do to make it take shape?" And the boys do not make things easy for him. They are noisy, they cause trouble, they stare at him with impudent curiosity. He is at once tempted to check this or that trouble-maker, to issue orders, to make compulsory the rules of decent behaviour, to say No, to say No to everything rising against him from beneath: he is at once tempted to start from beneath. And if one starts from beneath one perhaps never arrives above, but everything comes down. But then his eyes meet a face which strikes him. It is not a beautiful face nor particularly intelligent; but it is a real face; or rather, the chaos preceding the cosmos of a real face. On it he reads a question which is something different from the general curiosity: "Who are you? Do you know something that concerns me? Do you bring me something? What do you bring?"

In some such way he reads the question. And he, the young teacher, addresses this face. He says nothing very ponderous or important, he puts an ordinary introductory question: "What did you talk about last in geography? The Dead Sea? Well, what about the Dead Sea?" But there was obviously something not quite usual in the question, for the answer he gets is not the ordinary schoolboy answer; the boy begins to *tell a story*. Some months earlier he had stayed for a few hours on the shores of the Dead Sea and it is of this he tells. He adds: "And everything looked to me as if it had been created a day before the rest of creation." Quite unmistakably he had only in this moment made up his mind to talk about it. In the meantime his face had changed. It is no longer quite as chaotic as before. And the class has fallen silent. They all listen. The class, too, is no longer a chaos. Something has happened. The young teacher has started from above.

The educator's task can certainly not consist in educating great characters. He cannot select his pupils, but year by year the world, such as it is, is sent in the form of a school class to meet him on his life's way as his destiny; and in this destiny lies the very meaning of his life's work. He has to introduce discipline and order, he has to establish a law, and he can only strive and hope for the result that discipline and order will become more and more inward and autonomous, and that at last the law will be written in the heart of his pupils. But his real goal which, once he has well recognized it and well remembers it, will influence all his work, is the great character.

The great character can be conceived neither as a system of maxims nor as a system of habits. It is peculiar to him to act from the whole of his substance. That is, it is peculiar to him to react in accordance with the uniqueness of every situation which challenges him as an active person. Of course there are all sorts of similarities in different situations; one can construct types of situations, one can always find to what section the particular situation belongs, and draw what is appropriate from the hoard of established maxims and habits, apply the appropriate maxim, bring into operation the appropriate habit. But what is untypical in the particular situation remains unnoticed and unanswered. To me that seems the same as if, having ascertained the sex of a new-born child, one were immediately to establish its type as well, and put all the children of one type into a common cradle on which not the individual name but the name of the type was inscribed. In spite of all similarities every living situation has, like a new-born child, a new face, that has never been before and will never come again. It demands of you a reaction which cannot be prepared beforehand. It demands nothing of what is past. It demands presence, responsibility; it demands you. I call a great character one who by his actions and attitudes satisfies the claim of situations out of deep readiness to respond with his whole life, and in such a way that the sum of his actions and attitudes expresses at the same time the unity of his being in its willingness to accept responsibility. As his being is unity, the unity of accepted responsibility, his active life, too, coheres into unity. And one might perhaps say that for him there rises a unity out of the situations he has responded to in responsibility, the indefinable unity of a moral destiny.

All this does not mean that the great character is beyond the acceptance of norms. No responsible person remains a stranger to norms. But the command inherent in a genuine norm never becomes a maxim and the fulfilment of it never a habit. Any command that a great character takes to himself in the course of his development does not act in him as part of his consciousness or as material for building up his exercises, but remains latent in a basic layer of his substance until it reveals itself to him in a concrete way. What it has to tell him is revealed whenever a situation arises which demands of him a solution of which till then he had perhaps no idea. Even the most universal norm will at times be recognized only in a very special situation. I know of a man whose heart was struck by the lightning flash of "Thou shalt not steal" in the very moment when he was moved by a very different desire from that of stealing, and whose heart was so struck by it that he not only abandoned doing what he wanted to do, but with the whole force of his passion did the very opposite. Good and evil are not each other's opposites like right and left. The evil approaches us as a whirlwind, the good as a direction. There is a direction, a "yes," a command, hidden even in a prohibition, which is revealed to us in moments like these. In moments like these the command addresses us really in the second person, and the Thou in it is no one else but one's own self. Maxims command only the third person, the each and the none.

One can say that it is the unconditioned nature of the address which distinguishes the command from the maxim. In an age which has become deaf to unconditioned address we cannot overcome the dilemma of the education of character from that angle. But insight into the structure of great character can help us to overcome it.

Of course, it may be asked whether the educator should really start "from above," whether, in fixing his goal, the hope of finding a great character, who is bound to be the exception, should be his starting-point; for in his methods of educating character he will always have to take into consideration the others, the many. To this I reply that the educator would not have the right to do so if a method inapplicable to these others were to result. In fact, however, his very insight into the structure of a great character helps him to find the way by which alone (as I have indicated) he can begin to influence also the victims of the collective Moloch, pointing out to them the sphere in which they themselves suffer—namely, their relation to their own selves. From this sphere he must elicit the values which he can make credible and desirable to his pupils. That is what insight into the structure of a great character helps him to do.

•   •   •   •   •

This is where the educator can begin and should begin. He

can help the feeling that something is lacking to grow into the clarity of consciousness and into the force of desire. He can awaken in young people the courage to shoulder life again.

•   •   •   •   •

... He who knows inner unity, the innermost life of which is mystery, learns to honour the mystery in all its forms. In an understandable reaction against the former domination of a false, fictitious mystery, the present generations are obsessed with the desire to rob life of all its mystery. The fictitious mystery will disappear, the genuine one will rise again. A generation which honours the mystery in all its forms will no longer be deserted by eternity. Its light seems darkened only because the eye suffers from a cataract; the receiver has been turned off, but the resounding ether has not ceased to vibrate. To-day, indeed, in the hour of upheaval, the eternal is sifted from the pseudo-eternal. That which flashed into the primal radiance and blurred the primal sound will be extinguished and silenced, for it has failed before the horror of the new confusion and the questioning soul has unmasked its futility. Nothing remains but what rises above the abyss of to-day's monstrous problems, as above every abyss of every time: the wing-beat of the spirit and the creative word. But he who can see and hear out of unity will also behold and discern again what can be beheld and discerned eternally. The educator who helps to bring man back to his own unity will help to put him again face to face with God.

LOGICAL EMPIRICISM

Logical empiricism is said to be the sequel to eighteenth-century rationalism after philosophy had thrown off the grips of German idealism that had controlled English and continental thought since the days of Kant and Hegel. It is in the spirit of nineteenth- and twentieth-century experimental science and uses its advances and techniques. It had developed methods for the clarification of basic concepts, assumptions and procedures in the fields of value and knowledge, and uses the tools of linguistics and linguistic analysis to examine propositions to determine whether disagreements are matters of fact or language. It scrutinizes aims and ideas in education critically and empirically and formulates ways and means of accomplishing them. American analysts in this philosophy of education include B. O. Smith, Robert H. Ennis, Paul B. Komisar, James E. McClellan, and Israel Scheffler.

ISRAEL SCHEFFLER

Israel Scheffler was born in New York City in 1923. After receiving his A.B. and A.M. Degrees from Brooklyn College, he studied at the Jewish Theological Seminary, where he earned his M.H.L. and at the University of Pennsylvania where he took his Ph.D. in Philosophy in 1952. He has held numerous fellowships and has taught at universities in America and Europe. Presently he is the Victor S. Thomas Professor of Education and Philosophy at the Graduate School of Education of Harvard University, where he has trained young scholars and has written a number of books. In addition to contributing to the philosophy of education, he has made substantial contributions to the philosopny of science. IIis *The Language of Education* deals with certain recurrent forms of discourse relating to schooling and then offers an extended consideration of the concept of teaching. In his introduction Sheffler writes:

> ... there is an ambiguity in the notion of philosophical study that may prove misleading here unless explicitly resolved. This notion may, on the one hand, indicate inquiry into philosophical questions or the use of philosophical methods; it may, on the other hand, refer to historical study of what has been concluded by inquirers into philosophical questions or users of philosophical methods. These two sorts of enterprises are quite different in spite of the fact that they often have the identical label. If we undertake the first sort of enterprise, we need, ourselves, to philosophize—that is to take a stand on philosophical issues or to apply philosophical tools of inquiry. If we undertake the second sort of enterprise we do not, in the same sense, need to philosophize, but rather to try to understand the results and the course of past philosophizing. The present study in educational philosophy is an effort of the first sort. It is an attempt to apply philosophical methods to fundamental educational ideas, rather than an attempt to chart the growth and career of received educational doctrines of a philosophical kind.

Educational Slogans*

The following selection is from Chapter 2, which deals with

Source: Israel Scheffler, *The Language of Education* (Springfield, Ill.: Charles C Thomas Publishers, 1960), pp. 36-41.

educational slogans and is an analysis of the slogan "We teach children, not subjects."

Educational slogans are clearly unlike definitions in a number of ways. They are altogether unsystematic, less solemn in manner, more popular, to be repeated warmly or reassuringly rather than pondered gravely. They do not figure importantly in the exposition of educational theories. They have no standard form and they make no claim either to facilitate discourse or to explain the meanings of terms. We speak of definitions as clarifying, but not of slogans; slogans may be rousing, but not definitions.

Slogans in education provide rallying symbols of the key ideas and attitudes of educational movements. They both express and foster community of spirit, attracting new adherents and providing reassurance and strength to veterans. They are thus analogous to religious and political slogans and, like these, products of the party spirit. . . . No one defends his favorite slogan as a helpful stipulation or as an accurate reflection of the meanings of its constituent terms. It is thus idle to criticize a slogan for formal inadequacy or for inaccuracy in the transcription of usage.

There is, nevertheless, an important analogy with definitions, that needs to be discussed. Slogans, we have said, provide rallying symbols of the key ideas and attitudes of movements, ideas, and attitudes that may be more fully and literally expressed elsewhere. With the passage of time, however, slogans are often increasingly interpreted more literally both by adherents and by critics of the movements they represent. They are taken more and more as literal doctrines or arguments, rather than merely as rallying symbols. When this happens in a given case, it becomes important to evaluate the slogan both as a straightforward assertion and as a symbol of a practical social movement, without, moreover, confusing the one with the other. In the need for this dual evaluation lies the analogy mentioned between slogans and definitions.

In education, such dual evaluation is perhaps even more important than in the case of political and religious slogans, for, at least in Western countries, educators are not subject to the discipline of an official doctrine and are not organized in creedal units as are religious and political groups. Educational ideas formulated in careful, and often difficult, writings soon become influential among teachers in popularized versions. No official discipline or leadership preserves the initial doctrines or some elaboration of them, seeing to it that they take precedence over popular versions at critical junctures, as is familiar in religion and politics. Educational slogans often evolve into operational doctrines in their own right, inviting and deserving criticism as such. It is important to remember, at this point, that though such criticism is fully warranted, it needs to be supplemented by independent criticism of the practical movements giving birth to the slogans in question, as well as of their parent doctrines. We may summarize by saying that what is required is a critique both of the literal and the practical support of slogans; parent doctrines must, furthermore, be independently evaluated.

The example of John Dewey's educational influence is instructive. His systematic, careful, and qualified statements soon were translated into striking fragments serving as slogans for the new progressive tendencies in American education. Dewey himself criticized the uses to which some of his ideas were put, and his criticisms had the effect of inviting reconsideration and reflection. He was, after all, the acknowledged intellectual leader of the movement. Increasingly, however, progressive slogans have taken on a life of their own. They have been defended as literal statements and attacked as such. Critics, in particular, have often begun by attributing the literal defects of progressive slogans to Dewey's parent doctrines and gone on to imply that the progressive movement has thereby been shown unworthy in its aims and operation.

That the literal purport and practical purport of slogans require independent criticism may be illustrated by consideration of the slogan, "We teach children, not subjects." In view of the fact that this and closely analogous formulas have sometimes been treated as literal statements, and not merely as rallying symbols of the progressive movement, let us examine the statement literally. Does it make sense?

Suppose I told you I had been teaching my son all afternoon yesterday. You would have a perfect right to ask, "what have you been teaching him?" You would not necessarily expect some single type of answer, such as the name of some academic subject. If, instead of saying, "Mathematics," I were to answer, "How to play first base," or "To be polite," or "The importance of being earnest," you would be satisfied. But, suppose, in answer to your question, I said, "Oh, nothing in particular, I've just been teaching him, that's all," you would, I think, be at a loss to understand how we spent the afternoon. It would be as if you had asked me, "What did you have for dinner?" and got the reply, "Oh, nothing, I've just had dinner, but had nothing *for* dinner."

I might of course, say reasonably in the latter case, "I can't recall," or "I don't know the name of the dish," or "I don't think I can describe it to you." But in each such case, I am acknowledging that your question has some true answer naming or describing some food, though I am, for one or another reason, not supplying it. To say, however, "I had nothing *for* dinner, just had dinner," is to deny that your question has such a true answer in this case, and it is this denial that makes the assertion impossible to understand. Analogously, to revert to the teaching example, I might, of course, say "I can't recall the name of the book," "I don't know the name of the swimming stroke," or even "I don't think I can describe it to you now" (suppose it is a compli- cated chess strategy). If, however, I said none of these things but insisted rather that I had been teaching the boy nothing, you would fail to understand me, or, at least, fail to take me as uttering a literal truth.

This case must be distinguished from another in which you ask me, "What have you taught him?" that is, "What have you been successful in teaching him?" In answer to this question, it is quite possible for me to say, "Nothing." It is quite possible for me to have been teaching algebra to someone to whom I have been unsuccessful in teaching algebra. I have taught him nothing, though I have been teaching him algebra, I have been trying to get him to learn algebra but he has failed to learn. To ask, however, in the words of our original question, "What have you been teaching him?" is not to ask, "What is it that you have been successful in teaching him?" It is rather to ask, "What have you been trying to get him to learn?" As to this question, if I answered, "Nothing; I have just been teaching him, but have not been trying to get him to learn anything at all," you would, I think, be really puzzled. It would be as bad as if I had said, "I spent yesterday afternoon teaching swim- ming," and in response to your question, "To whom?" I had replied, "Oh, to no one; just teaching swimming, that's all." If no one teaches anything unless he teaches it to someone, it is equally true that no one can be engaged in teaching anyone without being engaged in teaching him something.

Let us return now to the statement, "We teach children,

not subjects." If we take 'subjects' as a general word without restriction to academic subjects it appears that the statement is not interpretable as both literal and true, since it seems to say, quite literally, "We teach children, but there isn't anything that we try to get them to learn." We have, indeed, previously seen that a denial that anything is taught is legitimate where the question concerns the success of teaching rather than its intent. But this fact is surely of no help in interpreting the slogan before us, as the resulting statement in such an interpretation would be, "We teach children, but we are not successful in teaching them anything." The latter statement, unlikely in any event, would hardly be claimed true by proponents of any educational movement. Taken literally, the slogan is a clear failure, and cannot be used as a serious premise in any argument.

To reach this conclusion, however, is not to evaluate the practical purport of the slogan, the aims it symbolized, the educational tendencies with which it was associated. What, in fact, was its practical purport? Briefly, its point was to direct attention to the child, to relax educational rigidity and formalism, to free the processes of schooling from undue preoccupation with adult standards and outlooks and from mechanical modes of teaching, to encourage increased imagination, sympathy and understanding of the child's world on the part of the teacher. To know the educational context in which such a practical message took shape is to grasp the relevance of its emphasis. Conversely, the relevance of the message cannot be seen without reference to the context. The story is a long one but a quotation from a recent study will serve to indicate the outstanding features. Citing Joseph Rice's report on the American public schools in 1892, based on a tour of 36 cities in which Rice talked with 1,200 teachers, L. A. Cremin writes:[41]

> "Rice's story bore all the earmarks of the journalism destined to make 'muckraking' a household word in America. In city after city public apathy, political interference, corruption, and incompetence were conspiring to ruin the schools. ... A principal in New York, asked whether students were allowed to move their heads answered: 'Why should they look behind

[41] L. A. Cremin, "The Progressive Movement in American Education: A Perspective," *Educational Review*, 27:251, (Fall) 1957.

when the teacher is in front of them?' A Chicago teacher, rehearsing her pupils in a 'concert drill,' harangued them with the command: 'Don't stop to think, tell me what you know!' In Philadelphia, the 'ward bosses' controlled the appointment of teachers and principals; in Buffalo, the city superintendent was the single supervising officer for seven hundred teachers. With alarming frequency the story was the same: political hacks hiring untrained teachers who blindly led their innocent charges in sing-song drill, rote repetition, and meaningless verbiage."

Given such a situation, the relevance of a renewed educational emphasis on the world of the child is obvious. It is, moreover, easy to see that a positive evaluation of this emphasis, representing the practical purport of our slogan,[42] is altogether independent of the criticisms we made of its literal sense. That is, one commits no logical error in accepting these criticisms and at the same time applauding the emphasis of the slogan. Whether or not one is to applaud this emphasis is a separate question, requiring consideration of practical and moral issues in relation to some given context. It is, finally, clear that the practical relevance of a slogan, as well as the applause accorded to it, may vary with context quite independently of its literal purport. In the case of the slogan before us, many feel, indeed, that its practical message is presently less urgent than it once may have been, that it is either irrelevant or considerably less warranted in the current educational situation. This variation in the fortunes of the slogan's practical purport is a function of changing times and changing problems; it cannot result from the failure of the slogan as a literal doctrine, which is invariant.

---

[42] By the relevance of a slogan's practical purport, I mean its applicability within the context of its use on a particular occasion. In speaking of the evaluation or warrant of this practical purport, I refer to the question whether or not such application ought indeed to be made. To illustrate, compare the case of imperatives. Consider the imperative, 'Put on the light!,' uttered on a given occasion. It is relevant on that occasion only if the light is not already on. Even if it is relevant, however, we may still ask whether or not the light ought to be put on.

BIBLIOGRAPHY

NEO-THOMISM
Abbott, S.J., Walter M. (ed.), *The Documents of Vatican II* (Racine Wis.: the American Press, Western, 1966).
*Donohue S.J., John W., *St. Thomas Aquinas and Education* (New York: Random House, 1968).
Gallagher, Donald, and Idella Gallagher, eds., *The Education of Man: The Educational Philosophy of Jacques Maritain* (Garden City, N.Y.: Double-day, 1962).
Guzie, S.J., Tad W., *The Analogy of Learning: an Essay Toward a Tho-mistic Psychology of Learning* (New York: Sheed and Ward, 1960).
*Maritain, Jacques, *Education at the Crossroads* (New Haven: Yale University Press, 1967). *
*——, *Man and the State* (Chicago: University of Chicago Press, 1966).
Mayer, Mary Helen, *The Philosophy of Teaching of St. Thomas Aquinas*, (Milwaukee: Bruce, 1929).

EXISTENTIALISM
*Buber, Martin, *Between Man and Man* (Boston: Beacon, 1955).
Burns, Hobart, and Charles J. Brauner, *Philosophy of Education* (New York: Ronald, Press 1962).
Friedman, Maurice S., *Martin Buber, The Life of Dialogue* (Chicago: University of Chicago Press, 1955).
*Hedley, W. Eugene, *Freedom, Inquiry and Language*, Part I (Scranton, Pa.: International Textbook, 1965).
Kneller, George F., *Existentialism and Education* (New York: Philosophical Library, 1966).
*Morris, Van Cleve, *Existentialism in Education* (New York: Harper & Row, 1966).
*——, *Modern Movements in Educational Philosophy* (Boston: Houghton Mifflin, 1969).
*Neill, A. S. *Freedom Not License* (New York: Hart, 1966).
*——, *Summerhill: A Radical Approach to Child Rearing* (New York: Hart, 1964).

LOGICAL EMPIRICISM
Archambault, Reginald D., *Philosophical Analysis and Education* (New York: Humanities, 1965).
Brown, L. M., *General Philosophy in Education* (New York: McGraw-Hill, 1966).
*Hardie, Charles D., *Truth and Fallacy in Educational Theory* (New York: Teachers College Press, 1962).
*Langford, Glenn, *Philosophy and Education* (London: Macmillan, 1968).
*Macmillan, C. J. B., and Thomas W. Nelson (eds.), *Concepts of Teaching* (Chicago: Rand McNally, 1968).
O'Connor, D. J., *An Introduction to the Philosophy of Education* (New York: Philosophical Library, 1957).
*Peters, R. S., *Ethics and Education* (Chicago: Scott, Foresman, 1966).
*Reid, Louis Arnaud, *Philosophy of Education, An Introduction* (New York: Random House, 1962).

Scheffler, Israel, *The Anatomy of Inquiry* (New York: Knopf, 1963).
———, *Conditions of Knowledge* (Chicago: Scott, Foresman, 1965).
———, *The Language of Education* (Springfield, Ill.: Charles C. Thomas, 1960).
*Smith, B. Othanel, and Robert H. Ennis, *Language and Concepts in Education* (Chicago: Rand McNally, 1968).

*Paperback editions.

Appendix
Contemporary Philosophies in the Classroom

ALTHOUGH THERE IS is no single philosophy of education in America, there is considerable agreement among educational theorists regarding ultimate goals or general aims. All philosophers of education are interested in the promotion of the democratic way of life, although definitions of these terms may differ slightly. All agree that the school is an important agency for the rearing of the young to become active participants in American life. All wish the youth to be well grounded in the fundamental tools of learning, to be at home in their cultural, social, physical, and biological environments, and to be productive members of the American economic system.

Although there is agreement on ultimate aims, philosophies of education disagree on proximate aims, methods, and the importance, selection, and use of subject matter. Many of these differences come about because educational theorists begin from different metaphysical and epistemological bases. The more traditional philosophies of education are likely to begin with a metaphysic that admits a fixed reality.

The idealist begins by affirming the existence of the self as an independent being and believes that the ultimate existent or reality is idea. Realists, on the other hand, believe that the external world is real. Natural realists are inclined to call reality "matter." Other types of realists are dualists who believe in the

existence of both mind and matter as separate entities, and plu-
ralists, who admit to variant existents in an ever-changing phenomenal world. The pragmatist, the progressive, and the existentialist
emphasize man and regard the world as process and reality as a
series of events. Ultimate reality takes several forms in contemporary educational philosophy: for the idealist it is idea; for the
realist it is matter or nature in its various forms which can be
logically or empirically demonstrated and verified; and for the
pragmatist it is the event.

Epistemology, the theory of knowledge, is basic to the
philosophy of idealism. The idealist predicates his knowledge upon
the consistency of his direct experience with ultimate reality and
in general supports the proposition that there is no knowledge
without a knower. The extent and exactitude of knowledge is
limited by the quality of the sense organs, the extent and kind of
experience the individual has had, and the involvement or implication of the individual therein. Hence, the idealist is likely to
entertain a skeptical attitude toward knowledge, and to believe
that absolute knowledge existing in pure forms can never be
completely known and can be best approached through the use of
logic, because reality is "a logically unified total system, a Universal Mind."[1]

The realist also believes in a fixed reality, but says that our
knowledge of the external world depends upon the correspondence of the real world with our sense impressions of it.
Some realists hold that in knowing, the knower and the object
known are closely identified, that the known is presented in
consciousness, and that the mind is a relationship between the
organism and the object.[2] On the other hand, critical realists
maintain that objects are represented in consciousness, that is, the
qualities that the object has in the mind are different in some way
from the object they represent.

The pragmatist's theory of knowledge lies somewhere between
the observed experience of the empiricist and the reason of the
rationalist. It is the pattern by which facts are organized, a
hypothesis that works, that is the basis for knowledge. A com-
pilation of facts, no matter how carefully gathered and statistically
treated, does not constitute truth for the pragmatist, unless these
data can be put to use for desirable ends. It is only in experience
with things, usually in a social setting, that knowledge is made.
That is, knowledge is experimented with and manipulated, rather

[1] J. Donald Butler, *Four Philosophies*, rev. ed. (New York: Harper, 1957), p. 200.
[2] *Ibid.*, p. 317.

than experienced passively. Knowledge for the pragmatist, then, must make changes and bring about needed results. Truth is insightfulness that accurately predicts subsequent behavior.

The idealist intuits ultimate knowledge; the realist discovers it by reason and observation; the pragmatist makes it, and it is always partial and relative.

All philosophies are concerned with values. Education is especially concerned with values that determine its aims. The idealist assumes values to be real existents. They become real to the individual as he realizes, possesses, and enjoys them for himself. Some realists believe that there is something in an object that has an immediate attraction for a person and therefore gives it a value. Others say that values arise from the special interest persons have in some characteristics of an object. For the pragmatist values do not exist in any final or complete form, but in their relation with individual and group activities.

PRAGMATISM: A CHANGING UNIVERSE

Pragmatism, also called instrumentalism and experimentalism, takes relativity seriously. It implies change, novelty, and interrelationships between persons and things. No person or thing can be considered an independent entity. To the learner the world is familiar because he is a part of it, but it is also full of novelty because it is always changing. Novel situations are brought under control by active thought. "The mind is conceived as . . . a capacity for active generation of ideas whose function it is to resolve the problems posed to an organism by its environment."[3]

Values likewise are never fixed, always immediate, changing, and situational. They are instrumental and useful in achieving good ends. Pupil interest is central in all phases of education, especially in curriculum building, where subject matter is considered to be the means whereby desired objectives are attained. The child must learn to maintain his interest and must stick to his task until the goal for which he set out has been reached so that ends and means may constitute a continuous learning process. Although pragmatic education stresses the social involvement of the individual, it considers the personality of each individual to be unique and provides for its development in a number of socially

---

[3] Israel Scheffler, *Conditions of Knowledge* (Chicago: Scott, Foresman, 1965), p. 5.

desirable directions. Unlike reconstructionism, pragmatism does not design elaborate plans for social progress but depends upon the free flow of ideas.

In a television broadcast, Professor H. Gordon Hullfish of Ohio State University described an eighth grade social studies classroom conducted by an experimentalist or pragmatist.

> The class is engaged in a project for the study of city government. Last week the students made a field trip to the local city hall to observe firsthand how their own city governed. Now they have divided themselves into specific interest groups for the purpose of more intensive study on particular aspects of the topic. The teacher moves quietly from group to group, offering assistance where needed and making suggestions to advance the work of the committees.
>
> Within each group there is appropriate division of labor. Some consult reference books, others prepare charts, still others analyze data and compile reports.
>
> One group is delving into how the city can best be governed. They have collected data from cities using various plans, noting the success or failure in each. After weighing all the evidence, they will bring it to the entire class so a decision can be made on what form of government will best serve the theoretical model city they are building.
>
> A second group is hard at work on the traffic problem. They have built a scale model of a proposed highway system, to demonstrate graphically the way in which existing traffic problems might be overcome.
>
> A third group is concerned with community services, and has prepared a set of specifications for medical, recreational, and educational services in their city.
>
> The room is a scene of quiet, coordinated activity. The students move about freely. They work at committee tables, going and coming as necessary to consult reference books on the shelves or to secure construction materials and talking with one another and with the teacher in pursuit of their plans.[4]

EXISTENTIALISM: CONDEMNED TO FREEDOM, BORN TO DIE

The existentialist is mainly concerned with two factors in the human predicament—individual freedom and death. The infant is born into the world—he exists, but he has no being. From the start

[4]Philip H. Phenix, *Philosophies of Education* (New York: Wiley, 1961), pp. 14-15.

he is enmeshed in a world of regulation. Social, political, and economic organizations and automation regiment men into particular places and functions in society with or without their consent. Men are treated as things, as expendable, interchangeable parts of a machine. Although they are herded together in crowds, they are lonely, homeless, full of anxiety, goal-seeking. Soon they will die, and others will be fitted into their places in the social and economic machine. What follows after death is uncertain, so it is only the small span between birth and death in which an individual has a chance to develop his own personality, his essence, his being, and to make it known to others.

The teacher's primary concern is to free the individual from the tyranny of others, to help him realize himself as an independent being and to assist him in forming an "I-thou," interpersonal relationship with his fellows.

> . . . there are three constituent awarenesses which make up the psychological content of "self"
>
>   1. I am a CHOOSING agent, unable to avoid choosing my way through life.
>   2. I am a FREE agent, absolutely free to set the goals of my own life.
>   3. I am a RESPONSIBLE agent, personally accountable for my free choices as they are revealed in how I live my life.
>
> The teacher's imperative is to arrange the learning situation in such a way as to bring home the truth of these three propositions to every individual.[5]

There is for each person an "existential moment," a time when, with a sudden flash, the individual recognizes himself as an independent being. His attitude becomes one of "Here am I. It's Me. What am I to make of myself?" Whenever this may be, it is the teacher's task to make it possible for the student to realize himself, paradoxically, as a free—responsible, individual—social being. He must inhibit his own actions so that nobody gets hurt, including himself. Education, like religion, is a race against death, which must be constantly kept in view.

Although existentialism is a frequent topic of discussion in educational circles, actual applications of existentialism to the practice of public education are limited. Examples of existentialism in the school situation are rather difficult to come by. Dr.

---

[5] Van Cleve Morris, *Existentialism in Education* (New York: Harper & Row, 1966), p. 135.

Morris remarks that:

A possible illustration of existentialism in education is Summerhill, a small private school in England at Leiston, Suffolk, about 100 miles from London.[6]

For forty years "Neill," as his students call him, has been testing a hazardous hypothesis. Does freedom work? Suppose you had a school in which there were no rules, no requirements, no homework, no regulations, no roll taking, no grades, no academic expectations, no tests, no institutional code of decorum, no social conventions. Suppose all you had were a small "campus," some living quarters, some classrooms, half a dozen teachers, and forty or fifty youngsters ranging in age from five to seventeen. It would be a small but thoroughly free and open society, with no institutional "ethos" to adjust to and no organizational hierarchy to please. It would be, rather, merely a collection of separate individuals dealing with one another, old and young alike, as free and autonomous persons. Could anything like "education" possibly occur there? Neill has found that the answer is "yes."

The school draws its students from an admittedly atypical clientele. For one thing, there are tuition, boarding, and rooming fees; these run about $500 per year, a figure which is low compared with that at many other independent schools, but which nevertheless exerts a selective influence over admissions. For another, the school seems to attract many youngsters who have been in revolt against other kinds of schools, who have failed to adjust to institutional life, and who have been transferred by their parents to Summerhill. In the telling, Mr. Neill finds the greatest satisfaction in the rehabilitation of these youngsters. They come to Summerhill full of hate—for parents, for teachers and principals, for authority. Their previous encounter with learning has been so thoroughly associated with compulsory duties that they are at war not only with adult authority but with the act of learning itself. They hate books, they hate study, they hate learning! . . .

Their enrollment in Summerhill represents a traumatic and sudden "decompression" in the scholastic environment. All the pressures associated with "going to school" are abruptly

[6] The Summerhill Society, with headquarters in New York City, has imported the idea and now sponsors a similar school, founded in 1962, at present operating in Mileses, New York.

lifted, and their customary response is precisely what one might expect—they play hooky, refuse to attend any class or do any work; they indulge to the full their child impulses to play and play all day long. Neill lets them. Sooner or later, though, they voluntarily take up their studies again. This interval Neill appropriately calls "recovery time"; it sometimes goes on for months. "The recovery time is proportionate to the hatred their last school gave them. One record case was a girl from a convent. She loafed for three years. The average period of recovery from lesson aversion is three months."

After the child is rehabilitated, he continues to be as free to determine his own routine and learning schedule as he was during his "recovery" period. He studies what he likes with the teachers he likes. He discovers himself in full responsibility for his own learning. . . .

Neill has created a remarkable community on the basis of an exceedingly simple but powerful idea. He admits it has a lot of Freud in it: A free child is a happy child. A happy child does not fear or hate; he can love and give. The loving, giving child can live positively. Neill would be a more thoroughgoing exemplar of Existentialist education if he were to make one further, final argument which is implicit in his work: The free child eventually becomes the RESPONSIBLE child; it is freedom itself which makes this awareness possible. He who becomes responsible becomes capable of authenticity. Neill is creating authentic individuals.[7]

IDEALISM: THE CONSISTENCY THEORY OF TRUTH

For the idealist educator there is a fixed reality found in the cultural heritage and in the application of reason. Reality is fixed in eternal ideas, molds, or forms, and morals are cast from these molds. The idealist is also an essentialist because he believes that there is an essential or necessary body of knowledge and moral precepts that must be transmitted to each succeeding generation. Although the idealist is often a perfectionist, he does not insist upon the same degree of proficiency on the part of each individual. Because the amount and quality of knowledge ultimately

[7]Morris, *op. cit.* pp. 147-150.

depends upon the powers of perception of the individual knower, the idealist educator is greatly concerned with individual differences. Experience begins with the senses, but is comprehended by the mind so that the mind must be disciplined to be able to interpret experience consistent with the eternal, unchanging ideas or forms that constitute ultimate reality and value. This absolute, which is God thinking, is never fully realized or comprehended, but the teacher must attempt to lead the pupil to attain as much of it as he can. Some idealists believe that what an individual will become is latent within him at birth, and that the teacher, like a gardener, cultivates or nurtures him through education to mature self-realization.

Russell Kirk, research professor of political science at C. W. Post College of Long Island University, cites the following explanation of a school program that aims to develop the individual toward self-realization in the highest ideals so that he can render useful service to humanity.

One of the major objectives of this academy is to provide boys with intellectual stimulation and to encourage them in scholarly pursuits. The library is an important resource in fulfilling these aims. Here the boys become familiar with the treasures of our written tradition and gain skill and discrimination in using them. But other pursuits also contribute to the development of individual ability.

Participation in sports teaches boys to work effectively with their fellows and to acquire such qualities as courage, self-reliance, respect for others, and the ideals that go into the making of strong character. The curriculum includes strong offerings in the basic traditions of Western Civilization, including classical language and literature. The study of Latin gives the boys an idea of some of the sources of our own cultural and linguistic heritage. We also have a modern language laboratory. Some of our graduates will assume positions of leadership in government, diplomacy, and business where the ability to speak a foreign tongue fluently will be essential.

This academy includes military discipline as part of its program—in the conviction that ready obedience to properly constituted authority is a significant element in the development of mature manhood. Furthermore, preparation for responsible citizenship in modern society demands thorough grounding in the basic sciences, for which extensive laboratory experience is provided. The arts, too, belong to the great traditions of our society. Some of the boys achieve a memorable dramatic experience through participation in the production of plays by Shakespeare and other great dramatists. The academy boys have the privilege of expert instruction in small classes. For example, we have a senior seminar in government, which will help to prepare the boys to serve as intelligent leaders in civic and national enterprises.[8]

REALISM: THE CORRESPONDENCE THEORY OF TRUTH

For the realist, reality simply *is*. It exists in the external world. Concepts are true to the degree that they correspond to this reality. The ontological base for realism is nature, which is presented to consciousness through the senses. Mind is an aspect or function of the brain. Education conforms to external reality and the curriculum is made up of the best data available. For the natural realist the method of education is the method of science, and activities are descriptive and quantitative of natural and social phenomena.

For the rational and classical realists, the emphasis is on the development of mental power. For them, man is always and everywhere the same. The power of reason is unique with man and therefore deserves more attention than any other factor in his makeup. Classical realists follow Aristotle in the belief that all men are equal and everywhere and at all times the same, and therefore should receive the same kind of education and should be exposed to the same mental processes and the same subject matter. However, Aristotle was undoubtedly thinking of the upper class only, a relatively small group. The classical realist, following Plato and Aristotle, stresses the freedom and importance of the individual and attempts to provide appropriate mental discipline. The natural realist, on the other hand, is inclined to explore the use of programmed instruction, automatic learning, and other methods of conditioning to bring about desired intellectual and social behavior.

[8] Phenix, *op. cit.,* p. 101.

Glossary

ABSOLUTISM
> The theory that there is always a relevant standard of belief, reality, and action.

AESTHETICS
> The study of beauty.

AGNOSTICISM
> The theory that the final answer to basic questions is always uncertainty.

ALTRUISM
> The theory that the good of others should always supercede one's own good.

ANTITHESIS
> The opposite of ideas or statements.

A POSTERIORI
> Refers to data of the mind that owe their origins to the outside world of human experience, and do not belong to the mind's native equipment.

A PRIORI
> A term applied to all judgments and principles whose validity is independent of all sense impressions. Whatever is a priori must possess universal and necessary validity.

ARCHAIC
> A style that is primitive and incomplete in comparison with a later or posterior style, which is considered perfect and complete.

ATOMISM
> The view that there are discrete irreducible elements of matter.

ASSOCIATIONISM
> A theory of the structure and organization of mind that asserts that every mental state is resolvable into simple discrete components. A

school of psychology based upon mental connections established by a process of learning.

ATHEISM

The belief that there is no God, or that there is no personal God.

AUTHORITARIANISM

The theory that truth is determined by its having been asserted by a certain esteemed individual or group.

AXIOLOGY

The modern term for the theory of values.

CARTESIAN DUALISM

The theory of René Descartes that reality consists of thinking substance or mind and extended substance or matter.

CATEGORICAL IMPERATIVE

The supreme, absolute moral law of rational self-determining beings.

CONSERVATISM

The belief that the school is a restraining and conserving force in the community, which keeps the basic traditions of society healthy and alive.

CONSISTORIUM

The papal senate.

COSMOPOLITANISM

World-mindedness, unprejudiced with regard to other nations than one's own.

COSMOLOGY

A branch of philosophy that treats of the origin and structure of the universe.

DEDUCTION

Reasoning from the general to the particular.

DEISM

Belief that God is a universal principle having no immediate relation with the world.

DETERMINISM

The doctrine that every fact in the universe is guided entirely by laws.

DIALECTIC

For the Greeks, the art of question and answer. For Hegel, a method of reconciling opposites.

DUALISM

The theory that reality is composed of two irreducible elements: matter and spirit.

ECLECTICISM

The principle, tendency, or practice of combining or drawing upon various philosophical or theological doctrines.

EGOISM

The view that each individual should seek as an end only his own welfare.

EMPIRICISM

The proposition that the sole source of knowledge is experience.

ENTELECHY

The realization of what a thing is by virtue of its form.

EPICUREAN SCHOOL

The school of thought that gave expression to the desire for a refined type of happiness that is the reward of the cultured man who takes pleasure in the joys of the mind, over which he can have greater control than over those of a material or sensuous nature.

EPISTEMOLOGY
The branch of philosophy that investigates the origin, structure, methods, and validity of knowledge.

ESSENTIALISM
The belief that it is the chief duty of the adult community to transmit the cultural heritage to the oncoming generation.

ETHICS
The study concerned with judgments of approval or disapproval, rightness or wrongness, goodness or badness, virtue or vice.

EVOLUTIONISM
The theory that later things develop from earlier things.

EXPERIMENTALISM
The resort to concrete experience as the source of truth.

EXISTENTIALISM
The theory that existence precedes essence. That the self is the ultimate reality and that its inner struggles are the basic stuff of existence.

HEDONISM
The theory that pleasure alone has positive, ultimate value.

HERACLETIANISM
The view that all things in the universe as a whole are in constant, ceaseless flux. Nothing is, only change is real.

HETERODOX
Belief contrary to accepted opinion or dogma.

HUMANISM
The theory that the human element is of prime importance in the universe.

HYPOTHESIS
A provisional assumption.

IDEALISM
A theory that ideas are the essentials of knowledge; that all reality is of the essence of spirit; that ideas are to be pursued in action.

INDUCTION
Reasoning from the particular to the general. The method of science.

INNATE IDEAS
The power of understanding given in the very nature of mind. Ideas that are inborn and come with the mind at birth.

INTUITION
Immediate, direct apprehension of truth.

INTUITIONISM
Any philosophy in which intuition is appealed to as the basis of knowledge or at least of philosophical knowledge.

KANT'S THING-IN-ITSELF
That which lies beyond human observation and experience.

LOGIC
The branch of philosophy that investigates the structure of propositions and of deductive reasoning; a study of the laws of thought, judgment, and reasoning.

LOGICAL EMPIRICISM (SCIENTIFIC EMPIRICISM, LOGICAL POSITIVISM)
A philosophy that emphasizes the unity of science. Stresses the application of scientific method to all problems of life. Employs method of logical analysis and verification to educational concepts.

LOGOS
A term denoting either reason, or one of the expressions of reason, or order in words or things.

MACROCOSM
The universe as contrasted with some small part of it that epitomizes it in some respect under consideration.

MARXISM
The theory of economic determinism based on the class struggle; sometimes referred to as Dialectical Materialism.

MATERIALISM
The theory that only matter is existent or real.

MENTALISM
The theory of the exclusive reality of individual minds and their subjective states.

METAPHYSICS
The branch of philosophy that deals with the nature of reality: its first cause, its nature, its purpose, and its existence.

MICROCOSM
A world in miniature. Man as an epitome of the universe.

MODALITY
Concerning the mode, actuality, possibility, or necessity in which anything exists.

MONADS
In Greek usage, originally the number one. Later, any individual or metaphysical unit. Leibnitz applied the term to unified, indestructible, self-motivated souls.

MONISM
The theory that there is only one ultimate reality.

NOMINALISM
The theory that abstract or general terms, or universals, represent no objective real existence, but are mere words or names, mere vocal utterances.

NORMATIVE
Constituting a standard; regulative.

ONTOLOGY
The study of existence, of the essence of things.

OPTIMISM
The theory that this is the best of all possible worlds, or that everything will happen for the best.

ORTHODOX
Beliefs which are declared by a group to be true and normative.

PANPSYCHISM
The theory that the whole of nature consists of psychic centers similar to the human mind.

PANSOPHIA
John Amos Comenius's plan for an institute of universal knowledge.

PANTHEISM
The belief that the universe as a whole is God.

PARMENIDESIAN
The theory that developed the conception of "being" in opposition to "becoming" of Heraclitus.

PERENNIALISM
> The belief in the power of the mind and the patterns of medieval thought as a basis for education.

PHENOMENALISM
> The theory that knowledge is limited to phenomena including physical phenomena, the totality of actual perception and mental phenomena, the totality of objects of introspection.

PHILANTHROPINUM
> School for boys organized by Basedow in 1774.

PLURALISM
> The theory that reality consists of certain irreducible elements.

PLURALISTIC SOCIETY
> A society in which many elements exist equally and harmoniously.

POLYTHEISM
> The belief that divine reality is multiple; that there are many gods.

POSITIVISM
> The theory that man can have knowledge only of phenomena, through the senses, and that only relatively.

PRAGMATISM
> The theory that the test of truth is how it works.

PREDESTINATION
> The doctrine that all events of man's life, even his eternal destiny, are determined beforehand by a deity.

PROBABILITY
> The quality or state of being likely true or likely to happen.

PROGRESSIVISM
> The belief that the well-being and the improvement of society lie with the young, who must be challenged and trained to accept shared responsibility for its continuing improvement.

PSYCHIC
> A characteristic of any mental phenomenon.

PURITANICAL
> A term referring, in general, to a purification of existing religious forms and practices. In America, the theological position of the New England colonists.

RATIONALISM
> The theory that thought is the clue to nature, reality, and values.

REALISM
> The theory that universals exist before things and that things exist independently of the knower. Reality is ultimately independent of any knowledge of its existence.

REASONING
> The faculty of connecting ideas consciously, coherently, and purposely. Thinking in logical form.

RECONSTRUCTIONISM
> The belief that the schools and other agencies of society should plan and work aggressively.

RELATIVISM
> The view that truth is relative and may vary from individual to individual, from group to group, or from time to time, having no objective standard.

REVELATION

The communication to man of the divine will.

SCHOLASTICISM

Both a method and system of thought. In its widest sense it embraces all the intellectual activities carried on in the medieval schools. Was grounded on Aristotelianism.

SEMANTICS

The science of the evolution of language and of the phenomena that mark its growth. (C. W. Morris)

SOCRATIC METHOD

A way of teaching in which the master professes to impart no information but draws forth more and more definite answers by means of pointed questions.

SOPHISTS

Those who, in ancient Greece, subordinated purely theoretical learning to its practical usefulness.

STOIC

One who believes that virtue alone is the only good and the virtuous man is the one who has attained happiness through knowledge.

SUPERNATURALISM

The belief in that which surpasses the active and inactive powers of nature.

SYLLOGISM

A certain form of valid inferences that involve as premises two categorical propositions having a term in common—the middle term.

SYNODS

Ecclesiastical councils or meetings.

SYNOPTIC

Giving a general view, often containing identical parts.

SYNTAX

The systematic statement of the formal rules of language.

SYNTHESIS

The general method of deductive reasoning that proceeds from the whole to the part. In Georg Wilhelm Hegel, the resolution of opposites.

TELEOLOGY

The theory of purpose, ends, goals, final causes, values, the Good. Teleology explains the past in terms of the future.

THEISM

The theory that conception of God can be accurately defined and acceptably used.

THEOLOGY

The study of the nature of God and the relation of God to the world of reality.

THEORY OF ORGANISM

That the universe is an integrated and unified whole.

THESIS

An undemonstrated proposition used as a premise in a syllogism. Any proposition capable of being supported by reason.

THOMISM

The official philosophical position of the Roman Catholic church as formulated by St. Thomas Aquinas and derived from Aristotle.

UTILITARIANISM
   The view that the right act is the act that will actually or probably produce at least as much intrinsic good as any other action open to the agent in question.
VOLUNTARISM
   The theory that reality is of the nature of will.

Index

Abbott, Walter M., 214
Abelard, Peter, 38
"Absolute," doctrine of the, 132-33
Academy at Geneva (established by Luther), 70
Achilles, 49
Action step in observation, 143, 145
Adler, Felix, 148-49
Adventures of Ideas (Whitehead), 193
Agassiz, Louis, 174
"Aims of Education" (Maritain), 210
"Aims of Education" (Whitehead), 193
Al-Farabi, 36
Albertus Magnus, 38
Alcuin, 36
Alexander the Great, 12
Andrea, Johann Valentin, 69-70
Anselm, St., 36
"Apperceptive mass," 141
Aquinas, St. Thomas, 36, 38-42, 62
    educational philosophy of, 38-42
    neo-Thomism and, 207-8
Aristotle, 6, 12-21, 53, 62, 161, 175, 218
    educational philosophy of, 15-16, 17-21

Aristotle *(cont.)*
    political theory of, 13, 15, 17-18
    reintroduction of theories, 36-38, 45
Arrowood, C., 125
Association, laws of, 177-82
Associationism, 142
Atomists, 1
Augustine, St., 6, 36n
    educational philosophy of, 30-35
Averroes, 36
Avery, Albert E., 39n
Avicenna, 38

Bacon, Francis, 96, 163
Bacon, Roger, 36
Barnard, Henry, 135
Basedow, Johann Bernhard, 90, 100, 107
Beales, A.C., 78
Beard, Charles, 62
Benedict, St., 35-36
Benedict XIII, Pope, 85
Bentham, Jeremy, 127
Bergson, Henri, 134, 156, 208
Berkeley, George, 100, 113
"Bill for the More General Diffusion of Knowledge" (Jefferson), 115-19

Bloy, Léon, 208
Bonaventura, St., 38
Book of the Courtier (Castiglione), 47
Book of Discipline, The (Calvin), 73-76
Borromeo, St. Charles, 77
Bradley, E.H., 134
Breeding, quality of, 104
Brightman, Edgar S., 159
Brubacher, John S., 147, 217
Bruno, 156
Buber, Martin, educational philosophy of, 220-28
Busby, Richard, 96
Butler, J. Donald, 159

Caesar, Julius, 82
Caird, Edward, 134
Caird, F.J.E., 165
Calasanctius, St. Joseph, 84
Calkins, Mary W., 134
Calvin, John, 30
    educational philosophy of, 69-77
Cambridge University, 70
"Cardinal Principles of Secondary Education," 165-66
Carlisle, 127
Carlyle, Thomas, 134, 156
Castiglione, Baldassare, 47
Catechism, 76, 83
Catholic orders in education, 84-85
Cave, Plato's allegory of the, 4-5
Charity, Sisters of, 84
Chaucer, Geoffrey, 45
Child and the Curriculum, The (Dewey), 187
Children, early education of, 54-57
    Calvin on, 75
    Comenius and, 90
    Luther on, 66-69
    Whitehead on, 198-99
Christian Doctrine, Fathers of, 84
Christian philosophy, 29-30, 32
Christian Schools, Brothers of, 85
Cicero, 6, 21, 46, 82, 93
Citizenship, education and
    Calvin on, 70
    Luther on, 68-69
    See also State
Classical studies, 46
Cohen, Herman, 156
Coleridge, Samuel, 127, 134, 156
Comenius, John Amos, educational philosophy of, 88-96, 147
Compulsory education, 76-77
Comte, August, 127, 163, 174
Confessions (St. Augustine), 31
Constantine, Emperor, 30
Constitutions of the Society of Jesus, 78-82

Content and process, 141
Contiguity, law of, 177-78
Corporal punishment, 30-31
Council of Trent (1545-1563), 77, 85
Counter Reformation, 85
Cremin, L.A., 233-34
Croce, Benedetto, 134, 156
"Cultural epochs" theory, 140
Culture, Hegel on, 136, 137
Curtius, 82
Cyclical process in education, 202-3

Dante Alighieri, 45
Darwin, Charles, 155, 156, 163, 174
Da Vinci, Leonardo, 47
Declaration on Christian Education, 207
Declaration of Independence, 113
Decree on the Apostolate of the Laity, 207
Decree on Ecumenism, The, 207
Defoe, Daniel, 104
Demand step in observation, 143, 144
Democritus, 1, 163
Depravity of man, doctrine of, 70, 97
Descartes, René, 96, 113, 194
Dewey, John, 135, 142, 147, 155, 156, 173, 176
    compared with Maritain, 213
    educational philosophy of, 183-93
Dialectic, 5, 53
Dialectical reasoning, 132-33, 174
Difficulty in order of subjects, 198-99
Divine Comedy, The (Dante), 45
Dominic, St., 36
Drawing, 125
"Dynamics of Education, The" (Maritain), 211

Eby, F., 125
Eckhart, Meister, 59, 65, 156
Edinburgh, University of, 70
Edman, Irwin, 183
"Education" (Emerson), 159-63
Education, Intellectual, Moral and Physical (Spencer), 163, 164
"Education of Character, The" (Buber), 223-28
Education of a Christian Prince (Erasmus), 51
Education at the Crossroads (Maritain), 209-19
Education of Man (Froebel), 147, 149-53
Ehlers, Henry, 214
Emerson, Ralph Waldo, 127, 134, 155, 176, 183
    educational philosophy of, 156-63
Emile (Rousseau), 105, 107-13, 123
Emotions, James-Lange theory of, 175
Empiricism, 96-97

Enchiridion or Manual of Christian Knight (Erasmus), 51
Ends in education, Maritain on, 210, 215-16
Enlightenment, the, 87-88, 123
Ennis, Robert H., 228
Epicurus, 6, 163
Erasmus, Desiderius, educational philosophy of, 51-57
Essay Concerning Human Understanding (Locke), 97
Essays (Montaigne), 47
Essays in Radical Empiricism (James), 176
Ethics and morality
    Aristotle on, 13
    Buber on, 221-22
    Dewey's theory of, 184-85, 187
    Hegel on, 135-36
    Plato on, 2-3
    Spencer's theory of, 164
Eudaemonia (happiness), Aristotle's concept of, 13, 16
Evolution, biological, 155, 156, 163, 174
Existentialism, 220
Expectation step, 143, 144

Feltre, Vittorino de, 46
Fichte, Johann Gottlieb, 107, 123-24, 127, 134
Fiske, John, 156
Fourier, St. Peter, 84
Francis, St., 36
Franklin, Benjamin, 100, 113
Freedom
    Buber on, 222
    in education, 106
    Hegel's concept of, 133, 136-37
    of religion, 114
Froebel, J., 90, 107, 123
    compared with Hegel, 147-48
    compared with Herbart, 148
    educational philosophy of, 145-53
"General Notion of Education" (Hegel), 135-38
Generalisation, stage of, 201
Gentile, Giovanni, 134, 156
Geography, 125
Girls, schools for, 63-65
Goethe, J.W. von, 156
Good Morals and School Studies (Vergerio), 46
Government, *see* State
Grammar, 76
Graves, Franklin Pierpont, 98
Great Didactic (Comenius), 89, 90-96
Greek language, 52-53, 76, 80, 83, 96, 99, 134, 166
Gregory, St., 39-41

Gymnastics, 5, 19, 125
    See also Physical education

Habit, James' five laws of, 177
Hall, G. Stanley, 176, 183
Harris, E.E., 156
Harris, William T., 135
Hartlib, Samuel, 90, 96
Harvard College, 70
Health, Locke on importance of, 101
Hebrew language, 80
Hegel, G.W.F., 107, 123, 127, 174, 200, 209, 220
    compared with Froebel, 147-48
    educational philosophy of, 132-38
Heine, Heinrich, 17
Heraclitus, 1, 183
Herbart, Johann Friedrich, 100, 123, 175
    compared with Froebel, 148
    educational philosophy of, 139-45
Hippocrates, 93
History, study of, 125, 134, 140
Hobbes, Thomas, 87, 96
Hocking, William E., 159
Horne, Henry Harrell, 134, 158-159
How Gertrude Teaches Her Children (Pestalozzi), 124
Humanities, 212
    Jesuit rules for teaching, 82-83
"Humanities in Education, The" (Maritain), 212
Hume, David, 100
Huss, John, 59
Huxley, John, 191
Huxley, T.H., 156

"I-thou" relationship, 221
Idealism, 127, 134, 155, 156, 173
Ignatius, St., 77-85
In Praise of Folly (Erasmus), 51
Individual will, Hegel on, 138
Instincts, theory of, 175
Institute for Adult Education, 220
Institutes of the Christian Religion (Calvin), 71-73
Institutes of Oratory (Quintilian), 21, 22-27, 46
Instruction, steps in, 143, 145
Instrumentalism, 135, 174
Islam in Europe, 61

James, William, 142, 156, 165, 184
    educational philosophy of, 173-82
James-Lange theory of emotions, 175
Jefferson, Thomas, 88, 113-19, 127
Jesuits (Society of Jesus), educational system of, 77-82
John of Salisbury, 38
Jowett, Benjamin, 134

Judeo-Greco-Christian ideals, 217-18

Kant, Immanuel, 107, 123, 127, 132, 134,
    139, 163, 175, 183
Kapital, Das (Marx), 134
Kierkegaard, S., 156, 220, 221
Kindergarten, founding of, 146, 147, 149
Kneller, George F., 220
Knowledge, Spencer's level of, 164
Knowledge, theory of
    Aristotle's, 13
    Aquinas', 38
    Dewey's, 184
    Herbart's, 140-41
    Locke's, 96-97
    Plato's, 5-7
Knox, John, 71
Komisar, Paul B., 228

Ladd, G.T., 156
Lamarck, J.B.P., 163
Lamprecht, Sterling P., 5, 30, 71
Language, childhood acquisition of, 199
Language of Education, The (Scheffler),
    229-34
Languages, 125, 134, 140, 146
La Salle, St. Jean Baptiste de, 65, 84-85
Latin language, 46, 52-53, 74, 80, 96, 99,
    134, 164, 167
    Comenius' theory for teaching, 89
Laurie, E.S., 88
Laws, The (Plato), 2
Learning, quality of, 104
Leibnitz, G.W., 100, 132
Leo XIII, Pope, 156, 207
Leonard and Gertrude (Pestalozzi), 124,
    127-32
Leonardo da Vinci, 47
"Letter to the Mayors . . . in Behalf of
    Christian Schools" (Luther),
    66-69
Leviathan (Hobbes), 87
Leyden, University of, 70
Liberal education, 165
    Maritain on, 212
    Whitehead on, 196-97
"Limen" threshold, 141
Literature, study of 4, 125, 134, 212
Livy, 82
Locke, John, 87, 90, 105, 113-14, 127,
    139, 163, 175
    educational philosophy of, 97-104,
    106
Logic, 53, 76, 134
    developed by Aristotle, 12
Logical empiricism, 228
Luther, Martin, 30, 45, 51, 61-69
    educational philosophy of, 63-69
Lyceum (founded by Aristotle), 112

McClellan, James E., 228
McDougall, W., 156
Machiavelli, Niccolò, 47-51
McMurray, Charles, 142
McMurray, Frank, 142
McTaggart, J.E.M., 156
Magistro, De (Aquinas), 39
Maimonides, Moses, 38
Man and the State (Maritain), 208-9
Mann, Horace, 135
Marcus Aurelius, 156
Maritain, Jacques, 156
    compared with Dewey, 213
    educational philosophy of, 208-19
Marsilius of Padua, 59
Marx, Karl, 133, 134, 156
Mathematics, 99, 125, 140, 146, 212
    as model of thinking, 16
Memory, 53, 98
Meno (Plato), 7-12
Mental growth, stages of, 199-201
Mercy, Sisters of, 84
Merici, St. Angela, 84
Method of education, Comenius on, 94-96
Military knowledge, 48-51
Mill, James, 127
Mill, John Stuart, 127, 163, 174
Milton, John, 46, 90, 99
Misconceptions in modern education,
    Maritain on, 210
Moerbeke, William, 38
Montaigne, Michel, 45, 47, 96, 99, 104,
    139
Morality, *see* Ethics and morality
More, Thomas, 51
Morris, G.S., 134, 183
Morris, Van Cleve, 220
Morrison, H.C., 142
Music, 4, 5, 125, 146, 212

Nationalism, 36*n*, 45
Natural science, 146, 212
Naturalism in education, 106-7, 160-61
Nature
    method of education compared to,
    95
    Rousseau's doctrine of, 105, 108
Nature and Life (Whitehead), 194-95
Neill, A.S., 220
Neo-Hegelianism, 134
Neoplatonism, 6, 30
Neo-Thomism, 207-8
New realism school, 176
Newman, Cardinal, 127
Nietzsche, Friedrich, 156, 220
Nominalism, realism and, 36*n*
Notre Dame, Sisters of, 84

Observation, steps in, 143-45
Of Christian Doctrine (St. Augustine), 32*n*

Of Education (Milton), 90
Olier, Jean Jacques, 84
"On Christian Philosophy" (Pope Leo XIII), 207, 208
On The Liberal and Moral Training of Children (Vegio), 46
Orbis Sensualium Pictus (Comenius), 89
Origin of Species (Darwin), 155

"Pansophia" plan of Comenius, 88, 90
Parker, Col. Francis Wayland, 142
Parmenides, 1
Pastors, role of, 72-73
Paul, St., 15n, 71-73
Paul, St. Vincent de, 84
Paul III, Pope, 76, 77
Paul VI, Pope, 207
Peabody, Elizabeth P., 149
Peirce, Charles S., 156, 174, 176
Perry, Ralph Barton, 176
Pestalozzi, J.H., 89, 100, 107, 139, 145-47, 156, 165
    educational philosophy of 123-32
    influence of, 125-27
Petrarch, 46
Philadelphia, College of, 114
Philopoemen, 49
Philosophy, study of, 134, 212
Phylogenetic theory, 164
Physical education, 5, 99-100, 125
    Rousseau on, 109-10
    See also Gymnastics
Pindar, 214
Pittacus, 90
Pius XI, Pope, 208
Plato, 29, 36n, 45, 46, 113, 156, 163, 183
    Aristotle and, 16, 17
    educational ideas of, 1-7
    Meno dialogue of, 7-12
Play, educational importance of, 147, 149
    Dewey on, 186
Plotinus, 6, 29, 30, 156
Poggio, Andrew, 46
Pole, Cardinal Reginald, 76
Poor relief, Locke's plan for, 99
Porphyry, 29
Port Royal order, 84
Porter, Noah, 156
Positivism, 127, 163, 174
Pragmatism, 174, 176
Pragmatism (James), 176
Precision, stage of, 201
Predestination, 70
Presentation, Sisters of the, 84
Prince, The (Machiavelli), 47-51
Principia Mathematica (Russell and Whitehead), 193
Principles of Psychology, The (James), 175, 176

Private tutoring, 99
Process and content, 141
Process and Reality (Whitehead), 193
Proclus, 36n
Progressive education, 148
"Project" method for subject matter, 189-93
Protagoras, 6
Psychology
    Aristotle's theories on, 15
    Herbart's contributions to, 140-41
    James' theories on, 174-75
Public education, 114-19
Pueris Instituendis, De (Erasmus), 54-57
Punishment and reward, 102, 131-32
Pythagoreans, 1

Quadrivium, 212
Quintilian, 53
    educational theory of, 21-27

Rabelais, Francois, 96, 99
Ratio Studiorum, 78, 82-83
Ratione Studii, De (Erasmus), 52, 53
Readiness for education, 98-99
Realism, nominalism and, 36n
Reformation, the, 59-61
Rein, Wilhelm, 142
Renaissance, 45-47, 60, 85
Republic, The (Plato), 2, 3-4, 5
Reward and punishment, 102, 131-32
Rhetoric, 76, 80, 99
"Rhythm of Education" (Whitehead), 198-204
Rice, John, 233
Robert of Lincoln, 36n
Rocellinus, 36
Romance, stage of, 200-1
Romanticism, 127
Rousseau, Jean Jacques, 88, 90, 123, 127, 139, 146
    educational philosophy of, 104-13
Royce, Josiah, 134-35, 156
Rusk, Robert R., 147
Russell, Bertrand, 176, 193

Sadoleto, Cardinal Jacopo, 76-77
St. Joseph, Sisters of, 84
Sallust, 82
Santayana, George, 165
Scheffler, Israel, educational philosophy of, 229-34
Schelling, F.W., 127
Schlegel, Friedrich, 127
Schleiermacher, Friedrich, 127
Schurz, Mrs. Karl, 149
Science of Education, The (Herbart), 142-45
Scipio Cyrus, 49

260   *Index*

Secondary education, 134, 165-66
Self, knowledge of, 90-92
Self-consciousness, reflective, 136
Self-love in children, 110
Sense perception, education and, 125
Sense realism, 88, 90
Sforza, Francesco, 48
Shaftesbury, Anthony Ashley Cooper, Earl of, 96
Similarity, law of, 178
Slogans in education, 230-34
Smith, B.O., 228
Social Contract (Rousseau), 88, 105
Social Darwinism, 155
Social Statics (Spencer), 163
Socrates, 2, 7-12, 46
Some Thoughts Concerning Education (Locke), 97, 100-4
Soul
    Aristotle's theory of, 15
    in Augustine's philosophy, 31
    Platonic division of, 5
Spencer, Herbert, 155, 156, 174
    educational philosophy of, 163-71
State, theory of the
    of Aristotle, 13, 15, 17-18
    of Calvin, 70
    of Locke, 87-88
    of Luther, 65
    of Machiavelli, 47
    of Maritain, 208-9
    of Plato, 4
    of Rousseau, 105
Statute of Virginia for Religious Freedom, 113
Stoicism, 6
Sulpician order, 84
Summa Theologica (Aquinas), 208
Summerhill school, 220
"Swan Song, The," 124

"Tabula rasa" doctrine of the mind, 96-97, 175
Talks to Teachers on Psychology (James), 175, 176-82
Teachers
    Buber on, 224-28
    Emerson's advice to, 158
    Erasmus on, 55-56
    Locke on necessary qualities of, 102
    role of, 73
Technical education, Whitehead on, 197
Theodosius, decree of, 30
Thomas Aquinas, *see* Aquinas, Thomas
Transcendentalism, 134, 156
"Trials of Present Day Education, The" (Maritain), 212 Trivium, 212
Trivium, 212

Unconsciousness and experience, 141
"Unity," Froebel's concept of, 149-50
Universality as goal of education, 137-38
Universities, 75
    Maritain on, 212
    spread of in Europe, 65
    Whitehead on, 197
Upanishads, 156
Upon the Method of Right Instruction (Erasmus), 51
Ursuline order, 84
Utilitarianism, 127
Utopia (More), 51

Vaihinger, H., 156
Varieties of Religious Experience, The (James), 175
Vatican II, 207
Vegio, Maffeo, 46
Vergerio, Pietro, 46
Vespasian, 21
Vincentian order, 84
Virgil, 82
Virginia, University of, 114
Virtue, quality of, 103
Visitandines order, 84
Vocational education, 124, 147, 197
Voltaire, 104
Von Fellenberg, Philipp E., 127

Wallace, Alfred, 155
Washington, George, 115
Watson, J.B., 156
"Way Out of Educational Confusion, The" (Dewey), 189-93
Wells, H.G., 191
"What is Man?" (Buber), 221
"What Knowledge is of Most Worth?" (Spencer), 166-71
Wheelwright, Philip, 70
White, Morton, 176
Whitehead, Alfred N., 1, 156, 173
    educational philosophy of, 193-204
Will to Believe, The (James), 175
William and Mary College, 115, 117, 119
William of Ockham, 59
William of Orange, 96
Wisdom
    obstacles to, 93-94
    quality of, 103
Woodbridge, G.E., 165
Wundt, Wilhelm, 156, 174
Wycliffe, John, 59, 65
Wythe, George, 113

Xenophon, 49

Zeller, Eduard, 142
Zeno of Citium, 6
Zoology, Aristotle on, 16-17